EXPLORING SUBLIME RHETORIC
IN BIBLICAL LITERATURE

EMORY STUDIES IN EARLY CHRISTIANITY

Vernon K. Robbins, General Editor
Roy R. Jeal, General Editor
Robert H. von Thaden Jr., Associate Editor
David B. Gowler, Associate Editor
Meghan Henning
Susan E. Hylen
Donghyun Jeong
Mikeal C. Parsons
Russell B. Sisson
Shively T. J. Smith

Number 28

EXPLORING SUBLIME RHETORIC IN BIBLICAL LITERATURE

Edited by

Roy R. Jeal

Atlanta

Copyright © 2024 by SBL Press

Publication of this volume was made possible by the generous support of the Pierce Program in Religion of Oxford College of Emory University.

All rights reserved. No part of this work may be reproduced or transmitted in any form or by any means, electronic or mechanical, including photocopying and recording, or by means of any information storage or retrieval system, except as may be expressly permitted by the 1976 Copyright Act or in writing from the publisher. Requests for permission should be addressed in writing to the Rights and Permissions Office, SBL Press, 825 Houston Mill Road, Atlanta, GA 30329 USA.

Library of Congress Control Number: 2024932872

Cover design is an adaptation by Bernard Madden of Rick A. Robbins, Mixed Media (19" x 24" pen and ink on paper, 1981).

Contents

Foreword vii
    Erika Mae Olbricht
Abbreviations xv

Introduction
    Roy R. Jeal 1

Part 1. Foundations: The Beautiful Sublime

The Rhetoric of the Sublime in the Narrative of Mary
    the Mother of Jesus (Luke 1–2)
    Roy R. Jeal 13

The Sublime and Subliminal in Romans 2–3
    Jonathan Thiessen 39

Divine Speech, Hebrews, and Sublime Rhetoric
    Christopher T. Holmes 65

Rhetorical Criticism of the Sublime
    Thomas H. Olbricht† 87

Coleridge's Sublime and Rhetorical Interpretation of
    New Testament Texts
    Murray J. Evans...111

Part 2. Development: The Terrifying Sublime

Terror and the Logic of the Sublime in Revelation
    Christopher T. Holmes 135

Sublime Terror in 1 Enoch
   Vernon K. Robbins 155

The Sublime Terror of Ignatius of Antioch
   Harry O. Maier 177

Subliming the Sublime: The Bible and the Sublime in
   Eighteenth-Century Britain
   Alan P. R. Gregory 189

Sublime Terror in Context: A Response
   Roy R. Jeal 215

Bibliography 227

Contributors 247
Ancient Sources Index 249
Modern Authors Index 258

Foreword

Erika Mae Olbricht

My father, Tom Olbricht, loved a mountain range—from the Ozarks, where he grew up, to the Rockies, which he loved to visit. Every summer when I was growing up, we lived in our travel trailer in New England, but we frequently traveled there from Texas on a wide detour through Yosemite, the Grand Tetons, or the Badlands. He was a hiker and loved chugging up the side of a mountain to take in the view. His particular favorite in New England was Mount Monadnock in southern New Hampshire, with its smooth bluffs of granite outcrops and blueberry bushes and vistas from the summit stretching forever. For him that enormous slice of the natural world was an encounter with the divine. I can hear his clear tenor singing hymns like "Let Every Heart Rejoice and Sing," which captured such moments, as in the chorus:

> While the rocks and the rills, while the vales and the hills,
> A glorious anthem raise,
> Let each prolong their grateful song,
> And the God of our fathers praise.

I'm sure he sang it on a mountaintop once or twice.

Of course, people have treasured the sheer grandeur of these majestic and sublime places for centuries; a deep appreciation for such landscapes instigated the creation of the US National Parks System (NPS) for their preservation as part of the national heritage. The NPS is the legacy of John Muir (and others) who famously championed preserving the wild, sublime landscapes of the American West. My father's love of these same

---

I thank John Wiehl and Steve Pinkerton for reading earlier versions of this foreword and Sarah Gridley for ruminating on etymology with me.

landscapes eventually led me to study landscape conservation, a decision also fostered by my love of gardens that I share especially with my mother. This range of landscapes, both the breathtaking and the intimate varieties, inform the visual rhetoric framework I explore here for understanding the response to and impact of actual places.

This collection explores a range of ideas about how the sublime works on the soul and the actions of the individual. While each author has a different description of the force of the sublime, in the words of Roy R. Jeal, "what is clear is that the sublime affects mind and body in ways not immediately, probably not ever, understood in completely systematic, rational ways."[2] This element particularly interests me in terms of how people experience landscapes. It is no peculiarity that art historians and landscape studies scholars, philosophers, and literary critics talk the most about the sublime, because those fields analyze objects that record and present, in various media, experiences that the authors and artists considered sublime, which is often understood as one impetus for artistic expression: the need to record an overwhelming experience or emotion. We inherit this idea from William Wordsworth's preface to his *Lyrical Ballads*: "Poetry is the spontaneous overflow of powerful feelings: it takes its origin from emotion recollected in tranquility."[3] But we rarely attend to the rest of the sentence, where Wordsworth insists that the original emotion returns upon further contemplation and writing: "the emotion is contemplated till, by a species of reaction, the tranquility gradually disappears, and an emotion, kindred to that which was before the subject of contemplation, is gradually produced, and does itself actually exist in the mind. In this mood successful composition generally begins, and in a mood similar to this it is carried on."[4] The effect of a successful record, then, is to capture and transmit the original passion, or something "kindred" to it, that occurred in the moment, which occurred in a particular physical place, often—particularly in the case of Wordsworth—in reference to nature or a landscape.

Landscape has its etymological origins in art: a *landskip* was a Dutch painting meant to show the view as a composed piece of art, and indeed, some landscapes were created for the explicit purpose of posing as subject matter for painters; many scholars have written about Lancelot "Capability"

---

2. See Roy R. Jeal's introduction to this volume.

3. William Wordsworth, *Lyrical Ballads: With Pastoral and Other Poems* (London: Longman & Rees, 1798), l.

4. Wordsworth, *Lyrical Ballads*, l–li.

Brown's park landscapes along these lines or about William Gilpin's designs and paintings or Humphry Repton's Red Books, which were created for his clients in order to explain visually the before and after of his proposed landscape changes.[5] These landscape design records are used to manage the historic landscapes themselves as well as the views they created for the visitor who then might recreate it through drawing or painting for both contemporary and future viewers. The visual representation can give access to profound emotions and insights, even if they are not the exact ones experienced by the painter or writer.

But these genteel and curated views are categorically not *sublime* views, which by definition exceed human activity in the landscape and privilege the force of nature. For example, the vast scene of apocalyptic mountains in John Martin's *The Great Day of His Wrath* (1851–1853) shows tiny people helpless against the raging landscape.[6] Caspar David Friedrich's *The Wanderer above the Sea of Fog* (1817–1818) invites us to see the same landscape and feel what the viewer in the image also sees, standing proud atop a misty mountain, looking out over an obscured but enormous landscape. The landscape is the subject of the painting rather than the figure of the man, who, positioned in the foreground but shown from the back—a composition device the German Romantics called *Rückenfigur*—is gazing along with us at the sublime landscape before him. But the size of the figure, his dominance in the very middle of the painting, moderates any sense that nature is overwhelming or that humans are subjected to it in any way. The figure contemplates nature from a place equal to it. On the other hand, Thomas Cole's *Kaaterskill Falls* (1826), like other Hudson River school paintings, presents the human as completely dwarfed by the enormity of mountain, sky, river—the ideal content of the imagined (and in some locations, real) American landscape. A viewer will likely miss the very tiny human figure in the center of the painting, insignificant in scale and at the whim of the giant landscape around it.

---

5. See, e.g., Peter De Bolla, *The Education of the Eye: Painting, Landscape, and Architecture in Eighteenth-Century Britain* (Stanford: Stanford University Press, 2003); John Phibbs, *Place-Making: The Art of Capability Brown* (Swindon: Historic England, 2017); Stephen Daniels and Lucy Veale, "Revealing Repton: Bringing Landscape to Life at Sheringham," *Landscape Research* 40 (2005): 5–22; and Andre Rogger, *Landscapes of Taste: The Art of Humphry Repton's Red Books*, Classical Tradition in Architecture (London: Routledge, 2008).

6. See Alan P. R. Gregory's essay in this volume.

But they will not miss the waterfall that dominates the foreground of the painting. A staple of the sublime landscape, the waterfall signals a powerful and potentially devastating rush of water. Its force can perhaps be signaled more effectively through the term *cataract*, though we rarely use it in that context any longer, as we mostly think of a cataract as an eye condition that hampers vision. According to the *OED*, both meanings overlap in time and are likely explained in part by the prefix *cata-*, which generally means down or downward, sometimes having the sense of reduction or waste (perhaps as in a reduction of eyesight). The earliest meaning of *cataract*, however, comes from the Latin and refers to heaven's floodgates ("cataract" def. 1) that *hold back* a devastating gush of water, in reference to Gen 7:11 and 8:2. These floodgates, these cataracts, are opened to allow the flood and closed to end it. They hold back or suppress the flood waters. Yet, cataract can also indicate a "violent downpour or rush of water" (def. 2b), either sudden or consistent, as in a waterfall, "one of considerable size, and falling headlong over a precipice" (note to def. 2a). In short, a cataract can indicate either the gate that holds back water or the violent cascade of water itself.

The connection between the gate, the cascade, and the eye condition is in the downward motion captured by the prefix, but also in the sense of a cataract as a portcullis (def. 3), something that comes down and gates the vision, though the *OED* notes that "the sense-development in Greek, Latin, and French-English, is not in all respects clear" ("cataract" etymology note). Definition 3 defines cataract as a "portcullis; also the grating of a window," and definition 4—the first that refers to the eye—notes that the pathological designation seems to be "a figurative use of the sense portcullis," or "'a web in the eye', the notion being that even when the eye is open, the cataract obstructs vision, as the portcullis does a gateway" (def. 4 note). Therefore, connected through the idea of downward movement, the cataract indicates a motion and movement visible in the landscape of those who see clearly, and at the same time an obfuscation of the visual as an access point.

This overdetermined confluence of visual meanings is linked with the sublime: The cataract in a landscape is meant to be looked at (though certainly its roar is also a sensory factor) and can even be the overwhelming natural aspect of a landscape that exceeds the human scale of apprehension—its scale and impact are what render it sublime. In 1826, Cole painted Kaaterskill Falls, in the Catskills (New York), from multiple perspectives, and the contrasting viewpoints are instructive. The more traditional view, captured in *The Falls of the Kaaterskill*, depicts the waterfall from a distance and centers it on the canvas as the subject of the painting. In contrast, *Kaaterskill Falls* is painted from the vantage point inside the cave over which the waterfall cascades, looking out over the river where the tumbling water rolls away from the viewer. In fact, the painting depicts a sort of eye, since the mouth of the cave frames the upper part of the canvas as though it were an eyelid, not just giving us an image, but dramatizing the act of seeing and apprehending the landscape. Rather than looking at the water, the viewer of the painting is placed within the cave looking out beyond the waterfall to the river valley. It's not that Cole created a painting that accounts for each of the meanings of the word *cataract* that I've presented here. After all, the waterfall is placed to the side—the landscape is not actually obscured by it. However, it is hard to discount the unusual vantage point as making a statement about the act of viewing itself. The subject of the painting is not (only) the waterfall, but what the viewer sees beyond. Writing about the painting in *Art History*, Michael Gaudio notes that "the entrance of the cataract disrupts the view and initiates a shift into an aural experience of nature."[7] Gaudio himself (even though he is most interested in the noise of the cataract) falls prey to the visual impediment implied in Cole's painting; he writes that the cataract "interrupts my visual progress through the painting, clouding my vision so to speak."[8] The visual pun on the clouded eye present in both the painting and the historian's explication of it shows that we are being asked intentionally to understand the landscape from the viewpoint of the artist; and while the same could be true of any painting, the framing and the pun on cataract in this particular painting makes the visual obviously central to the sublime experience, encapsulated—or perhaps negated—by the word *cataract*'s different meanings.

 The cataract makes an appearance in "Lines Composed above Tintern Abbey" as well—one of Wordsworth's most frequently quoted poems and one my father explicates in this collection.[9] For my purposes here, I want to follow the trajectory Wordsworth traces from viewing the original place to recalling the view later in life (five years later, as he tells us in the first line of the poem), as he reflects on the role played by nature in his earlier

---

 7. Michael Gaudio, "At the Mouth of the Cave: Listening to Thomas Cole's *Kaaterskill Falls*," *Art History* 33 (2010): 457.
 8. Gaudio "At the Mouth of the Cave," 457.
 9. See Thomas H. Olbricht's essay in this volume.

years and on the maturation process he has since undergone. This passage begins with a waterfall:

> The sounding cataract
> Haunted me like a passion: the tall rock,
> The mountain, and the deep and gloomy wood,
> Their colours and their forms, were then to me
> An appetite; a feeling and a love,
> That had no need of a remoter charm,
> By thought supplied, nor any interest
> Unborrowed from the eye. (78–85)

His original vision of the place was through sound, color, and form—the last two insights borrowed "from the eye." But now he has changed, and "I cannot paint / What then I was" (77–78). The mature poet has instead "learned / To look on nature, not as in the hour / Of thoughtless youth; but hearing oftentimes / The still sad music of humanity" (90–93). Therefore, he has felt

> A presence that disturbs me with the joy
> Of elevated thoughts; a sense sublime
> Of something far more deeply interfused,
> Whose dwelling is the light of setting suns,
> And the round ocean and the living air,
> And the blue sky, and in the mind of man:
> A motion and a spirit, that impels
> All thinking things, all objects of all thought,
> And rolls through all things. (96–104)

The moral movement in this passage, spurred by nature, takes the poet from himself—"me" in the first quoted line—to "all things." My father quotes these exact lines in his essay in this volume, to point out that "The sublime occurs in the natural world when the invisible intellectual forms penetrate the realm of sense … [and] creates wholeness at a transcendental level in a living soul resulting in harmony and joy."[10] In both the painting and the poem, visiting a place results in sensitive connection with nature, with the divine, with "all thinking things, all objects of all thoughts."

---

10. See the essay by Thomas H. Olbricht in this volume.

A physical place like Tintern Abbey is something to be experienced and something that works on the self when one is attuned to it; it can be interpreted and processed into text or image in the same way as other experiences, with more or less recognition of the ineffableness of the moment. A landscape painting (or poem or diary entry) is a way of taming and containing the ferocity of the actual place—to frame it and hang it on a wall rather than cling to a tree in a storm, as John Muir famously claimed to do in California.[11] The text, the painting, lives to be reencountered, perhaps to work on readers or viewers in the same way the original physical place had worked in that moment, in that weather, on that day with a particular slant of sun or rain, never to be recreated in physical actuality but approximated in text or image.

For many experiences, that recounting of the moment then becomes an object of analysis—a task undertaken by the contributors to this volume, for example. Particularly persuasive in this collection is the concern with where the experience of the sublime leads the viewer: Are they incited to moral fortitude? To spiritual ecstasy? (Are those mutually exclusive?) While the conclusions reached in the collection along those lines are not univocal, the contributors nevertheless insist on the possibility that the sublime pushes us toward good things—in the spirit of Longinus. What does one *do* with a sublime experience? For a reader of Scripture, perhaps one possible answer is obvious: the experience of the sublime is as close to the divine as one (conceivably) could get and thus an action (repentance, conversion, etc.) befitting a moral life could be warranted.

Wordsworth's poem demonstrates the same motion. In recounting through poetry the importance of the place to him, the poet finds nostalgia and yet moral maturity: in "nature and the language of the sense" the poet locates "the anchor of my purest thoughts, the nurse, / The guide, the guardian of my heart, and soul / Of all my moral being" (110–113). While I did not go to Tintern Abbey with my parents, I have been there twice, each time aware of the history of the abbey and the extent to which the immortalization of it in Wordsworth's poem has guaranteed its conservation status because of that connection. (Such were the things I learned in my conservation degree.) But the setting (my father calls it *numinous* in his essay) in its shallow river valley and the peaceful drift of mist from the tops of the hills, dimming the shafts of sunlight on the grass floor of the

---

11. See "A Wind-Storm in the Forest," in Muir, *The Mountains of California* (New York: Century, 1894), 244–57.

nave, obscuring the changing leaves of a Welsh autumn: these images stay with me and connect me to the place, to my mother and father, and provide space for contemplation and respite as well as a sense of all that has passed and a hope for what will come.

Abbreviations

1 En.	1 Enoch (Ethiopic Apocalypse)
2 Bar.	2 Baruch (Syriac Apocalypse)
AB	Anchor (Yale) Bible
ABRL	Anchor (Yale) Bible Reference Library
A.J.	Josephus, *Antiquitates judaicae*
AJP	*American Journal of Philology*
Ann.	Tacitus, *Annales*
Ant. rom.	Dionysius of Halicarnassus, *Antiquitates romanae*
Apol.	Apuleius, *Apologia* (*Pro se de magia*)
BDAG	Danker, Frederick W., Walter Bauer, William F. Arndt, and F. Wilbur Gingrich. *A Greek-English Lexicon of the New Testament and Other Early Christian Literature*. 3rd ed. Chicago: University of Chicago Press, 2000.
BECNT	Baker Exegetical Commentary on the New Testament
B.J.	Josephus, *Bellum judaicum*
BNPSup	Brill's New Pauly Supplements
CBQ	*Catholic Biblical Quarterly*
ClAnt	*Classical Antiquity*
Claud.	Suetonius, *Divus Claudius*
ClQ	*Classical Quarterly*
ConBNT	Coniectanea Biblica: New Testament Series
CP	*Classical Philology*
CR	*The Classical Review*
Cyr.	Xenophon, *Cyropedia*
def.	definition
Dem.	Dionysius of Halicarnassus, *De Demosthene*
De or.	Cicero, *De oratore*
Deus	Philo, *Quod Deus sit immutabilis*
Dial.	Tacitus, *Dialogus ad oratoribus*
Eloc.	Demetrius, *De elocutione*

Eph.	Ignatius, *To the Ephesians*
Epict. diss.	Arrian, *Epicteti dissertationes*
ESEC	Emory Studies in Early Christianity
ESV	English Standard Version
Evag.	Isocrates, *Evagoras* (Or. 9)
ExpTim	Expository Times
GBS	Guides to Biblical Scholarship
Hist.	Herodotus, *Histories*
Hist. eccl.	Eusebius, *Historia ecclesiastica*
HSCP	Harvard Studies in Classical Philology
HvTSt	*Hervormde teologiese Studies*
ICB	Interpretation: A Bible Commentary for Teaching and Preaching
ICC	International Critical Commentary
Il.	Homer, *Iliad*
Inst.	Quintilian, *Institutio oratoria*
Ios.	Philo, *De Iosepho*
IVBS	International Voices in Biblical Studies
JBL	*Journal of Biblical Literature*
JCH	*Journal for Cognitive Historiography*
JHI	*Journal of the History of Ideas*
JJMJS	*Journal of the Jesus Movement in Its Jewish Setting*
JSNTSup	Journal for the Study of the New Testament Supplement Series
JTS	*Journal of Theological Studies*
LCC	Library of Christian Classics
LCL	Loeb Classical Library
LD	Lectio divina
Leg.	Philo, *Legum allegoriae*
LNTS	Library of New Testament Studies
LSJ	Liddell, Henry George, Robert Scott, and Henry Stuart Jones. *A Greek-English Lexicon*. 9th ed. with revised supplement. Oxford: Clarendon, 1996.
Magn.	Ignatius, *To the Magnesians*
Mart. Pol.	Martyrdom of Polycarp
Mid.	Demosthenes, *In Midiam*
NA[28]	Aland, Barbara, et al., eds. *Novum Testamentum Graece*. 28th ed. Stuttgart: Deutsche Bibelgesellschaft, 2012.
NICNT	New International Commentary on the New Testament

NRSV	New Revised Standard Version
NS	new series
NTL	New Testament Library
NTS	*New Testament Studies*
OED	*Oxford English Dictionary*
Opif.	Philo, *De opificio mundi*
OM	*Opus Maximum*
PatSt	Patristic Studies (Lang)
PCPS	*Proceedings from the Cambridge Philological Society*
Phaedr.	Plato, *Phaedrus*
Phld.	Ignatius, *To the Philadelphians*
Prog.	Theon, *Progymnasmata*
QJS	*Quarterly Journal of Speech*
Rhet.	Apsines, *Ars rhetorica*; Aristotle, *Rhetorica*
Rhet. Alex.	Anaximenes, *Rhetorica ad Alexandrum*
Rhet. Her.	Rhetorica ad Herennium
Rom.	Ignatius, *To the Romans*
RRA	Rhetoric of Religious Antiquity
RSQ	*Rhetorical Society Quarterly*
SBS	Stuttgarter Bibelstudien
SCJud	Studies in Christianity and Judaism/Études sur le christianisme et le judaïsme
Sib. Or.	Sibylline Oracles
SNTSMS	Society for New Testament Studies Monograph Series
Somn.	Philo, *De somniis*
SRI	sociorhetorical interpretation
STAC	Studien und Texte zu Antike und Christentum
StPatr	*Studia Patristica*
StPT	Studies in Philosophical Theology
Subl.	Longinus, *De sublimitate*
SymS	Symposium Series
TAPA	*Transactions of the American Philological Association*
TU	*Texte und Untersuchungen*
TynBul	*Tyndale Bulletin*
VCSup	Supplements to Vigiliae Christianae
WBC	Word Biblical Commentary
WUNT	Wissenschaftliche Untersuchungen zum Neuen Testament
ZAC	*Zeitschrift für Antikes Christentum/Journal of Ancient Christianity*

Introduction

Roy R. Jeal

The sublime is usually overlooked by biblical scholars. Interpreters of the rhetoric of the Bible in earlier times considered the sublime carefully, but only a few of more recent days (e.g., Wilhelm Wuellner; J. David Hester; Christopher T. Holmes; the contributors to this volume) have given it careful attention.[1] This volume addresses the need to study the sublime in the documents of religious antiquity. The essays together offer an introduction to the sublime and provide careful description, analysis, and commentary on passages in the Gospel according to Luke, Romans, Ephesians, Hebrews, Revelation, Ignatius to the Romans, and 1 Enoch. To this is added a discussion of how the sublime was employed in ways that obscured the Bible by the eighteenth century. Response essays discuss how Samuel Taylor Coleridge's analysis of the sublime is relevant to New Testament interpretation, particularly to sociorhetorical interpretation, and the implications of the contributions on sublime terror. The point is to demonstrate that it is important to recognize, analyze, and evaluate the force of sublime rhetoric in the texts we study and to encourage interpreters to take it into account.

Sociorhetorical interpretation (SRI) explores the "textures of texts" that interweave to produce *rhetography* (graphic rhetorical imagery evoked in readers and listeners minds), *rhetorolects* (rhetorical dialects), *rhetology* (rhetorical argumentation), and *rhetorical force* (the texts *do* things to audiences in their contexts).[2] In the explorations it has become clear

---

1. For those who studied it earlier, see the essays in this volume by Thomas H. Olbricht, Murray J. Evans, and Alan P. R. Gregory.

2. See the glossary and the introduction in Vernon K. Robbins, Robert H. von Thaden Jr., and Bart B. Bruehler, eds., *Foundations for Sociorhetorical Exploration: A Rhetoric of Religious Antiquity Reader*, RRA 4 (Atlanta: SBL Press, 2016), xv–xxv, 1–26.

that the rhetoric of the sublime is an important texture to be identified and analyzed in biblical and related documents. The sublime is powerful. It moves people toward deep, internalized emotion and understanding. Two sessions of the Rhetoric of Religious Antiquity (RRA) Seminar at the Annual Meetings of the Society of Biblical Literature in Denver (2018) and San Diego (2019) investigated the rhetoric of the sublime in a range of New Testament, early Christian, and pseudepigraphal texts. Participants in the seminar sessions were requested to consider the nature, contexts, and effects of sublime rhetoric and describe where and how it functions in texts in our purview. The essays in this collection stem from the work done for those sessions.

Part 1, "Foundations: The Beautiful Sublime," takes on the difficult task of explaining what the sublime is and how it works in selected New Testament texts. Roy R. Jeal in his essay "The Rhetoric of the Sublime in the Narrative of Mary the Mother of Jesus (Luke 1–2)" describes the sublime by drawing on the work attributed to Longinus, *On the Sublime* (Περὶ Ὕψους; *De sublimate*), the ancient text closely contemporaneous with the New Testament, and on more recent descriptions and discussions. Defining the sublime depends more on informed and experienced good judgment than Longinus's descriptions and examples. Understanding of sublime rhetoric occurs when one is prompted to grasp the force of language and metaphor, of images, of amazing things, apart from a high level of mental analysis. The sublime cultivates the human spirit, hence has a spiritual component. The difficulty of coming to a clear and straightforward definition reaches some resolution, Jeal suggests, in understanding the sublime as "a rhetoric of the moment" when there is an immediate effect where a text communicates beyond itself. The essay examines "Mary's moments" in Luke 1–2 employing the SRI analytics of rhetography, argumentative texture, sublime texture, and rhetorical force. Mary's moments are the Annunciation (Luke 1:26–38); Mary, Elizabeth, and the Magnificat (1:39–56); the visit of the shepherds (2:15–20); Simeon (2:25–35); and the time in the temple (2:41–51). The sublime moments described seem not humanly reasonable,

---

See also Robbins, *The Tapestry of Early Christian Discourse: Rhetoric, Society and Ideology* (London: Routledge, 1996); Robbins, *Exploring the Textures of Texts: A Guide to Socio-rhetorical Interpretation* (Valley Forge, PA: Trinity Press International, 1996); Robbins, *The Invention of Christian Discourse*, vol. 1, RRA 1 (Dorset: Deo, 2009); Robbins and Roy R. Jeal, eds., *Welcoming the Nations: International Sociorhetorical Explorations*, IVBS 13 (Atlanta: SBL Press, 2020).

yet Mary is herself a believer who righteously follows up on what she was told and what she observed. The sublime textures reveal information that otherwise is impossible to know. For Mary the cause must be God and so must be true. Audiences are drawn in with Mary, moved to accept the truth of the things visualized and heard, apart from rational analysis. The sublime effect is difficult to resist. It is rhetoric on the edge that moves people to certainty that God has done a wonderful thing in Mary, that there is an intersection of the human and the divine.

With classicist Jonathan Thiessen's "The Sublime and Subliminal in Romans 2–3," we continue to consider Longinus but from a much different perspective. Thiessen addresses the apparent contradictory statements regarding advantages of Jews in Rom 2–3. Despite the contradictions, lack of proofs, and even incoherence in the chapters, Thiessen indicates that Paul's argument succeeds in an indirect way by means of its use of the rhetoric of the sublime. He introduces Longinus's sublime as a literary phenomenon, pointing out that "for Longinus, the sublime resides in the *words* used to describe overwhelming phenomena more than in the phenomena themselves." Longinus imagined the sublime as *elevated* (ὕψος) language produced by skilled use of rhetorical figures. Thiessen analyzes six sublime rhetorical figures described by Longinus (pathos; change of person; question and answer; asyndeton and anaphora; disorder; concealment and calculated omission) and demonstrates that they occur as features of Rom 2–3 that allow Paul to hide aspects of his message subliminally (noting that sublimity and subliminal have differing etymologies so are not synonyms) to make his point without causing major offense. By overwhelming his audiences in Rome with sublime figures and without real proof of his point, Paul gives the impression that he has made a convincing argument. The point is made indirectly and succeeds by its effects, not by rational argumentation. It functions at a level beneath full consciousness. The sublime in Rom 2–3 thus functions in a subliminal way. Thiessen helpfully points out that the sublime rhetoric "operates primarily through sensory and aesthetic mechanism," so in SRI terms forms a sensory-aesthetic texture.

In "Divine Speech, Hebrews, and Sublime Rhetoric," Christopher T. Holmes also draws on Longinus's *On the Sublime*, relying on it as foundational for his analysis of Heb 12:18–29. Holmes points out that sublime rhetoric steps beyond the usual goals of ancient rhetorical theory. It is distinguished by "nonrational or suprarational effects" that aim to lead audiences to ἔκστασις, to being transported, and mentally and emotionally resituated.

The sublime uplifts the soul. Holmes looks particularly at God's speech in Hebrews, showing how this rhetoric has the sublime effect of moving audiences to view their life-situation in a new way. His chapter is laid out in three parts. The first section provides an orientation to *On the Sublime*. According to Longinus, sublime rhetoric is designed to have striking effects so that its audiences are reoriented to good things. The second part examines Longinus's discussion of the creation story in Genesis. Perhaps surprisingly, Longinus viewed the creation account as an impressive example of sublime rhetoric. Holmes uses the discussion of Genesis to shape a framework for interpreting the description of God's speech in Hebrews. Part 3 examines the sublime speech in Heb 12:18–29. In this passage God's speech is immediate, effective, and powerful. It aligns neatly with Longinus's description of the nature of sublime language and sound. The graphic language describing the presence of God who speaks fearfully—in fire, darkness, storm, the sound of a trumpet—whose voice "shook the earth," has the sublime, dislocating, and relocating effect that Longinus described. Such divine speech is preeminently sublime.

Thomas H. Olbricht's "Rhetorical Criticism of the Sublime" strikes out in a different direction by examining the views of eighteenth century Scottish rhetorician Hugh Blair, Romantic era poet William Wordsworth, and twentieth century New Testament scholar Wilhelm Wuellner. Olbricht offers some personal history of his own education where he was introduced to Longinus but eventually became acquainted with Wordsworth and several Scottish rhetoricians. Later he interacted with Wuellner's views of sublime rhetoric. In his essay, Olbricht considers the ideas of Blair, Wordsworth, and Wuellner and from them proposes a rhetorical criticism of the sublime that he applies to the letter to the Ephesians. Blair believed that "the ultimate sublimity pertains to God." The sublime therefore must be found in religious discourse. Wordsworth imagined that the sublime was grasped by the human spirit in ecstatic moments, not by conscious thought. The sublime moment provides a sense of "peace, fulfillment, and wholeness." Wuellner believed that analysis of the sublime builds on conventional rhetorical analysis based in classical rhetoric. He was interested in how "the power of the sublime integrates the esoteric with the exoteric," when a "spiritual component" provides a sense of balance. For all three rhetoricians, as with Longinus, the sublime produces a powerful ecstatic moment when people are "elevated … to a transcendental, mystical reality." Olbricht's analysis of the sublime in Ephesians follows where, among other things recognizable to rhetorical critics, he considers the transcendental intentions of the discourse, the macrocosm sublime aspects, the sublime moments, sublime terror, and the effects of sublime discourse. He concludes that there is a "rapprochement of the divine and the human" where humans are raised to a sublime reality.

Murray J. Evans, a scholar in English literary studies strongly grounded in rhetoric, the sublime, the Bible, and theology, interacted with the essays presented in Denver in 2018. His work brings a wonderfully helpful interdisciplinary perspective to the work of biblical scholars who are interested in rhetoric and in the sublime. In his article "Coleridge's Sublime and Rhetorical Interpretation of New Testament Texts," Evans brings to the foreground of our work in biblical studies the thought and writing of Samuel Taylor Coleridge. In his essay, Evans does four things: (1) presents aspects of Coleridge's biography, his influential ideas, and understanding of the sublime; (2) discusses hermeneutical concerns regarding using Coleridge's sublime for the analysis of ancient texts; (3) discusses ideological implications for sublime rhetoric in theology and issues of power; and (4) provides a sample and analysis of one of Coleridge's "devices of sublime rhetoric." Along the way, Evans interacts with essays in part 1 of this volume. Coleridge described the sublime by distinguishing it from other figures. He imagined the sublime, Evans points out, not by a clear and concise definition, not by imagery or wording that has clear boundaries, but by the vaguer language of "a 'hazy apprehension' of 'boundless or endless *allness*'" with which vagueness observers or readers engage intensely. Evans views Coleridge's sublime as useful for biblical interpreters and Christian theologians because Coleridge always had the Bible and theology in sight. He had a view toward transcendence where language means more than it says. Evans points out that Coleridge had in sight what in SRI are called *textures* in texts. So Coleridge's sublime "is not so much a strange country somewhere else, but instead, something close by, perhaps next door."

Part 2, "Development: The Terrifying Sublime," probes the sublime language in our range of texts that prompts the inherent emotion and experience of terror. Terror is evoked by threatening and fearsome religious experiences, by words, ideas, and visions that shock, dismay, and horrify, sometimes causing panic and other emotional and physical responses. In his article, "Terror and the Logic of the Sublime in Revelation," Christopher T. Holmes draws again on Longinus to analyze the nature and force of terror in Revelation. Holmes's aim is to explore the logic of the sublime in Revelation and to show how terror is evoked in a number of scenes in Revelation. The essay argues that the effects of sublime terror support the hortatory goals of Revelation. This is more than persuasion; it is ἔκστασις, dislocation. What Longinus describes as "impressive ideas" and "vehement emotion" are presented in words that function as symbolic images of superhuman creatures and catastrophic judgments that strike terror in people and create an "overwhelming experience" meant to move audiences away from fear of merely temporal Roman demands for obedience to trust in God who judges empires. Holmes points out that the deep emotions of terror provoked by the visions of Revelation dislocate audiences from the pressures of inevitable suffering as Christ-believers to continuing trust and obedience. Sublime rhetoric points them toward awe and respect for Christ (Rev 1), for God seated in the throne room (Rev 4), for terror at scenes of judgment (Rev 6–16), and for the terror aroused by the beasts (Rev 12–13). The terrible things stretch thinking to disturbing heights. Yet the displacing terror pushes audiences to recognize the similarly overwhelming power of God for their own good and the security they have in the assurance of faith. Hence, the sublime effect of terror.

Vernon K. Robbins's "Sublime Terror in 1 Enoch" shifts our attention away from the Longinian sublime to Immanuel Kant's philosophy, particularly as it is presented and interpreted by Robbins's colleague, philosopher Rudolf Makkreel. Kant carries us deeply into thinking about the sublime. Kant described the human mind engaging in "pure and practical reason" when it makes "determinant judgments" in understandable, linear ways. He described "reflective judgment" as what occurs when the mind "experiences nature imaginatively." Pure and practical reasoning is deductive while reflective judgment is inductive. Pure and practical reasoning *erases* emotions and understands while reflective judgment *assesses* emotions and interprets aesthetically. The sublime leads to aesthetic comprehension. Kant defines the sublime as a "state of mind," which means that it is interpretation that is sublime, not physical objects or things. Robbins proceeds to analyze 1 En. 21.1–10 and 62.1–14, employing Kant's descriptions of the mathematical sublime and the dynamical sublime. The mathematical sublime interprets according to magnitude while the dynamical sublime interprets according to power. First Enoch 21.1–10 presents the mathematical sublime in its sense of immeasurable time and spaces. First Enoch 62.1–14 presents the dynamical sublime of the powerful chosen son of man. Both of these texts evoke sublime terror with the fearsome senses of deep cosmic space-time and the judgment of God. Robbins goes on to consider how the sublime empowers or builds up people by presenting Kant's *Bildungsvermögen*, which Makkreel translates and analyzes as "the formative faculty in the imagination." Robbins points out that Kant's view of the effect of the sublime is what SRI describes as the *rhetorical force* of texts. He considers how the rhetorical force of sublime terror might energize the moral resources of agapeic communities for good in the world. In the end, he wonders how well it will work in self-interested societies.

Harry O. Maier, in "The Sublime Terror of Ignatius of Antioch," takes us to the bizarre horror of the letter of Ignatius to the Romans. Ignatius longs for his own martyrdom, for being attacked, mutilated, and killed by wild beasts in the arena in Rome. He adjures the Christ-believers in Rome not to intervene for him. Maier's analysis of the rhetoric of the letter demonstrates that it is "designed to transport listeners from their everyday experiences to the arena, to invoke in them an experience of sublime terror." This is the sublime force. Ignatius wants his audience in Rome to feel the emotion of his suffering and death, thereby being shocked into silence by the sense of being dragged along with him into the arena to watch and hear the tearing of his flesh and the crushing of his bones. Ignatius is crazy, a madman, pushing people to imagine that such horrid suffering is good and desirable, that the gruesome mutilation and death will bring him to Christ. Maier explains that this strange sublime rhetoric sparks fear but simultaneously agreement. This, of course, is what Ignatius wants, drawing his listeners into silence and awe. The effect is to transport audience members to a terrifying mental location, to bring about the silent ἔκστασις. The sublime produces the silence that prevents the Roman believers from intervening so that Ignatius himself can be a "word of God." Allegiance is to Christ, not to saving Ignatius and avoiding the horrors. Usually expected good judgment is lost. Ignatius looks forward to the pain.

In "Subliming the Sublime: The Bible and the Sublime in Eighteenth-Century Britain," Alan P. R. Gregory takes us on a journey through an era of developed interest in the sublime. The Bible was imagined by eighteenth-century critics to have within it the most sublime of all texts. This led to "an account of how the Bible … worked, how it affected readers in ways that were religiously formative, even salvific." The Bible was imagined to contain the greatest examples of the sublime because it addresses the most sublime object, God. The critics also believed that the Bible employed a range of sublime topoi including terror, which was seen as a powerful motivator for order. Gregory considers how the sublime was accorded religious authority; how it influenced the reading and interpretation of the Bible; how it was connected with notions of biblical authority; and how the sublime affected the popular religious imagination. He discusses the sublime particularly as it was understood by Edward Young, John Dennis, and Edmund Burke. Dennis considered terror to be so "irresistible" that it forces out all other passions and drives people to God. It is such an "invincible force" that it leads to the renovation of minds and hearts. Burke saw terror as one of the "passions that serve 'self-preservation.'" Sublime texts, including those that evoke terror, were argued to be "religiously formative." Gregory suggests that eighteenth-century critics "sublimed the sublime" so as to have salvific power, to have the ability to restore humans to their "paradisal origins." Frightening people with a little horror was viewed as one of the sublime functions. God is known as a fearsome force not to be opposed. This does, as Gregory points out, obscure the complexities of scripture and skews understandings of God, a rhetorical force that continues in the language and thinking of some popular traditions.

The volume closes with Jeal's "Sublime Terror in Context: A Response," a commentary on the articles in part 2. This essay begins by reminding us that terrifying rhetography causes dislocation. The language and imagery of terror touches minds and bodies, transporting them to the emotional realm of fear and anxiety. Terror draws people in—it can move them to feel that they are participants in the terrifying places and pains. Jeal goes on to explain that, in terms of SRI, this is the *rhetorical force* of the sublime terror in texts. Thinking, belief, and behavior are shaped by the dynamics of terror. While the rhetorical force of sublime terror is, ostensibly, meant to move people toward good things, it can be used both to thrill them and to brutalize them into a fearful submission. It can be a friend or an enemy. It closes with consideration of sublime terror texture as one of many "arrangement[s] … of threads" that interweave with others to form "network[s] of meaning and meaning effects" that can be explored and analyzed.

The essays in this volume point toward the approach to interpretation that SRI has in sight. They offer views of a *texture* that is evident in texts and deserves recognition and analysis. To identify and analyze sublime textures is to study and learn about a fascinating aspect of the rhetorical, social, and cognitive nature of texts that reveals much about how they function to influence thinking and behavior. It is an important feature of a full-bodied interpretation. These essays expand the scope of what SRI examines, explores, and discovers. What is clear is that the sublime has what SRI calls *rhetorical force*. The sublime textures are effective. They function, as the essays point out, to transport minds and bodies to trust, to act, and, in most if not all situations, to thrive. While not all of the essays employ SRI explicitly or implicitly, they demonstrate that the sublime has rhetorical, religious, and moral power. There is a modest amount of overlap in discussions of Longinus's *On the Sublime* as a starting point for analysis, but this is not a distraction. Longinus provides an important contextual frame from which to garner ideas and figures and a grasp of the power of elevated, ὕψος language. The essays by Olbricht, Evans, Robbins, and Gregory draw in the deep thinking of others who have described and analyzed the sublime and its effects from the eighteenth to twenty-first centuries. There are differing explanations of the sublime. What is clear is that the sublime affects mind and body in ways not immediately, probably not ever, understood in completely systematic, rational ways.

Perhaps in some ways there is a mystical aspect of the sublime, a kind of illumination. Certainly the texts in our purview imagine, indeed anticipate, unmediated contacts with God, Jesus Christ, the Holy Spirit, angels, and a range of apocalyptic creatures and events. The sublime insists that readers of the texts think about the sacred and the sacred realm. Still, it does not call us to abandon the intellect. It is just that human intellect does not always get it, does not quite know how it works. Some things are known apart from intellectual understanding. Perhaps, for example, the value and force of "speaking to each other in psalms and hymns and spiritual songs, singing and praising in your hearts to the Lord" (Eph 5:19) does not need more rationality than what the sublime notions convey. Humans can become convinced by the actual practice.

Sincere thanks to the contributors for their essays and the scholarly work. Special thanks to Dr. Erika Olbricht, Thomas H. Olbricht's daughter, who kindly worked through her late father's essay and, later, prepared the foreword to this volume. The essays are offered in the hope that readers and interpreters of the texts will notice, study, and analyze the *sublime verses* as a piece of what we do to understand meanings. They are also offered with memories of two rhetoricians, scholars of the Bible and rhetoric who were good friends and supporters: Tom Olbricht and David Hester. Tom and David were persons who loved their work, made major contributions, and loved and cared for their colleagues among whom we may count ourselves. We have learned and inherited much from them and are grateful.[3]

---

3. See now Lauri Thurén, ed., *Rhetoric and Scripture: Collected Essays of Thomas H. Olbricht*, ESEC 23 (Atlanta: SBL Press, 2021).

Part 1

Foundations: The Beautiful Sublime

The Rhetoric of the Sublime in the Narrative of Mary the Mother of Jesus (Luke 1–2)

Roy R. Jeal

Introduction

A foundational notion of sociorhetorical interpretation (SRI) that becomes profoundly clear in the practice of textural analysis, one that seems obvious and that we have always known in some sublime sense, is that you cannot (= must not) reduce anything, certainly not the texts and ideas we work with, to unidimensional explanation. There are multiple textures, and a single text can and must be analyzed in multiple ways. One of these textures is the sublime. It is not privileged above other textures; indeed, it is a subtexture of *sensory-aesthetic texture* (though more sensory than aesthetic), but it does need consideration and careful analysis.[1] This essay aims to describe what the sublime is and how it has what SRI refers to as *rhetorical force*, through an analysis of passages that portray Mary, the mother of Jesus, in the birth narrative of Luke 1–2.

Defining the Sublime

While the sublime, whether in ancient Mediterranean contexts or modern, is regularly defined and described relative to the essay *On the Sublime* (Περὶ "Υψους; *Peri Hypsous*, "Concerning Height"; *De sublimate*), attributed to

---

1. See Thomas H. Olbricht, "Wuellner and the Promise of Rhetoric," in *Rhetorics and Hermeneutics: Wilhelm Wuellner and His Influence*, ed. James D. Hester and J. David Hester, ESEC 9 (London: T&T Clark, 2004), 98: "The effort is not to claim ontological privilege for the sublime, but a certain viable mapping." On sensory-aesthetic texture, see Vernon K. Robbins, *Exploring the Textures of Texts: A Guide to Socio-rhetorical Interpretation* (Valley Forge, PA: Trinity Press International, 1996), 29–36.

someone named Longinus but probably written by another author during the first century CE, it is remarkably difficult to define with precision.[2] It seems to be easier to describe and analyze the rhetorical force of the sublime than to say exactly what it is, to understand the effect without (or before) understanding the mechanism. So it is with many realities. There is no precise *technē* of the sublime.[3] Longinus begins *On the Sublime* by stating that an "author must first define his subject" (*Subl.* 1.1) and that it "consists in a consummate excellence and distinction of language" (*Subl.* 1.3), but the essay offers many descriptive analogies rather than a clear and precise statement of definition.[4] Longinus points out the difficulty, noting that it "is not an easy thing to grasp: judgment in literature is the ultimate fruit of ripe experience" (*Subl.* 6.1). Definition of the sublime is to a significant extent subjective, but it must come out of informed and experienced good judgment (i.e., developed critical skill). It relates to taste and skill developed over much time. It is recognized by minds informed of their cultural milieux. So, to the question, "What is (the) sublime?," the first direct answer is "It depends." Sometimes you get it, and sometimes you don't. Timothy Costelloe, in the context of the sublime in Hegel, writes of it as "the relationship between experience and the attempt to grasp, explain, and express it in philosophical terms."[5] Philip Shaw says that

> sublimity, then, refers to the moment when the ability to apprehend, to know and to express a thought or sensation is defeated. Yet, through this very defeat, the mind gets a feeling for that which lies beyond thought

---

2. Hence frequent references in the literature to the author as Pseudo-Longinus. See Donald Russell, "Introduction," in Longinus, *On the Sublime*, trans. W. H. Fyfe, rev. Donald Russell, LCL (Cambridge: Harvard University Press, 1995), 145–58. All references to and quotations from *On the Sublime* are from the LCL edition.

3. J. David Hester, "The Wuellnerian Sublime: Rhetorics, Power, and the Ethics of Commun(icat)ion," in Hester and Hester, *Rhetorics and Hermeneutics*, 20.

4. See James I. Porter, *The Sublime in Antiquity* (Cambridge: Cambridge University Press, 2016), xxi.

5. Timothy M. Costelloe, "The Sublime: A Short Introduction to a Long History," in *The Sublime From Antiquity to the Present*, ed. Timothy M. Costelloe (Cambridge: Cambridge University Press, 2012), 1. Costelloe provides helpful etymological descriptions of "sublime" (from Latin *sublimis*: "high up; aloft; elevated; exalted; illustrious; eminent; those of noble or heroic character") (2–3). For a detailed history of the sublime, see the monumental work of Porter, *Sublime in Antiquity*. See also Gary S. Selby, *Not with Wisdom of Words: Nonrational Persuasion in the New Testament* (Grand Rapids: Eerdmans, 2015).

and language. At this point the person experiencing the sublime undergoes a strange transformation.⁶

Significantly, Shaw claims here that sublimity is a *moment* rather than a material or literary thing. This points to the experiential nature of the sublime and suggests that sublime language is rhetorical language that moves people toward a level of understanding. Some modern scholars suggest that study of the sublime is no longer useful, that the sublime is dead, while others question whether a clear theory of the sublime is possible and conclude that it is not.⁷

But there unquestionably *is* a sublime, the moment or consciousness that resists rationalized understanding (though is not wholly impervious to it), for our purposes in language and in texts, when words of grandeur elicit notions, senses, and emotions that are unmistakably exceptional, astonishing, possibly shocking and terrifying, pleasing, even intellectually, morally, and religiously transformational. The words themselves are sublime. Sublime words can produce what classicist James I. Porter refers to as profound mental or spiritual disruption and are "at the limits of the humanly conceivable" and what poet and critic Ezra Pound imagined as "a flash of understanding" and "an affective psychological event."⁸ The sublime can elicit a "disposition of mind" that moves people to be amenable to, indeed to be fully convinced about, beliefs and behaviors. Sublime language is the language of grandeur that "points beyond itself," that transports and produces ecstasy.⁹ "Sublime rhetoric creates," according to Porter, "the verbal equivalent of an illusion of height and depth, a *trompe l'oeil*."¹⁰ The sub-

---

6. Philip Shaw, *The Sublime*, 2nd ed. (London: Routledge, 2017), 3–4.
7. On the sublime as dead, see Costelloe, "Sublime," 1, 7. For whether a theory of the sublime is possible, see esp. Jane Forsey, "Is a Theory of the Sublime Possible?," in *The Possibility of the Sublime*, ed. Lars Aagaard-Mogenson (Cambridge: Cambridge Scholars Press, 2017), along with other essays in the volume that argue in favor of a theory of the sublime.
8. Porter, *Sublime in Antiquity*, 5, 6. On Pound, see Marianne Korn, *Ezra Pound: Purpose, Form, Meaning* (London: Pembridge, 1983), 78. It seems clear from reading Pound's remarks in *How to Read* (New York: Haskell House, 1971) that he was very familiar with Longinus. It is made explicit in his poem "Invern."
9. Porter, *Sublime in Antiquity*, 5. By ecstasy I mean a sense of joy, of elation.
10. Porter, *Sublime in Antiquity*, 91. *Trompe l'oeil*, a "trick of the eye," is a two-dimensional painting that creates the illusion of a three-dimensional object. Except that in the case of the sublime the effect is not an illusion but a reality.

lime "is a quality which amazes and astonishes rather than persuades in ordinary, gentle ways."[11] The sublime seizes the imagination, not with propositional information, but with the metaphor of language. The intention is to bring about a kind of metamorphosis, a transformation of understanding, hence of living (cf. *Subl.* 1.1). The effect of the sublime is what S. T. Coleridge called "a vague appetency," a longing, desire, or tendency toward an exceptional understanding that "humans can only apprehend but not comprehend."[12]

Longinus claims there are "five most productive sources of the sublime in literature": the power of grand perceptions; the inspiration of vehement emotion; proper construction of figures; nobility of language; and dignified and elevated word arrangement (*Subl.* 8.1). He goes on to describe each source. These sources or structures are rhetorical features familiar to ancient and modern rhetoricians.[13] In his study of the sublime in Greco-Roman antiquity, Porter offers a typology of markers of the sublime gathered from Longinus in order to show a logical structure of the sublime.[14] The typology indicates "an underlying logic … that is composed of extremes, contrasts, intensities, and incommensurabilities, of transgressed limits, excesses, collisions, and structures on the edge of collapse or ruin…. The sublime is not so much found in these sorts of causes as it is *provoked* by them."[15] This all demonstrates that the sublime is fundamentally rhetorical, anticipating human conceptual and ethical

---

11. Donald Russell, "Greek Criticism of the Empire," in vol. 1 of *The Cambridge History of Literary Criticism: Classical Criticism*, ed. George Kennedy (Cambridge: Cambridge University Press, 1989), 307.

12. "A vague appetency" is discussed in Murray J. Evans, *Sublime Coleridge: The "Opus Maximum"* (New York: Palgrave Macmillan, 2012), xiv et passim. Second quotation from Evans, *Sublime Coleridge*, 57. It would be better, certainly now, to use the word *prehend* rather than *apprehend*. Prehension more closely suggests perception but not necessarily cognition. The sublime is prehended *before* attempts are made at working it out rationally and logically. It is qualitative reasoning that aims to persuade audiences that a portrayal is real, rather being directly and logically argumentative. In music, a term that describes the sublime is *jubilus*, which refers to a melody or group of melodic tones that indicate great joy. It indicates something that the heart grasps joyfully, in *jubilation*, but cannot put into words. On this see the commentary of Augustine on Ps 32. I thank Professor Karen Jensen for this information.

13. As Porter points out, the sublime was well-known in Mediterranean antiquity and Longinus was a witness to it rather than an innovator (*Sublime in Antiquity*, 618).

14. See the typology in Porter, *Sublime in Antiquity*, 51–54.

15. Porter, *Sublime in Antiquity*, 53, emphasis original.

outcomes. Another way of saying this is that the sublime (as a cultural phenomenon) cultivates the human spirit.

In New Testament studies, interest in the sublime was discussed and promoted by the late Wilhelm Wuellner (d. 2004).[16] Wuellner's ideas, or at least some of them, are a little discomfiting for biblical scholars—or for some of them. He is himself "opaque" and "elusive" in his promotion of consideration of the subtle and difficult sublime.[17] For Wuellner, there was more to rhetoric and rhetorical interpretations than considering rhetorical theory and method or of speaking artistically, persuasively and movingly.[18] He was interested in what he called "a certain spiritual component … equated with the sublime."[19] To have this interest, he believed, is to be more human. Loss of concern for sublime things meant, for Wuellner, "the erosion, if not the downright eclipse, of the full scope of human consciousness."[20] On the other hand, he believed the sublime as *grandeur* inspires wonder and transformation in humans and that this is the rhetoric of power in the sublime.[21] Wuellner refers to rhetorician Kenneth Burke's descriptions of "the goadings of mystery" and "the radiance of the divine" as crucial notions.[22] Wuellner reacted to a unidimensional exegesis. He was concerned that biblical scholarship and rhetorical interpretation of the New Testament not devolve to being a mere commodity. Interpretation should not be just what we *do* but who we *are*.

The Rhetoric of the Sublime: A Rhetoric of the Moment

So the sublime is inherently rhetorical because it aims and is designed to be persuasive, to have effects on people. But it is not a systematic rheto-

---

16. For our purposes here, see esp. Wuellner, "Reconceiving a Rhetoric of Religion: A Rhetoric of Power as the Power of the Sublime," in Hester and Hester, *Rhetorics and Hermeneutics*, 23–77. For recent work, see Christopher T. Holmes, *The Function of Sublime Rhetoric in Hebrews: A Study in Hebrews 12:18–29*, WUNT 2/465 (Tübingen: Mohr Siebeck, 2018).

17. These descriptive terms from Olbricht, "Wuellner and the Promise of Rhetoric," 103.

18. Wuellner, "Reconceiving a Rhetoric of Religion," 26–27.

19. Wuellner, "Reconceiving a Rhetoric of Religion," 28.

20. Wuellner, "Reconceiving a Rhetoric of Religion," 33.

21. E.g., in Wuellner, "Reconceiving a Rhetoric of Religion," 41–42.

22. Wuellner, "Reconceiving a Rhetoric of Religion," 53. Wuellner is careful to note that for Burke this is not the same as mysticism.

ric of persuasion as it is usually imagined according to the Aristotelian tradition. It is what may be called "a rhetoric of the moment."[23] It is not a rhetoric where listeners or readers have a level of control over being persuaded, where they move forward (or are moved forward) knowingly, where arguments are recognized and understood, where there is a high level of mental analysis and comprehension during significant length of time while listening or reading. The rhetoric of the sublime is sudden, momentary, where listeners are transported outside of themselves (ἔκστασις):

> I almost feel freed from the need of a lengthy preface showing how the sublime consists in a consummate excellence and distinction of language, and that this alone gave the greatest poets and prose writers their preeminence and clothed them in immortal fame. For the effect of genius is not to persuade the audience but to transport them out of themselves [ἀλλ' εἰς ἔκστασιν ἄγει τὰ ὑπερφυᾶ].[24] Invariably what inspires wonder, with its power of amazing us, always prevails over what is merely convincing and pleasing. For our persuasions are usually under our own control, while these things exercise an irresistible power and mastery and get the better of every listener. Again, experience in invention and the due disposal and marshalling of facts do not show themselves in one or two touches but emerge gradually from the whole tissue of the composition, while, on the other hand, a well-timed flash of sublimity shatters everything like a bolt of lightning and reveals the full power of the speaker at a single stroke. (*Subl.* 1.3–4)

It is a rhetoric of καιρός, not of χρόνος. Longinus describes the sublime as the immediate effect of pieces of grand language, not as the persuasive process of argumentation (see also *Subl.* 12.4; 15.9; 17.2).[25]

---

23. Cf. these lines from the novel by Anthony Doerr, *All the Light We Cannot See* (New York: Scribner, 2014), 245: "Sublimity.... It's the instant when one thing is about to become something else. Day to night, caterpillar to butterfly. Fawn to doe. Experiment to result. Boy to man."

24. τὰ ὑπερφυᾶ is neuter plural of ὑπερφυής, "overgrown, enormous, monstrous, marvelous, extraordinary." A reasonable translation here is "but the extraordinary things lead to ecstasy."

25. Porter, *Sublime in Antiquity*, 611–17. Porter however, notes that sometimes the moment is planned, designed by speaker or author in advance. While sublime language has immediate effects, it is not necessarily itself *ex tempore* (611).

Porter lists terms, "a veritable lexicon of the sublime," in addition to ὕψους that Longinus uses to describe the sublime and that help indicate the range of rhetorical possibilities.[26] Aristotle had already spoken of the emotional effects of language on audiences (*Rhet.* 1.2.3) and of the beauty of words in persuasion:

> Metaphors should also be derived from things that are beautiful, the beauty of a word consisting, as Licymnius says, in its sound or sense, and its ugliness in the same.... Metaphors therefore should be derived from what is beautiful either in sound, or signification, or to sight, or to some other sense. (*Rhet.* 3.2.13 [Freese, LCL])

So the words and the idea of the sublime were not new with Longinus. Humans have virtually always been skillful and experienced at, even if not conscious of, prehending sublime material realia, stimuli of various kinds, and immaterial things, ideas, and data that they do not understand and cannot clearly describe. They are regularly moved, even psychologically transported, by such prehensions.

The rhetoric of the moment begins with the material.[27] It works from memory of things of the material (created) realm even as it draws the mind, the passions, and the body to the sublime planes of the emotions and the divine. Its interest, though, is not to deny the material, sensory realm, but, as Porter points out, "it is *an excess that is immanent* to some local texture of language or reality."[28] The sublime aims to speak at the recognizable limits of the material, to stretch the edges, to look just over the horizon but not past the material realm toward "a more morally informed, higher, and godly mission."[29] The goals of the sublime are pragmatic or, in SRI terms, *wisdom* goals. Longinus seems to be interested in employing sublime language that benefits audiences by helping them to be better people.[30]

The effect of sublime rhetoric is like the remarkable phenomena described by psychologists Daniel Kahneman and Gerd Gigerenzer. Kahneman describes how words can elicit responses that occur "quickly,

---

26. Among these words formed from ὕψος-, μέγ-, δεῖν-, ὑπέρ-, ἐκ-, ὄγκ- (Porter, *Sublime in Antiquity*, 180–82).
27. Porter, *Sublime in Antiquity*, 391.
28. Porter, *Sublime in Antiquity*, 614, emphasis original.
29. Porter, *Sublime in Antiquity*, 615. See Longinus, *Subl.* 35.3; 36.2; 44.8.
30. On this, see Porter (*Sublime in Antiquity*, 616–17) on Longinus's opening and closing usage of ὠφέλεια, "assistance, benefit, advantage."

automatically and effortlessly" causing remarkable brain activity as it attempts to make sense of things, leading to a high level of understanding.[31] Gigerenzer describes how humans make inferences and decisions based on minimal information using rules of thumb that they are able to follow from experience rather than complete knowledge.[32] The point is that the rhetoric of the moment, the grandeur of the sublime, is effective. The sublime moves people to accept and believe in many things and to behave accordingly. Texts can communicate beyond themselves.[33]

Mary's Moments

1. Annunciation, Luke 1:26–38

Rhetography

Luke makes the encounter between the angel Gabriel and Mary visible in the mental/visual imagination. Longinus recommends this in *Subl.* 15:

> Weight, grandeur, and urgency in writing are very largely produced … by the use of "visualizations" (*phantasiai*).… Others call them "image productions" [εἰδωλοποιΐα]. For the word phantasia is applied in general to an idea which enters the mind from any source and engenders speech, but the word has now come to be used predominantly of passages where, inspired by strong emotion, you seem to see what you describe and bring

---

31. Daniel Kahneman, *Thinking Fast and Slow* (New York: Farrar, Strauss & Giroux, 2011), 51.

32. Gerd Gigerenzer, *Gut Feelings: The Intelligence of the Unconscious* (London: Penguin, 2008) and many other publications. See http://tinyurl.com/SBL4831e. Gigerenzer is a critic of Kahneman's views. See Roy R. Jeal, "Visual Interpretation: Blending Rhetorical Arts in Colossians 2:6–3:4," in *The Art of Visual Exegesis: Rhetoric, Texts, Images*, ed. Vernon K. Robbins, Walter S. Melion, and Roy R. Jeal, ESEC 19 (Atlanta: SBL Press, 2017), 70–71. I thank my colleague Evan Curtis for pointing me to Gigerenzer.

33. Harry Maier points out that "*Enargeia* invites listeners to fill in details prompted by vivid description" (Harry O. Maier, "Paul, Imperial Situation, and Visualization in the Epistle to the Colossians," in *The Art of Visual Exegesis: Rhetoric, Texts, Images*, ed. Vernon K. Robbins, Walter S. Melion, and Roy R. Jeal, ESEC 19 (Atlanta: SBL Press, 2017), 177. Things are subliminally absorbed. Cf. the effects of much commercial advertising. *Enargeia* is vivid language that invites listeners to complete the details of images not mentioned in narrations (Maier, 177–78).

it vividly before the eyes of your audience.... The object of the poetical form of it is to enthrall, and that of the prose form to present things vividly, though both indeed aim at the emotional and the excited. (*Subl.* 15.1–2)[34]

The "most perfect effect of visualization [φαντασία] in oratory is always one of reality and truth" (*Subl.* 15.8). Longinus comments on the effect of visualization:

What then is the use of visualization in oratory? It may be said generally to introduce a great deal of excitement and emotion into one's speeches, but when combined with factual arguments it not only convinces the audience, it positively masters [δουλοῦται, "enslaves"] them. (*Subl.* 15.9)

The rhetograph portrays the angel/messenger Gabriel, who evidently looks like a human and has a human voice (cf. Dan 8:15–17; 9:20–22), appearing in Nazareth of Galilee to the young woman, Mary, who is promised in marriage to a man named Joseph of the house of David and designated a virgin.[35] The geographical scene in Galilee is far from the presumed holy and sublime center of priestly activity and power in the temple of Jerusalem in a virtually unknown and certainly unimportant village. Mary is visualized as a girl of perhaps twelve or thirteen years, who, while properly (socially and bindingly) promised to Joseph, does not yet live with him and who is quite aware that she does "not know a man" (or husband; ἐπεὶ ἄνδρα οὐ γινώσκω, 1:34), idiomatically meaning she has never engaged in sexual intercourse. She is pretty clearly seen as a pubescent though knowledgeable young woman. Gabriel greets Mary with the sound of effusive joy—"Rejoice, favored one! The Lord (is) with you."[36] To this sublime appearance and greeting Mary is observed to be perplexed and confused (διεταράσσομαι), and she reasons (διαλογίζομαι) about the kind of greeting this might be. Mary's confusion is not immediately removed by Gabriel's pluriform statement about God's

---

34. For explanation, see Jeal, "Visual Interpretation," 59–61.
35. In Dan 9:21 the angel/messenger is called a male.
36. Alliteratively Χαῖρε, κεχαριτωμένη. The translation "Rejoice" is admittedly debatable. Most interpreters and translations render the imperative verb χαῖρε as "Greetings" or, more archaically, "Hail." But it can be intended to evoke joy ("Rejoice!" or "Be joyful!"). See John Nolland, *Luke 1–9:20*, WBC 35A (Dallas: Word, 1989), 49; Joel B. Green, *The Gospel of Luke*, NICNT (Grand Rapids: Eerdmans, 1997), 86. Scripture translations are mine except where noted.

favor: that she will conceive and bear a son to be named Jesus who will be remarkably important and who will reign on the throne of King David over an unending kingdom.³⁷ So she is portrayed asking, logically, even for a young girl, how this is possible since she is a virgin (1:34). While what Mary has heard seems incomprehensible and whatever it may mean, the language envisions an elevated, grand, indeed astonishing coming pregnancy of a peasant girl who has God's favor and an as yet unborn child who will be given a name meaning "God saves" and is already visualized as someone tremendously great (οὗτος ἔσται μέγας καὶ υἱὸς ὑψίστου κληθήσεται, 1:32). Mary will not become pregnant in the ordinary way but is told that the Holy Spirit will come upon her, that the power of the Most High will overshadow her, and that the holy child will be called the son of God (1:35). Mary's question to the angel is not answered directly or in a directly comprehensible human way, but with the sublime promise of sublime events and situations. The Holy Spirit is not envisioned as taking the place of a male impregnating Mary but engages in the action of sublime creativity.³⁸ Audiences (Theophilus and others including ourselves) prehend but do not comprehend all this in any kind of systematically rational way. Mary, for her part, hears Gabriel's subtle, elusive, but for her convincing argument, that her much older relative Elizabeth has conceived a son (1:36) and that "nothing is impossible with God" (lit. "because no word from God will be impossible," 1:37). The sublime suggestion seems to be that if old Elizabeth can have a baby, then virginal Mary can have one too. Mary is a believer. Upon her very quick conviction, she declares herself "the slave of the Lord" (ἰδοὺ ἡ δούλη κυρίου) with her complete acceptance of Gabriel's words.

Sublime Texture

The scene is sublime from the outset. Although there are a number of encounters between angels and humans presented in the Bible, they are

---

37. Some have called Mary's confusion a "wordless question." See Nolland, *Luke 1–9:20*, 51.

38. What Raymond E. Brown refers to as "the surprise of creation" (*The Birth of the Messiah: A Commentary on the Infancy Narratives in Matthew and Luke*, ABRL [New York: Doubleday, 1993], 314). See also Vernon K. Robbins, "Sociorhetorical Criticism: Mary, Elizabeth, and the Magnificat as a Test Case," in *Foundations for Sociorhetorical Exploration: A Rhetoric of Religious Antiquity Reader*, ed. Vernon K. Robbins, Robert H. von Thaden Jr., and Bart B. Bruehler, RRA 4 (Atlanta: SBL Press, 2016), 51.

still exceptional and grand incidents experienced by only a few persons. Such encounters typically speak to a situation of the moment and are grasped quickly, in a rhetorical moment, even if they have lasting and dramatic effects. Gabriel is an apocalyptic messenger who sets up the sublime scene and message by revealing information to Mary that she could not otherwise have known or even imagined, as both her confusion and recognition of the obstacle of virginity make clear.[39] Then, in what seems like only minutes, Gabriel departs (1:38b). What is quite clear is that God is acting, via the angel, the encounter with Mary, and the conception of the child in her virginal womb, to bring about an amazing and utterly exceptional, astounding series of events that are *meant* to have what would normally be thought to be impossible outcomes. The cause of the sublime events and circumstances is found in God.[40] The narrative is in the tradition of the sublime events of Israel indicated in the Hebrew Bible: Sarah, Samson's mother, Hannah, and now of Elizabeth and Mary.[41] Barrenness and virginity are not obstacles to the power of God. The Holy Spirit will come upon Mary and the power of the *Most High* will overshadow her (1:35). The news that her relative Elizabeth is also miraculously pregnant drives the sublimity of the ideas home for Mary.[42] It must all be true. What is meant to move audiences from Theophilus onward is this intersection of the divine and the human. God is at work. So, a major feature of the sublime texturing is the sensory-aesthetic apprehension of the scene and the effects it aims to have on people. You do not talk with and accept the word of an angel every day, nor do you read (or listen to) narratives about such encounters that are presented in order to know with certainty the words that have been heard about the gospel (Luke 1:4).

According to Longinus, the sublime is about admiring genuine greatness, not deceptive forms of false greatness indicated by mere external appearances (*Subl.* 7.1).[43] The sublime is not about noise and bombast.

---

39. That Gabriel sets it up is to say Luke sets it up.
40. See Green, *Gospel of Luke*, 84–85; Nolland, *Luke 1–9:20*, 40, 49. Robbins, "Sociorhetorical Criticism," 42.
41. Cf. later stories such as the narrative about Anna and the annunciation of Mary (which clearly draws on Luke) in the Protevangelium of James.
42. See Green, *Gospel of Luke*, 91. This is not a logical, empirical argument, but works on the partially parallel situation of Elizabeth.
43. He refers to wealth, position, reputation, sovereignty as being only a "grand exterior" (7.1).

Rather than outward shows of grandeur, genuine sublime elevates the lowly and "naturally elevates us: uplifted with a sense of proud exaltation, we are filled with joy and pride, as if we had ourselves produced the very thing we heard" (*Subl.* 7.2). Mary is described as being favored by God, as the very young Galilean peasant woman who will bear the son of the Most High. The narrative is about a quiet, apocalyptic encounter between an angel and a woman. It is an incident unexpected by Mary or, in any kind of usual circumstances, by anyone at all. It is the kind of sublime event that, according to Longinus, should be repeated as Luke apparently does because "what is truly great bears repeated consideration: it is difficult, nay, impossible, to resist its effect; and the memory of it is stubborn and indelible" (*Subl.* 7.3).[44] It draws readers and listeners into Mary's story and the story of Jesus. Christ-believers retell it year-by-year, and scholars continue to study it.

Argumentative Texture

Is there an articulated argument clearly understood by Mary or by audiences of the annunciation narrative? There are certainly explanations that are meant to address Mary's confusion regarding her encounter with Gabriel. The angel encouraged Mary not to fear (Μὴ φοβοῦ, 1:30)—so Luke suggests her fear was evident—but her question, "How can this be, since I do not know a man?" opens the way for an argumentative rationale. At best, however, the argument is indirect and implicit. There are allusions but no direct argumentative connections made to Jewish or Hellenistic texts or cultural knowledge.[45] The answer to "How can this be?" is "Nothing is impossible with God." In other words, it can be so because God says so ("because no word from God will be impossible," 1:37). The angel tells Mary "the Lord is with you" (1:28), already suggesting but not explicating the sublime point that the message and the eventualities have the ultimate sublime source and causation. This kind of argumentation draws on Mary's and audiences' religious assumptions, understandings, and expectations. Luke does present Gabriel saying that the virgin girl Mary will

---

44. "To speak generally, you should consider that to be beautifully and truly sublime which pleases all people at all times" (*Subl.* 7.4).

45. See Nolland, *Luke 1–9:20*, 44–46. There are accounts in ancient Mediterranean literature of gods impregnating virgins. Theophilus might have known of them. See Robbins, "Sociorhetorical Criticism," 49–50.

conceive a son who will be great and a powerful ruler. All will come about by the Holy Spirit and the power of the Most High, language apparently grasped by Mary and presumably by Theophilus. But rather than explicit, rational argumentation, Mary, as she is described, seems moved by that vague appetency, that is, the tendency toward what she prehends about what she is told, rather than by full comprehension of it. In the narrative as we have it, she, along with many audiences of Luke ever since, was moved by the sublime effects of the language.

Rhetorical Force

There is nothing exactly like this elsewhere in biblical narration. Matthew's version of the birth events does not include the annunciation scene. It is presented as a real description of events, without argumentative proofs, to impress the mind with the intersection of the human and the divine in Mary's body. The entire scene exalts Mary and announces that she is raised up as the woman favored by God from poverty and abjection to bear the one who saves. The obscure girl willingly accepts what is to be done to her along with its responsibilities, indeed referring to herself straightforwardly as the slave of the Lord. Its sublime language exalts Mary. It is not about the glory of the powerful and wealthy, but about the sublime work of the Most High (ὕψιστος, 1:32) who uses weak things and seemingly weak people for good. The effect—and here we come to close recognition of the sublime—is difficult to resist. Audiences are moved to acceptance of the scene and its ideas. The ideas are perceived as realities.

The rhetorical force is in the striking, emotional, astonishing, pictorial presentation, not in rational argumentation. It reasons experientially, presenting Mary's experience with Gabriel, her confusion, and her conviction that things will happen as the angel has stated. The effect is to draw Theophilus and other audiences into the symbolic world of the annunciation scene, to see it and hear it as it moves along (φαντασία; εἰδωλοποιΐα). Theophilus has been told that he is being presented with "the truth concerning the things about which [he has] been instructed" (1:4) and what he is given is an astounding story of things on the edge of possibility. He and engaged audiences, although they might respond with a bewildered "What?," are invited in their imaginations to identify with the sublime situation, thus making it meaningful to them. They are drawn into an established realm of belief so that they do not think yet of things apart from what has been described. The sublime itself takes control and the tendency is to accept it uncritically.⁴⁶ Like Mary, audiences take on what is narrated as true, "according to your word" (γένοιτό μοι κατὰ τὸ ῥῆμά σου).

2. Mary, Elizabeth, and the Magnificat: Sublime Recognition and Praise, Luke 1:39–56

Rhetography

Mary is here visualized getting up and rushing off from Nazareth in Galilee to a southern Judean town where she enters the house of Zechariah and greets Elizabeth.⁴⁷ The greeting establishes visual and audible connections directly between Mary and Elizabeth. They interact without the presence of a male, though their sons may be imagined in fetal form. As the sound of Mary's greeting meets Elizabeth's ears, her baby leaps in her womb. There is a kind of direct body-to-body physicality between Mary (she voices a greeting) and Elizabeth (she hears the greeting and experiences fetal movement). This physicality has deep sublime force in the way it suggests a connection among women and fetus that is meant to be prehended to have a direct link to features of the narration. The body-to-body connection may be attributed to the sublime action of the Holy Spirit who fills Elizabeth resulting in her great cry (καὶ ἀνεφώνησεν κραυγῇ μεγάλῃ, 1:42):

> Blessed are you among women, and blessed is the fruit of your womb. And why has this happened to me, that the mother of my Lord comes to me? For as soon as I heard the sound of your greeting, the child in my womb leaped for joy. And blessed is she who believed that there would be a fulfillment of what was spoken to her by the Lord. (1:42–45 NRSV)

Elizabeth could scarcely know that Mary was coming nor could she expect that such a young, virginal relative could be pregnant, nor could she have knowledge of who Mary's child was to be or of what had been spoken by the Lord. Yet she does know and so does her baby! Their sudden and astounding response to Mary's arrival and voice is revelatory. It is also rhetorically astounding to Luke's audiences, drawing them further into the story.

---

46. See again *Subl.* 7.2 and 15.9, quoted above.
47. Likely near Jerusalem, more than one hundred kilometers from Nazareth. See Green, *Gospel of Luke*, 94–95. The house is explicitly Zechariah's.

In a not dissimilar way, though Luke presents it rather matter-of-factly ("And Mary said," 1:46), Mary is heard to break out in her dramatic poem of praise about what is occurring. She is seen here in a proclamatory, prophetic space and role.[48] She exults (Μεγαλύνει ἡ ψυχή μου, 1:46) in praise and joy in God. She voices two reasons for her joy in ὅτι statements that imagine actions performed by God: "because" God "has looked with favor on the humiliation of his slave" (δούλη, 1:48) and "because the Mighty One has done great things for me" (1:49). Luke portrays Mary proclaiming the powerful actions of God in a range of verbs that demonstrate both mercy and judgment. She addresses how she will be viewed in the future ("from now on all generations will call me blessed," 1:48) and closes her prophetic word by recalling and emphasizing that God remembers his promises to her Israelite ancestors (1:55).

Sublime Texture

This pericope presents sublime, exceptional notions throughout. It would be very unlikely and socially questionable for a betrothed girl of Mary's age to travel off quickly unaccompanied, even if headed for the home of a relative. While Luke does not say she traveled alone or without permission, presumably from her father, the journey is, implicitly, completely Mary's initiative. This exceptional situation opens the passage and sets the scene for ongoing and intensifying sublimity. The sensory, somatic effects of Mary's greeting to Elizabeth are very dramatic and suggestive. Both Elizabeth and her fetus are imagined to be conscious of Mary and of the fact of her pregnancy, that the child she will bear will be great—indeed referred to as "my Lord" (1:43)—and that Mary believes that what was spoken to her by the angel was from the Lord (God) and that it would be fulfilled (1:45). This is altogether astonishing.

Mary's poem praises and rejoices in God seemingly because she herself is astounded at the sublime situation. She sees herself as a humiliated, lowly, probably impoverished slave of God who is raised to the height above any possible expectation or thought.[49] She is to be remembered and called blessed (μακαρίζω, 1:48). Everything is attributed to God, a point that audiences are not to miss. That a young Galilean girl would break out

---

48. Prophetic discourse/religious texture (rhetorolect).
49. On Mary as humiliated, see Robbins, "Sociorhetorical Criticism," 54.

in or plan such profound poetry, even if heard personally, runs against what could be imagined.⁵⁰ The scene and the language are completely sublime. The sublime Mary stays on with Elizabeth for three months, implicitly, once again, at her own initiative and also implicitly until just before Elizabeth's child is born.

This texturing again points to the intersection of the human and the divine. It draws audiences more deeply into the visualization of sights and sounds of the encounter between Mary and Elizabeth. Sublimity touches both women. They have insider knowledge that has not come to them in usual human, cognitive, or experiential ways. Elizabeth is described as crying out because she is filled with the Holy Spirit (1:41). She, like, Mary, inhabits a prophetic space and has a prophetic voice. The women in bodily form are mentally, cognitively, and emotionally transported outside of themselves into the realm of the sacred. Audiences are to imagine this as true and as imparting truth.

Argumentative Texture

Except for two ὅτι statements (1:48 and 49) and a καθώς clause (1:55), there is no explicit argumentation in this section. The force of the narrative is made almost entirely implicitly.⁵¹ Mary rejoices, explicitly, "because [God] has looked with favor on the humiliation of his slave" (1:48) and anticipates that future generations will see her as a blessed one "because the mighty one has done great things" for her (1:49). God's actions are certain "just as he spoke to our fathers" (1:55). Apart from this, audiences are meant to conclude certain things by, at best, enthymematic argumentation rather than explicated rationales. Elizabeth speaks what she knows, being filled with the Holy Spirit. The child leaps in her womb presumably also by the filling of the Holy Spirit in Elizabeth's body. Mary responds with the poetry of the Magnificat indicating that she knows what is occurring, recognizes the power and promises of God, knows that God reduces the powerful from their exalted positions, raises up the humble, and keeps

---

50. Redaction and historical critics, along with us, attribute exact speech to Luke rather than to the speaker named.

51. For an extended discussion of argumentation see Robbins (with consideration of the work of Lucy A. Rose), "Sociorhetorical Criticism," 45–47. Longinus does not address logical argumentation as such but is concerned largely with stylistic matters.

his promises. This remarkable language and thought reverses cultural and hierarchal understandings that Mary herself personifies.[52] Mary is a full participant in the promises to Israel, of nation-making, and will not be barren like Elizabeth had been for a long time. The blessed fruit of her womb indicates that the barren and humiliating times are about to end. This knowledge, though, is not received in usual human ways. God is at work in the bodies and cognitive senses of Mary and Elizabeth (and her fetus). Consideration of argumentation succumbs to a *somatic knowledge* that belies rationality in an older, formerly barren woman, in a very young, inexperienced Galilean girl, and in audiences listening to the narration. Rather than argumentation there is an implicit cultural understanding that is not spelled out. Theophilus is expected to grasp the sublime truth regarding the things he has heard.

Rhetorical Force

The astonishing nature of the narrative continues intensely in this section. The rhetoric moves Theophilus and extended audiences deeper into the envisioned storyline. Understandings of Mary, Elizabeth, and the unborn children are intensified by humanly unlikely events and words. The bodily (somatic) sublime strikes audiences as the women are transported outside of ordinary human experiences and expectations to things that give them joy, amazement, a forward-looking understanding of the work of God, and words to express it. Their intense emotional levels may be felt bodily and sensorily by listeners and readers who are drawn into understanding apart from rational analysis. The effect is to move people to deepened acceptance in rather full bodily ways of what they already believe, namely, that "the events that have been fulfilled among us" (1:1) are prehended to be truth and worth trusting. The power driving the rhetorical force of the language is the power of the Holy Spirit and God. Things have been and will be done by God, indicated in a series of third-person singular verbs and some pronouns. Then it all ends straightforwardly but still surprisingly by stating that Mary returned home after remaining with Elizabeth for about three months. All these sublime things occur without the presence of a male figure.

---

52. See Robbins, "Sociorhetorical Criticism," 64.

3. The Visit of the Shepherds, Luke 2:15–20

Rhetography

These verses display a continuation of the scene that begins in 2:8–9 following the birth of Mary's child. Shepherds, at night, are watching over their flocks. Like what has been observed previously, an angel appears (lit. "stood over them"), and the glory of the Lord shines around them. The shepherds are terrified, apparently unlike Mary, unable, at least initially, to grasp what is occurring when an angel appears. The upshot of this sublime encounter is that the shepherds decide to move quickly and find Mary, Joseph, and the newborn (2:15–16). We clearly observe them telling other people what they have been told and what they have witnessed about the child (2:17). The result of what the shepherds report is amazement (ἐθαύμασαν, "they are amazed, astonished," 2:18). The scene immediately shifts from the reporting shepherds and persons who are amazed back once again to focus directly on Mary, to her moment and her response. Nothing is mentioned (once again) about Joseph who remains a tangential, though still noted, figure. "But Mary preserved [lit. was keeping together] all these words, considering them [lit. throwing them together] in her heart" (2:19).[53] Unlike the others, she is not visibly amazed. Mary is visualized in a cognitive mode, quietly ruminating over "the utterances" (τὰ ῥήματα) she has heard from the shepherds. She already knows things about what is occurring and she seeks deeper understanding. The shepherds, for their part, are seen returning to their flocks, glorifying and praising God. They, unlikely as it may seem, have grasped something of the nature and glory of the events.

Sublime Texture

Everything is sublime, lofty here. Nothing is ordinary. An angel appears and speaks to terrified shepherds in the field. The angel announces that a "savior, who is the Messiah, the Lord" has been born (2:11). This Savior-Messiah-Lord arrives not as a powerful man but as a baby. The shepherds rush off to see about what they had been told and in turn they tell others

---

53. ἡ δὲ Μαριὰμ πάντα συνετήρει τὰ ῥήματα ταῦτα συμβάλλουσα ἐν τῇ καρδίᾳ αὐτῆς. Note that the verbal forms are συν- compounds.

in the area who are astonished at what they hear. Mary, in contrast, is not so amazed. She, the knowledgeable and believing, accepting girl, is exceptionally quiet, thinking things over. The unlikely shepherds return to their flocks, worshiping as they go along. All of this speaks to a sublime, indeed holy, encounter. Everything is exceptional, unexpected to the point of arousing terror in the shepherds and amazement among others. It transports people outside of themselves (ἔκστασις) and elicits worship. Mary is the sublime exception, though her lack of astonishment is itself astonishing. She has engaged in praise language previously but does not do so here. Her knowledge of divine encounter evokes careful thinking about what is going on. She is herself sublime, calm, seeking understanding while others are amazed.

Argumentative Texture

There is no explicated argument in this pericope, only a narration of events that has argumentative implications. The argument is entirely implicit, left for audiences to grasp rather than comprehend consciously. The implied argument functions on the reality of the newborn child. The angel announces it, resulting in the shepherds' visit, people's amazement, and the shepherds' praise of God. The implied rationale is that the child is Savior-Messiah-Lord. Mary's moment stands in contrast to the implied argument. This makes her stand out as the sublime, quiet, concentrated character.

Rhetorical Force

The rhetoric of these verses emphasizes the exceptional nature of the truth Theophilus is meant to grasp. Mary continues to be the young woman who accepts the task given to her by God. Her individual interior responses are recognized but not explained. No other human receives this level of recognition. She is not described as bewildered but appears to have a depth of understanding. The effect is to continue to draw audiences into the narration and to make Mary stand out as particularly important, perhaps as a model for how Theophilus and other audience members should behave. There is a sublime and exemplary strength in Mary that suggests the appropriate way forward.

4. Simeon, Luke 2:25–35

Rhetography

This rhetograph is dramatically different. The righteous, devout, and expectant Simeon, in a way like Mary and Elizabeth, is moved by the Holy Spirit from whom he had received a message of the Messiah (2:25–26) and comes "in the Spirit" into the temple in Jerusalem. Like Mary, he knows things. Simeon, as Mary had done, breaks into vocal blessing of God (the Nunc Dimittis), in joyful declaration that he has seen God's salvation, which is for gentiles and for Israel (2:30–32). The parents, Joseph and Mary, are astonished (θαυμάζοντες, 2:33) at what Simeon says. There is a moment of sublime amazement. But then, in his prophetic-priestly mode and space, Simeon utters a startling, frightening prophecy directly to Mary. Her child will have a profound and widespread influence and will experience opposition and suffering. Mary herself will suffer with her own soul being pierced with a sword (2:35). Those who know the storyline, like Theophilus, immediately envision what they already know about the eventual suffering of Jesus.[54] The impression is given that the suffering is inevitable. Though the text does not explicate it, Mary is visualized taking this in, having her moment of recognition of what Simeon states. Simeon functions here in the spaces of prophet and priest since he is both speaking and mediating. Mary stands in an anticipated priestly space herself since she will experience suffering as will her son, and her suffering will relate directly to his. The suffering of Jesus and, by sublime extension, her own, will function to reveal (ὅπως ἂν ἀποκαλυφθῶσιν) the thoughts (διαλογισμοί) of the hearts of many persons. She will share the painful future moment with far-reaching effect. Mothers can prehend the notion of suffering with their children, as 2:35 states, in their souls.

Sublime Texture

The holy and Spirit-led man Simeon appears at just the right, though entirely unexpected, sublime moment when Joseph and Mary bring the child Jesus into the temple, the holy location in Jerusalem where God and

---

54. Various interpretations have been proposed.

humans meet.[55] He appears as a completely trustworthy character who has special and clear insight into the situation, mediating information about Jesus that could scarcely have been guessed at otherwise.[56] What he says about Jesus is not described as coming from his own investigation but must have come directly from the Holy Spirit (2:26). Joseph and Mary are properly astonished at the unexpected declaration he provides about who Jesus is and what he brings for all people. This child will create a salvific connection between God and humans. Mary, however, becomes the direct recipient of Simeon's prophetic word (2:34): he knows that her baby is destined for (κεῖται εἰς, "set up for, proposed for, appointed for") the falling and rising of many persons and destined to be a sign who is opposed. This baby will have a profound effect on people. Joseph is conspicuously left out of this declaration. Mary, it is predicted, will feel the pain of what her son encounters.

It is all a striking scene. Mary is assumed to have heard and apprehended notions she does not yet comprehend in any full sense. The prophetic word about identity is sublime, the poetry is sublime, the predictions are sublime and frightening. Mary does not speak in these verses, but she and audiences of Luke know that she has heard Simeon. There is no immunity from suffering for Mary. Grief is anticipated. She alone is portrayed as standing with Jesus, sharing suffering in the moments of the intersection of the human and divine as she has been presented heretofore. Now she stands on the edge of the intersection of divine and human things where excruciating pain occurs, where choices are to be made. Theophilus and audiences of Luke are surely meant to pick up on this. The arrival of salvation is also the arrival of suffering, pain, and sorrow.[57] Mary will not be able to control what happens in the future. The language and the scene described touch the "thoughts of the heart."

Argumentative Texture

Explicit argumentation occurs only in 2:30 (ὅτι) and in 2:35 (ὅπως). Neither has a direct connection with Mary. Mary and audiences of Luke will

---

55. Simeon may well have been a priest. See Nolland, *Luke 1–9:20*, 120.
56. For Simeon as a trustworthy character, see Beverly Roberts Gaventa, *Mary: Glimpses of the Mother of Jesus* (Columbia: University of South Carolina Press, 1995), 62.
57. See Green, *Gospel of Luke*, 149.

grasp the ideas by engaging the context of the scene, interacting with the ideas presented abductively.[58] Audiences familiar with the narrative of the life of Jesus, particularly of the arrest, trial, and crucifixion, may well presume Mary's suffering is to come in that context. The passage, however, does not offer any explanation or argumentation about it.

Rhetorical Force

Luke provides a narration about a sublime scene that alludes to the direct influence of the Holy Spirit through Simeon and not to human reason. Audiences are left to surmise what Mary's moment is about and what the predicted piercing of her heart will be. Mary herself is left in the same situation. What will happen to her? There is no certainty at this point. She can only ponder, wonder, and anticipate without knowing what will happen. But this rhetoric helps contextualize audiences to the storyline being presented. But the story is not finished yet. The rhetorical effect of the sublime situation and language is to draw Mary and readers and listeners more deeply into the narrative, urging them to wonder what will happen, encouraging them to keep following the narration. The divine coming in which Mary has had her role since her visitation by Gabriel will inevitably be opposed. Mary can only continue to be the woman who will remember and wait.

5. In the Temple, Luke 2:41–51

Rhetography

Joseph and Mary are observed to be very pious, observant people who take Jesus once again to the sublime and holy temple, this time for the sublime and holy Passover festival. Most of the actions in this pericope are performed by Joseph and Mary.[59] After Joseph and Mary have traveled away from Jerusalem, they become aware that Jesus is not in the caravan (συνοδία, 2:44). Jesus, of course, is visualized back in the temple sitting among the teachers, listening and asking questions (2:46). The picture makes it clear that Jesus, an unusual, rather intellectual and holy

---

58. Where reasoning allows inferring something as an explanation of something else.
59. Many verbs indicate their actions.

twelve-year-old to say the least, answers questions, too (2:47), with listeners being sublimely astounded (ἐξίσταντο, "they were amazed"; "beside themselves"; "without understanding") at him.[60] What a boy! Three days later, when Joseph and Mary see him they too are astonished (ἐκπλήσσω, "overwhelmed," 2:48).[61] Mary, singled out again and noticeably stressed, incredulous, says, "Child, why have you treated us like this?" That she does not understand makes a palpable obstacle between herself and Jesus and what she now seems not to remember from earlier days. While behaving like parents do, worried about their apparently missing child, Mary and Joseph simply do not comprehend who Jesus is and what he is doing (2:49). They are perplexed: "And they did not understand the utterance [τὸ ῥῆμα] he spoke to them" (2:50). Still, Mary is made visible again as a woman who recognizes she is having another grand encounter that evokes deep feelings of wonder in her even though it is only vaguely understood. She has seen it before: the angel; promises of a child; virginal conception; her own youth and lowliness; the Holy Spirit; Elizabeth and her bounding fetus; the shepherds; Simeon; the temple; the prophetic word. She is trying to grasp the allusions and hints of what she hears and sees. "His mother carefully kept [διετήρει] all these utterances in her heart" (2:51).

Sublime Texture

The setting in the high and glorious location of the temple in Jerusalem at and following Passover time, the teachers, and the intellectual religious thinking and discussion make this pericope sublime throughout. Specific words employed emphasize the exceptional nature of what is described: all who heard Jesus are "without understanding" (ἐξίσταντο, 2:47); Mary and Joseph are "overwhelmed" (ἐξεπλάγησαν) and "in anguish" (ὀδυνώμενοι, 2:48);[62] Mary and Joseph "did not understand" (οὐ συνῆκαν) what Jesus said to them (2:50).[63] Mary is a genuine mother, distressed, emotional, worried, possibly slightly angry, wondering where her boy has gone. She

---

60. Growing up, but prior to bar mitzvah and not yet an adult. Nolland, *Luke 1–9:20*, 129. Jesus is here referred to as τέκνον, "child," no longer as παιδίον, "little child" or "infant."
61. Gaventa, *Mary*, 48.
62. Gaventa, *Mary*, 67.
63. The form συνῆκαν is from the verb συνίημι, more literally, "they did not have it together."

does not understand everything, certainly not why Jesus cannot be located in the caravan. This lack of knowledge, though, is from prehension, not comprehension. After Jesus has been located and given what many have considered to be a somewhat terse reply, and after the narrator points out Joseph's and Mary's lack of understanding, the short focus on Mary makes her stand out as a sublime character who evokes an emotional, heightened response among audience members: She carefully keeps all the utterances in her heart (2:51).[64] Her thoughts are internalized. She does not speak but is remembering and carefully thinking things over. They are amazing, confusing things that many people would reject. The emotional sublime radiates from Mary. It is the experience of a young woman who remembers some things, has just experienced more, and knows not how or does not wish to speak about them. What she has heard and seen astonishes again and again. Believing in them as truth, even if they are reminiscent of stories of events from the Bible and understandings of God or the Holy Spirit working, is something that requires pondering in the heart rather than broadcasting. Sublime Mary remains modest. Her issues are not resolved, vagueness remains. The conclusion to the pericope presents inconclusion on her part.[65] What does she anticipate? We do not know. Yet the vague notions evoke wonder and the possibility of some future grandeur (and suffering) for the boy Jesus and for Mary herself. This is the nature of sublime texture. It is vaguely grasped, not fully comprehended. Mary knows some things but she does not know everything. She is left in partial light.

Argumentative Texture

These verses are narrational and the lines that present Mary do not have explicit argumentation. The implied (and vague) argument runs like this: Joseph and Mary are confused, but the boy Jesus is not confused. Jesus is not confused and remains obedient to Joseph and Mary. Mary ponders all that has occurred and been stated. From this, Theophilus and audiences of Luke are meant to have what they have heard about the gospel message reinforced. What they come to understand is picked up not from clear argumentation, but from the movement of ideas and images as they go along.

---

64. The verb describing Mary's mental action is διατηρέω, "carefully keep, faithfully keep, maintain."

65. Gaventa, *Mary*, 69.

Rhetorical Force

This passage closes the birth narration in Luke. The leading rhetorical force is found in how the text sets things up to draw audiences along. It develops intrigue. What will happen next in the amazing series of incidents that Luke records and makes visible in the imagination? Mary's moment is about her continuing search for understanding. The parental confusion of Joseph and Mary together encourages audiences to continue on in their own contemplation of the narration. But Mary is presented as coming back after the confusion to a faithful keeping in her heart of all the utterances that have been made. She knows that she has had lofty experiences including the one just described. She knows what she has been told and she is known by audiences as the young woman who refers to herself as "the slave of the Lord" (1:38). Still, she draws audiences in with her search for understanding about what she prehends only in sublime and vague ways. She knows she has had lofty experiences. She knows what she has been told, yet things remain elusive. The audiences of the narration are meant to respond like Mary does: no hasty conclusions; remain open; remember and think things over carefully.

Conclusion: Rhetoric on the Edge

Murray Evans speaks of the sublime in the thought of S. T. Coleridge "as the means of systematically feeling and thinking along the edge of what readers can conceive."[66] This kind of rhetoric on the edge is what is observed in the Mary sequences. Luke is leading Theophilus and extended audiences along with astounding stories at the edge of comprehension and belief. Much of what Luke says resists rational understanding. The appearance of an angel; a virginal conception of a holy child who will be called the son of God; a formerly barren relative, filled with the Holy Spirit whose own child leaps in her womb; magnificent praising poetry; socially low shepherds recognizing the child; Simeon; Mary herself holding amazing events and ideas together in her heart. This is all sublime stuff. It runs right along the edge of what humans can believe. Luke offers it as certain (ἀσφάλεια, 1:4).

---

66. Evans, *Sublime Coleridge*, 153.

It begins in the material realm. Mary is a real bodily person, and the pregnancy, delivery, and the thoughts held in the heart are things of material realia. There is the memory of interactive encounters in the material, hence, recognizable realm. The material is raised to the sublime, though, to make the larger point. There is a psychology of the sublime Mary because the rhetoric of the moment and the rhetoric on the edge are meant to affect people. Theophilus is encouraged to come to a deepened certainty of the sublime events. The point is not so much to offer historical narration in some modern, scientific sense, but to convey the notion that God has done a great, momentous thing through the grand events described. This is the rhetoric of the sublime. It moves people to believe in the intersection of the human and the divine. Perhaps Theophilus knew it already, but Luke's narration helps drive it home. The rhetoric of the sublime creates realities in audience members' minds. Mary is clearly imagined keeping all the utterances in her mind and heart, pondering them, turning them over, trying to understand what she only prehends. The moments of encounter have moved her to at least this depth. It "awakens pleasure and awe in readers."[67] Mary and Luke's language about her draw people in; they transport them so that they respect the young woman who is intelligent, thoughtful, and accepting of what seems to strike her as amazing and confusing, despite the pain it will bring to her. She sees good coming into the world even as she does not understand it.[68]

Where the sublime goes, in SRI terms, is to wisdom. This is the space and language of living life in some level of developing understanding with all the ideologies, behaviors, and locations with which we live. The sublime seizes the imagination as the mind tries but often does not succeed to process information so as to make some sense of it. It nevertheless shapes, orients, and nuances life in particular ways.

---

67. Evans, *Sublime Coleridge*, 30.

68. My daughter, Bethany, a nurse and university professor, says of her clinical work, "Sometimes you get it before you figure it out. You know before you understand."

The Sublime and Subliminal in Romans 2–3

Jonathan Thiessen

> This Epistle, like all the others of the group, is characterized by a remarkable energy and vivacity.... There is a rush of words, rising repeatedly to passages of splendid eloquence; but the eloquence is spontaneous, the outcome of strongly moved feeling.... The language is rapid, terse, incisive; the argument is conducted by a quick cut and thrust of dialectic; it reminds us of a fencer with his eye always on his antagonist.
> —William Sanday and Arthur C. Headlam, *A Critical and Exegetical Commentary on the Epistle to the Romans*

Introduction

In this study, I make the case for the presence of a Longinian sublime in Rom 2–3. In doing so, I place the emphasis on the sublime as described by the imperial period text Περὶ ὕψους and ways in which it differs from the modern concept of the sublime. The treatise Περὶ ὕψους, generally translated *On the Sublime*, though it has had significant influence on western literary criticism and philosophy since its translation into French in 1674 by Nicolas Boileau, was almost unknown in antiquity.[1] The work is not cited in any ancient text that has survived.[2] The manuscript tradition ascribes the treatise to a certain Longinus, but scholars have not come to a consensus as to his identity or period, and the work has been variously dated to the Augustan age, to the first century CE, and to the

---

1. Unless otherwise indicated, quotations from Longinus are from Longinus, *On the Sublime*, trans. W. H. Fyfe, rev. Donald Russell, LCL (Cambridge: Harvard University Press, 1995). New Testament and French translations are my own.

2. See Martin Vöhler, "Pseudo-Longinus, *Peri hypsous*," in *The Reception of Classical Literature*, ed. Christine Walde, BNPSup 1/5, online ed. (Leiden: Brill, 2012): http://dx.doi.org/10.1163/2214-8647_bnps5_e1012470.

third century CE.³ Περὶ ὕψους, the Greek title of the treatise, refers to "that which is elevated, high, great." Longinus never precisely defines the sublime, and Boileau was forced to paraphrase: "that extraordinary and marvelous effect that strikes the reader and enables a passage to carry the reader away, ravish and transport."⁴

The theory of the sublime described by Longinus is the key proposed here for interpreting Rom 2–3, seeking to answer the following questions: Is there a way to reconcile the seemingly contradictory statements Paul makes about the advantages of Jews in Rom 2–3?⁵ Why avoid explaining what those advantages are? Through an analysis of techniques associated with the sublime, I offer this reading: Paul seeks to communicate a message that would be offensive to his audience: Jewish advantages are empty. Specifically because his message might offend, Paul chooses to communicate in an indirect manner using techniques best described by Longinus's treatise Περὶ ὕψους, in particular, hiding it subliminally beneath his apparent emotion (*pathos*).⁶ In the context of sociorhetorical interpretation, I

---

3. Following common practice, I refer to the unknown author as "Longinus." See also Malcolm Heath, "Longinus, 'On Sublimity,'" *PCPS* NS 45 (1999): 43–73, who argues for authorship by third-century Cassius Longinus.

4. Nicolas Boileau-Despréaux, *Oeuvres diverses du Sieur D*** avec le traité Du Sublime ou Du Merveilleux dans le discours, traduit du Grec de Longin* (Paris: Billaine, 1674), preface: "Cet extraordinaire et ce merveilleux qui frappe dans le discours et qui fait qu'un ouvrage enlève, ravit, transporte."

5. This approach, which studies the New Testament using ancient literary criticism, finds support in Longinus himself. According to Christine Oravec ("Sublime," in *Encyclopedia of Rhetoric*, ed. Thomas O. Sloane [Oxford: Oxford University Press, 2001], 757), "Longinus' treatment also differs [from other rhetorical treatises] by positioning its readership as critics, rather than as producers, of public speeches and literature." Longinus does provide advice for the active production of the sublime (e.g., his criticism of Caecilius's treatise for lacking advice for practical application [1.1] or his mention of usefulness for public speakers in 1.2). My point is that this is not the sole purpose in the treatise, which cites only examples from the ancient canon of what was already classical in his day. In this he differs from most rhetorical handbooks, which describe techniques for active persuasion. Using the concepts described in Περὶ ὕψους to interpret a text such as a Pauline epistle accords with the intentions of the treatise's author.

6. There is no evidence of direct influence of Longinus on Paul and no reason to imagine the apostle had knowledge of the treatise. Why then apply the notion of the sublime, as conceived by Longinus, to Paul? First, as Longinus's criticism of previous treatments of the sublime shows, the theory was present well before the first century in rhetorical circles Paul may have known. Second, the connection between the sublime and the divine, regularly expressed by Longinus throughout the treatise, points to a link with

suggest that the subliminal manner of eliciting agreement through the ubiquitous presence of pathos points toward sensory-aesthetic texture.

The sublime, productively employed in philosophy and aesthetics, has not been widely applied to the study of the New Testament, though it has been used commonly in other classical literary study.[7] At least two studies, however, have used the sublime in New Testament interpretation: Mark Schoeni applied the notion to Romans in 1993 and, more recently, Gary Selby has made extensive use of Περὶ ὕψους in his analysis of nonrational persuasion in the New Testament.[8] But, as is shown by Sanday's and Headlam's 1902 commentary on Romans quoted above, it is not necessary to reference the sublime to describe Paul's language in terms very similar to those used by Longinus.

The Roman Context

Before examining the difficulties in Rom 2–3, it is important to consider the context of the letter.[9] The letter is addressed "to all those in Rome"

---

biblical writing, which often relies as much on divine authority as on rhetoric. For the link between the sublime and the divine, see Casper C. de Jonge, "Dionysius and Longinus on the Sublime: Rhetoric and Religious Language," *AJP* 133 (2012): 271–300; for an example of nonrhetorical authority of religious discourse, see Robert G. Hall, "Paul, Classical Rhetoric, and Oracular Fullness of Meaning in Romans 1:16–17," in *Paul and Ancient Rhetoric: Theory and Practice in the Hellenistic Context*, ed. Stanley E. Porter and Bryan R. Dyer (Cambridge: Cambridge University Press, 2016); on the transcendental nature of religious rhetoric, see Laurent Pernot, "The Rhetoric of Religion," *Rhetorica* 24 (2006): 236. Achieving conviction through overwhelming effect rather than through logical argument is appropriate for the analysis of biblical literature. See Gary S. Selby, *Not with Wisdom of Words: Nonrational Persuasion in the New Testament* (Grand Rapids: Eerdmans, 2016). Finally, and more specifically to Rom 2–3, the series of rhetorical effects, the technical means of achieving them, and the psychological process that makes them successful, as described in Longinus, match the actual results and effects produced by Rom 2–3.

7. See, e.g., James I. Porter, "Lucretius and the Sublime," in *The Cambridge Companion to Lucretius*, ed. Stuart Gillespie and Philip Hardie (Cambridge: Cambridge University Press, 2007), on Lucretius or, more recently, Anne Lagière, *La Thébaïde de Stace et le sublime* (Brussels: Latomus, 2017) on Statius.

8. Mark Schoeni, "The Hyperbolic Sublime as a Master Trope in Romans," in *Rhetoric and the New Testament: Essays from the 1992 Heidelberg Conference*, ed. Stanley E. Porter and Thomas H. Olbricht, JSNTSup 90 (Sheffield: Sheffield Academic, 1993), 171–92; Selby, *Not with Wisdom of Words*, esp. 34–38.

9. Paul is probably writing in 56 CE, following a rich and varied ministry across the northeastern Mediterranean. He addresses a Christian community that he did not found himself and where he knows only a few members (Rom 1:13).

without specifying the church to which Paul writes. In fact, throughout the letter he avoids using the word ἐκκλησία to refer to the community in Rome. This has led scholars to conclude that Paul is writing to a network of Christian communities, divided over some fundamental conflict.[10] What that conflict was is also a matter of debate. One possibility is that it was between Jewish and gentile groups within the community, which raises the issue of the make-up of the Roman churches and thus the intended audience of Romans.[11] That Romans was written to a mixed community appears likely.[12] At the least, Paul could expect that his letter would be read and discussed by Jewish Christians. Even scholars who adhere to the view that the letter's intended audience was exclusively gentile must admit that it is unreasonable to imagine that his letter would never circulate among Jewish readers.[13] This is indeed assumed, given that many of Paul's letters were intended for general circulation and that there is no reason to deny

---

10. See Stanley E. Porter, *The Letter to the Romans: A Linguistic and Literary Commentary*, New Testament Monographs 37 (Sheffield: Sheffield Phoenix, 2015), 6–10 for an overview of positions. More specifically, see Paul S. Minear, *The Obedience of Faith: The Purpose of Paul in the Epistle to the Romans* (London: SCM, 1971) for arguments about distinct churches; for discussion of the "weak" and the "strong" in Rom 14, see Francis Watson, *Paul, Judaism and the Gentiles: A Sociological Approach*, SNTSMS 56 (Cambridge: Cambridge University Press, 1986), 94–98, as well as the revised version, Watson, *Paul, Judaism and the Gentiles: Beyond the New Perspective* (Grand Rapids: Eerdmans, 2007), 175–82. See also Peter Lampe, *From Paul to Valentinus: Christian at Rome in the First Two Centuries*, trans. Michael G. Steinhauser (Minneapolis: Fortress, 2003), 359–408 for archaeological evidence and discussion of the absence of ἐκκλησία.

11. It is important to remember that the historical composition of the Christian communities in Rome is related to but not identical with the intended audience of Romans.

12. This is the majority opinion currently, e.g., Robert Jewett, *Romans: A Commentary*, Hermeneia (Minneapolis: Fortress, 2007), 70; Peter Lampe, "Paul and the Church's Unity with Israel," in *Unity of the Church in the New Testament and Today*, ed. Lukas Vischer, Ulrich Luz, and Christian Link, trans. J. E. Crouch (Grand Rapids: Eerdmans, 2010), 69; Porter, *Letter to the Romans*, 9–10.

13. Scholars who argue for an intended audience that is exclusively or predominantly gentile include Stanley K. Stowers, *A Rereading of Romans* (New Haven: Yale University Press, 1994); Runar M. Thorsteinsson, *Paul's Interlocutor in Romans 2: Function and Identity in the Context of Ancient Epistolography*, ConBNT 40 (Stockholm: Almqvist & Wiksell, 2003); A. Andrew Das, *Paul and the Jews*, Library of Pauline Studies (Peabody, MA: Hendrickson, 2003); Das, *Solving the Romans Debate* (Minneapolis: Fortress, 2007); and Rafael Rodríguez, *If You Call Yourself a Jew: Reappraising Paul's Letter to the Romans* (Cambridge: Clarke, 2015). For an overview and other references to both sides of the debate, see Porter, *Letter to the Romans*, 6–10.

the presence of some Jewish Christians in Rome at the time of the writing. For ancient Mediterraneans, to whom indirect language came naturally, it would seem reasonable to ask whether beyond Paul's message to gentile readers there may be instruction intended for Jewish ears.[14] Primary audiences in antiquity were usually imagined in the social, physical, and discursive presence of secondary and tertiary audiences, or "accidental auditors." Society was deeply segmented, but the segments lived in constant interaction with each other.[15]

The Offensive Message: Jews No Longer Have the Advantage

Paul's position vis-à-vis Judaism has animated vigorous discussion for decades.[16] A new look at an old problem may deepen our understanding of Paul's argument in Rom 2–3. Paul's overt position on the advantages of Jews seems to be clearly expressed several times in the letter, as in 3:9: "What then? Are we Jews any better off? No, not at all. For we have already charged that all, both Jews and Greeks, are under sin" (ESV; repeated in various forms in 1:16; 2:9, 10; 3:22, 29; 4:9; 5:12; 10:12). Thus it seems that

---

14. On the indirect nature of ancient communication, see Thiessen, "Les lettres de l'apôtre Paul et la rhétorique du discours figuré" (PhD diss., Université de Strasbourg, 2020), 99–195. There must have been some mix of identity in the Roman communities or Paul would not have dedicated so much time and space to Greek-Jewish relations, which are not just a question of abstract theological discussion of the respective places of Greeks and Jews in the church but practical ones of everyday interaction. That there was indeed a community of Christian Jews in Rome is almost certainly indicated by Suetonius's mention of the expulsion of Jews from Rome due to their disputes over a certain Chrestus (*Claud.* 25.4; and Acts 18:2). James D. G. Dunn, *Romans 1–8*, WBC 38A (Dallas: Word, 1988), xlix, dates this expulsion as two actions, in 41 and 49, as does Simon Légasse, *L'épître de Paul aux Romains*, LD 10 (Paris: Cerf, 2002), 35. Outside observers assumed that it was only an internal dispute among Jews. It is doubtful whether at this time the Christian Jews themselves saw their identity as separate from their Jewish origins, though there is some indication that by the reign of Nero the Christians saw themselves as a separate entity, as the use of the term "Christians" shows (Tacitus, *Ann.* 15.44; Suetonius, *Nero* 16; see Dunn, *Romans*, xlix). Additionally, the quotations from the Septuagint in Rom 2–3, and the manner in which Paul's argument is built around these quotations imply knowledge of these passages by his readers.

15. I thank Professor Ian Henderson for this formulation (pers. comm.).

16. In particular in the forty-five years years since the publication of E. P. Sanders, *Paul and Palestinian Judaism* (Philadelphia: Fortress, 1977).

Paul considers Jews and Greeks to be in exactly the same position. But this message of equality is not so straightforward as an initial reading suggests, for through a series of ironies we can discern another message in contradiction to the overt one: the idea that the advantages of Jewish heritage cannot be counted on for remaining in God's covenant.

It may not be possible to reconcile Paul's contradictory statements and form a coherent system of thought. Rhetorical critics might conclude that a text as self-contradictory as this does not deserve to persuade. Nevertheless, critics may be astounded by the persuasion achieved despite the apparent incoherence and be led to question how it could be. Though the first effect of Paul's swerving argument is that he offers coherent and intelligent proof, in what follows I wish, first, to show that this facade hides a lack of real proof and betrays Paul's offensive opinion (offensive, that is, for certain Jews). Second, I will examine, through use of Longinus's sublime, how the argument succeeds. With this in mind, let us explore a series of five ironies in Rom 3:1–2 that, through arguments whose lack of logic remains subtle, hint at Paul's personal position.[17]

The first irony involves Paul's logically faulty proof for the advantages of Jews. Paul affirms forcefully in 3:1 that Jewish advantages are great because they have been entrusted with the oracles of God. But in the following verse, he declares that some have been unfaithful to these oracles. If by λόγια Paul refers to the Jewish prophetic tradition calling on Israel to turn away from idolatry and be faithful to God, Rom 3:3 refers to Israel not having done so. Despite having received these divine oracles, they failed

---

17. In addition to these ironies, other passages in Romans seem to indicate that Paul thought gentiles were in a position of advantage. First, in 1:18–32 Paul must be addressing all humanity, not just the non-Jews. It is as much an attack on them as on the gentiles and should not be taken to show that Paul considers gentiles to be at a disadvantage (see Jewett, *Romans*, 152). Indeed, nowhere in Rom 1 does Paul indicate the accusations in this passage are limited to pagans. If they were, his sudden accusation of a Jew in 2:1 would not make sense. Second, in 2:14 we see that though Jews, who are under the law, are to be judged severely by it, gentiles, who are not under the law, actually obey it. Third, in 2:25–29 Paul emphasizes the superiority of the circumcision of the heart to physical circumcision. Thus, in the end, the Jew by birth, law, and circumcision has no advantage, because the true Jew is a Jew by heart and faith; even this part, which appears to praise Jews deprives them of their advantage. Fourth, the collage of citations in 3:11–18 are passages Jews would not typically have applied to themselves but to gentiles; here they are turned subtly against them.

to obey and continued in unfaithfulness and idolatry.[18] Paul implies that refusing to trust (ἠπίστησαν) God's oracles calling on Israel to come back to him, or ignoring those predicting Jesus as the Messiah, results in rejecting those oracles. Paul does not explain how it is possible for Jews to have advantages if they have rejected God's words. After declaring that some have rejected God's oracles, Paul asks: "Does their faithlessness nullify the faithfulness of God?" This is not the expected question, which would be: "If they have been unfaithful, how could they receive the advantages of the oracles?" Paul's explanation in 3:4 shows how God can be considered faithful but does not explain what Jewish advantages are. The whole demonstration is presented as the beginning of a list of arguments illustrating the advantages of Jews: Paul begins what appears to be an enumeration, as the word πρῶτον, "first," shows, implying that he had in mind a list of advantages that he intended to enumerate.[19] That, at any rate, is what someone listening to the letter would assume. Paul probably had no intention of finishing the list. Πρῶτον gives the impression that more proofs are to come, but they never do.[20] In the verses that follow, Paul is carried away (or appears to be carried away) in the defense of his own preaching. Many of Paul's original hearers would have been struck by his argument for Jewish advantages through enumeration without recognizing that he does not follow through with a list of proofs. Despite this absence, the impression of strong argument would have remained. In fact, Paul never continues his list of Jewish advantages, nor does he finish arguing for the first of them. He turns away from the subject at hand, the advantages of Jews, and addresses the question of his own defense against his accusers;

---

18. For this use of λόγιον, see LXX Isa 28:13. Paul may also be implying (though he does not say so clearly) that refusing to recognize Jesus as the Messiah would be a continuation of that unfaithfulness to God's oracles. He may be thinking specifically of passages that prophesy the messiah (Rom 9:33; 11:26; 15:3, 13).

19. For examples in Hellenistic literature of lists beginning with πρῶτον, see 2 Macc 14:8; Sir 23:23; Philo, *Opif.* 41.3; Philo, *Somn.* 2.69; Philo, *Ios.* 216; Josephus, *A.J.* 6.55; 11.36.

20. As C. H. Dodd already remarked, Paul does appear to list some advantages of Jews in 9:4. Dodd, *The Epistle to the Romans* (London: Hodder & Stoughton, 1932), 43. This verse, however, does not immediately affect the interpretation of chs. 2–3 as they were read aloud to the original audience. Even the short list given in 9:4 is overshadowed by 9–11 where Paul is particularly concerned with the role of Jews in gentile salvation. In fact, this role turns out to be their rejection of God's revelation, enabling the gentiles to receive it first.

this occupies him until 3:8. Many commentators have considered, with C. H. Dodd, that Paul's argument is "obscure and feeble."[21]

Second, the irony of the advantages of Jews goes beyond the idea that they have rejected God's oracles. The word itself, περισσόν, is ambiguous. Its general meaning is "out of the common, extraordinary, remarkable, superfluous," but also "excessive, extravagant."[22] The word commonly has a negative and often ironic connotation in Hellenistic Greek.[23] Indeed, Paul's hearers will have been expecting a negative answer to the question "What is the advantage of the Jew?" following Paul's aggressive attack on the hypocritical Jew in 2:17–29. This expectation may cause the ironic meaning of περισσόν to remain uppermost in their minds. This ironic situation is reinforced by the second part of the question ("What is the usefulness [ὠφέλεια] of circumcision?") when it is compared with Paul's other statements regarding that question in Gal 5:2 ("See, I, Paul, say to you: if you circumcise yourselves, Christ is of no use [ὠφελήσει] to you!"). The fact that here Paul uses the same terms with precisely the opposite meaning is striking. It reveals another aspect of Paul's thought, one much more negative toward circumcision, and it confirms the ironic interpreta-

---

21. See Dodd, *Romans*, 44, 46 on the obscurity and weakness of Paul's argument, and Jewett, *Romans*, 240 for a summary of previous commentators' opinions. John W. Marshall maintains the opposite, arguing that here "Paul defends vigorously the benefit of circumcision to Jews and the loyalty of God to his people." See Marshall, "From Small Words: Reading Deixis and Scope in Romans," *JJMJS* 4 (2017): 9. I disagree: Paul *affirms* vigorously something that he does not defend well, or prove at all. Marshall rejects previous conclusions that the first verses of ch. 3 constitute a "wild goose chase."

22. LSJ, s.v. "περισσός."

23. Two passages in the New Testament illustrate the ironic usage of the word. In Matt 5:47 Jesus asks ironically: "And if you greet your brothers only, what *remarkable* thing [τί περισσόν] are you doing? Don't the nations do as much?" In Mark 14:31, Peter, after being told he will deny Jesus three times, exclaims "vehemently" (ἐκπερισσῶς, NRSV) that he is willing to die with Jesus. The following chapters show how this statement is much more "excessive" than "vehement." Septuagint Eccl 6:11 is an example of the ironic use with close parallels to Rom 3:1: "What is the advantage [τίς περισσεία] for the wise person over the fool? Indeed, the poor person knows how to walk in front of life.... Many words increase vanity. What advantage [τί περισσόν] is there for a person?" The irony of this passage is clear: there is no advantage, for all is vanity. For other ironic usage of the word in Hellenistic literature, see Philo, *Somn.* 2.132; Josephus, *B.J.* 1.111; Arrian, *Epict. diss.* 3.5.2. For negative occurrences of the word, see Eccl 7:16; Sir 3:23; Pss. Sol. 4.2; Philo, *Leg.* 3.140; Matt 5:37.

tion of Paul's answer to his own question: "What is the advantage of the Jew, or what is the usefulness of circumcision? Much in every way!"

Third, as Rom 3:9 shows, though Paul feels compelled to begin chapter 3 with a vigorous affirmation of Jewish advantage, his argument quickly comes back to bringing the Jewish reader down from his superior position. "What then? Are we any better off [προεχόμεθα]?" translates the NRSV, but the word προεχόμεθα could equally be translated "Do we have the advantage?" (as NIV), an allusion to Paul's initial question in 3:1.[24] That question was answered with a resounding "Much!" Here, in the heart of Paul's apology, it is answered with an equally resounding "Not at all!" Though Paul began chapter 3 with an emphatic affirmation of Jewish advantage, by 3:9 he appears to be arguing precisely against such an idea.

A fourth irony is the play on words in 3:2–3. Jews had been *entrusted* (ἐπιστεύθησαν) with God's oracles, but they refused to *trust* those oracles (ἠπίστησάν). In the first occurrence of the verb, the passive voice of God's action remains impersonal; in its second occurrence, the active voice, describing Jews' unfaithfulness, contrasts sharply and emphasizes the intentionality of their action.

Fifth, there is a similarity in Paul's statements in 1:16 and 2:9. In the former, Paul declares that the gospel "is the power of God for salvation to everyone who believes, to the Jew first and also to the Greek." But a little later, in 2:9, this expression is repeated with a subtle reversal: "There will be tribulation and distress for every human being who does evil, the Jew first and also the Greek." Here Jews remain in the position of first importance, but now for judgment, no longer for salvation.

---

24. Neither the meaning nor the reading are entirely sure. Προέχω in the active means "hold before, have already, have the advantage, surpass, be superior" and, in the middle voice: "offer, put forward" (LSJ, s.v. "προέχω"). According to BDAG (s.v. "προέχω"), if in Rom 3:9 the sense is "have the advantage," this would be a meaning not found elsewhere in the active (despite this affirmation by BDAG and others, such as Douglas Moo, *The Epistle to the Romans*, NICNT [Grand Rapids: Eerdmans, 1996]; see Dionysius of Halicarnassus, *Ant. rom.* 10.38.1). For this meaning in the active, see Philo, *Leg.* 1.30; Philo, *Deus* 44, in addition to passages cited by BDAG. A middle form with active meaning is the most common interpretation (Moo, *Romans*, 199–200) and that which I adopt here. As for the textual transmission, several manuscripts, including the sixth-century codex Claromontanus (D) read προκατεχομεν περισσον, a reading that is clearer, and connects explicitly to τὸ περισσόν in 3:1. It may be the result of a scribe clarifying the meaning of προεχόμεθα and tends to reinforce the interpretation of a middle voice with active meaning.

This series of ironies relating to Paul's opinion of Jewish advantages leads us to question whether his personal position was much more negative than it first appears. If that is the case, why communicate so subtly what could be stated more clearly? If we recall the mixed audience Paul is addressing, we begin to discern his motivations.

It is likely that Paul writes to deeply divided communities in Rome. The discussion of the weak and the strong in chapter 14 refers to this conflict, which Paul must have had in mind. If Paul's message is that if Jewish Christ-believers rely more on the torah than on Christ, their advantages are wasted, it may be an offensive message. Paul is not against torah observance as such, assuming one accepts that works of the law do not justify, but if he were to say to torah-respecting Jews that this means one does not have to obey dietary and purity laws or be circumcised, they would find him strongly opposed to the torah.[25] The subtle ironies of this passage show what is going on in Paul's mind as he chooses his words carefully; often the assumptions or implications that underlie a discussion can be as important for understanding as what is said openly.[26]

---

25. The degree to which Paul's disrespect of the torah generated opposition from traditional Jewish milieux is debated. Paula Fredriksen has argued that opposition to Paul in diaspora synagogues was not due to his disrespect of the torah at all but to fear by Jews that some gentiles would react violently when they saw others abandoning their traditional gods. Fredriksen, "Judaism, the Circumcision of Gentiles, and Apocalyptic Hope: Another Look at Galatians 1 and 2," *JTS* 42 (1991): 532–64; Fredriksen, "Why Should a 'Law-Free' Mission Mean a 'Law-Free' Apostle?," *JBL* 134 (2015): 637–50. Even if we were to accept this argument, or the idea that Paul approved of Jews continuing to respect the requirements of the torah, the fact remains that he had a reputation for disrespecting it. Acts 21 shows that the crowd in Jerusalem was strongly opposed to the idea that non-Jews could access the temple without adhering to Jewish requirements (21:28–29) and that Paul was willing to go to some length to counter the reputation he had for disrespecting them (21:20–24). Furthermore, violent affirmations against circumcision in Gal 5:2–12, even though addressed to non-Jews, may have offended Jewish audiences by their vehemence, as would remarks such as those in Phil 3:2–3 or 1 Thess 2:15–16.

26. Though division between Jews and gentiles comes up most clearly in Rom 14–15, it is important enough an issue for Paul to end his letter on it. The final position is particularly important in Greco-Roman rhetoric and reveals Paul's preoccupations. It may not be the main purpose for writing Romans, but it is one of the reasons. For discussion of the importance of that which is left unsaid, see Thiessen, "Les lettres de l'apôtre Paul et la rhétorique du discours figuré," 127–30.

Which Sublime?

Having examined the difficulty present in Paul's argument in Rom 3, we turn now to a possible key to understanding his rhetoric: the sublime. As we use Longinus's theory of the sublime to illuminate Paul, it is worth recalling that there are links between the sublime and the Jewish milieu: Paul and Longinus are likely contemporaries. The author is familiar with Jewish texts and ideas, as the citation of Genesis (*Subl.* 9.9) shows; and Caecilius, whom Longinus criticizes, was a Jew, according to the Suda (K 1165).

What is the sublime? Since the word has inspired a vast amount of literary and artistic production and is a common word in English ("Last night's pizza was sublime!"), it is important to specify which sublime we are discussing. The word is used in areas ranging from rhetoric to aesthetics, through the philosophy of art, political philosophy, ethics, anthropology, and French romanticism.[27]

In the midst of such a wealth of interpretation, particularly in common parlance, it is sometimes forgotten that *sublime* originally refers to height and that for Longinus τὸ ὕψος is primarily a question of literary criticism rather than of philosophy or art. Modern use of the concept goes far beyond the rhetorical sublime, and its source is not words but much more vast. This is shown by Philip Shaw's recent discussion of the definition of the sublime in his introductory work on the subject: in the five pages dedicated to defining the term, it is applied to a mountain, a thought, a deed, a monument, a revolution, a catastrophe, and a statue.[28] The only allusion Shaw makes to the sublimity of language is a passing mention of "a mode of expression" and "King Lear's dying words."[29] Similarly, in the introductory article by the French philosopher and literary critic Philippe Lacoue-Labarthe, the literary nature of the sublime is barely mentioned, for "it is, of course, the *spectacle* of power that is sublime," namely, "nature in all its power, of production as well as destruction."[30] Works discussing

---

27. For use in aesthetics, see Alexander Gottlieb Baumgarten, *Aesthetica* (Frankfurt an der Oder: Kleyb, 1750). For philosophy of art, see Immanuel Kant, *Observations on the Feeling of the Beautiful and Sublime*, trans. John T. Goldthwait (Berkeley: University of California Press, 1960).

28. Shaw, *The Sublime*, 2nd ed., New Critical Idiom (London: Routledge, 2017), 1–5.

29. Shaw, *Sublime*, 1.

30. Philippe Lacoue-Labarthe, "Sublime," in *Encyclopædia Universalis*, online ed.

the sublime in areas such as art and aesthetics often fail to emphasize that, for Longinus, the sublime resides in the *words* used to describe overwhelming phenomena more than in the phenomena themselves.[31] This is even the case in studies exclusively concerned with ancient literature. In his treatment of the sublime in Lucretius, James Porter, for example, discusses the natural sublime of "storm-tossed seas, earthquakes, jagged mountains, impending clouds, the yawning abyss between heaven and earth."[32] As indicated in the introduction to Baldine Saint Giron's study of the sublime, Western tradition of the idea quickly moved away from Longinus's rhetorical sublime, which does not appear among the disciplines she lists as having a distinct concept of the sublime.[33]

The sublime described by Longinus, however, applies primarily, perhaps entirely, to language. This is apparent from the opening words of the work and remains the case throughout. The goal of the treatise, affirms Longinus, is to furnish readers with the tools to *produce* the sublime themselves (*Subl.* 1.1). The structure, as well as the content and tone of the entire work are guided by this intention: the numerous examples taken from literature are intended to enable readers to produce sublime speech

---

(Paris, 2004): "La description empirique s'attache par prédilection aux phénomènes qui révèlent la nature dans toute sa puissance, de production ou de destruction: paysages grandioses, écrasants (montagnes, déserts), éléments déchaînés (tempêtes, orages, mer en furie). Mais c'est bien entendu le spectacle de la puissance qui est sublime" (emphasis added).

31. The only mention made by Michael Clarke ("Sublime," in *The Concise Oxford Dictionary of Art Terms*, 2nd ed. [Oxford: Oxford University Press, 2010], 238–39), e.g., is the statement that the concept was "originally derived from rhetoric and poetry." Marc Gotlieb emphasizes the natural phenomena described in *Subl.* 35 without observing that Longinus does not qualify them as sublime per se, but rather the language describing them. See Gotlieb, "Sublime," in *Encyclopedia of Aesthetics*, ed. Michael Kelly, online ed. (Oxford: Oxford University Press, 2014). See below for discussion of *Subl.* 35.

32. Porter, "Lucretius and the Sublime," 172. Porter, specialist in the ancient sublime, certainly shows in his 2016 study that he is aware that Longinus is primarily concerned with the rhetorical sublime, though he extends the definition of the sublime so widely as to embrace almost any expression or allusion to the grandiose in ancient thought. See Stanley E. Porter, *The Sublime in Antiquity* (Cambridge: Cambridge University Press, 2016).

33. Saint Girons, *Le Sublime, de l'antiquité à nos jours* (Paris: Desjonquières, 2005), 9–15. Saint Girons lists the sublime in the following disciplines: aesthetics, philosophy of art, political philosophy, ethics, and anthropology (9).

themselves, as are the analyses of five sources of the sublime. Each of the sources listed in *Subl.* 8.1 applies strictly to the production of the sublime in language and literature:[34] (1) the power of producing grand conceptions (τὸ περὶ τὰς νοήσεις ἁδρεπήβολον), (2) the inspiration of vehement emotion (τὸ σφοδρὸν καὶ ἐνθουσιαστικὸν πάθος), (3) proper construction of figures (τῶν σχημάτων πλάσις), (4) nobility of language (ἡ γενναία φράσις) and (5) dignified and elevated word-arrangement (ἡ ἐν ἀξιώματι καὶ διάρσει σύνθεσις). Discussion of the sublime throughout the work makes it clear that the theme is the production of the sublime in speech.[35]

One cannot deny that the "natural sublime" exists and that Longinus recognizes that natural phenomena may inspire astonishment. But an examination of the work shows that Longinus does not describe these phenomena as sublime in themselves. There are numerous allusions to breathtaking natural phenomena in the treatise, as has often been recognized. Usually this is taken as confirmation that, for Longinus, these phenomena are sublime. It has rarely been noted, however, that Longinus's description of natural wonders are comparisons whose goal is to illustrate how words, rather than nature, may be sublime. Longinus states in *Subl.*1.4, "a well-timed flash of sublimity shatters everything like a bolt of lightning and reveals the full power of the speaker at a single stroke."

Here, the orator's sublime rhetoric produces a shocking effect similar to lightning. The lightning serves as a metaphor and is not in itself described as sublime. Other occurrences of lightning (34.4) and raging fire (12.4) are similar. Though impressive features of the natural world described by Homer in passages quoted throughout *Subl.* 9–10 are cer-

---

34. As is indicated also by the use in *Subl.* 8.1 of ὑψηγορία, "elevated language." Fyfe translates, "the sublime in literature."

35. Examples could be multiplied showing that the sublime concerns language specifically. I mention several here. In 1.3, Longinus affirms that "the Sublime consists in a consummate excellence and distinction of language." The discussion in 2.1–2 concerns the question of whether sublimity is produced by art or nature. Here, *nature* is not what is described as sublime, but rather it is natural genius that enables an orator to produce sublime language. "Judgement in literature is the ultimate fruit of ripe experience," declares Longinus in 6.1. Again in 7.3: "If, then, a man of sense, well-versed in literature." Chapter 14 recommends the emulation of the great authors, such as Homer, Thucydides, or Demosthenes, for training the writer in producing the sublime in a passage. The entire discussion in *Subl.* 33–36 on whether faulty genius or impeccable mediocrity is superior presupposes that the sublime is a question of literary production.

tainly awe-inspiring, what Longinus considers sublime, or "elevated," is the diction of the authors. The same may be said of the passage in Περὶ ὕψους most often cited as a description of the natural sublime (*Subl.* 35–36). The mention in 35.4 of admiration for great rivers such as the Nile or the Rhine and for volcanoes such as Mount Etna is not an affirmation that these phenomena in and of themselves produce τὸ ὕψος. These spectacles, which are indeed "great," "extraordinary," and "beautiful," are not, in fact, described as "sublime" (*Subl.* 35.3).[36] Rather, it is the author's *description* of them that reaches the level of τὸ ὕψος, "the sublime" (*Subl.* 36.1–2).[37] This is confirmed by a look at the wider context: *Subl.* 35.2–4 is inserted into the discussion of whether a writer's impeccable mediocrity is better than genius despite its mistakes, and the discussion goes from a comparison of Lysias's and Plato's styles (35.1) to "writers of genius" generally (36.1) and thus is found in the heart of a discussion of literary characteristics.[38]

Beyond the application of the sublime to language, Longinus's sublime differs from modern usage in the very definition of the word. As noted earlier, τὸ ὕψος refers to the elevated. Under the entry "sublime," the *Oxford English Dictionary* declares the meaning "set or raised aloft, high up" to be "now rare" or "archaic in later use." The word often means: "of a feature of nature or art: that fills the mind with a sense of overwhelming grandeur etc." Though the "sense of overwhelming grandeur" corresponds to Longinus's conception of τὸ ὕψος if applied to language, the passages he gives illustrating the sublime may sometimes surprise readers expecting the word to be used as it is in aesthetics and art. One striking difference is that, for Longinus, sublimity is often produced by nothing more than skillful use of rhetorical figures, or sometimes a single figure. This source of the sublime occupies a third of the treatise in the (incomplete) form that has come down to us (16–29). In the examples given in these chapters, the sublime often lies in slight rhetorical elements.

---

36. τὸ περιττὸν … καὶ μέγα καὶ καλόν.

37. ὕψος … ὕψει.

38. For those with the presupposition that the sublime refers primarily to natural phenomena, aesthetics, or art, certain passages of Περὶ ὕψους appear to confirm this usage. In 36.3 Longinus states: "we admire accuracy in art, grandeur in nature." But the rest of the passage shows that here it is a question of comparison: just as one admires grandeur in nature, one admires sublimity in literature. Nature itself is not what is sublime, but the description of it.

According to *Subl.* 18.1, for example, merely transforming a statement into a question can create a sublime effect. Unexpected use of the second person and the vivid present do the same, as well as use of plurals for singulars and asyndeton (the omission of connecting particles).[39] These passages, when read against modern conceptions of the aesthetic or artistic sublime, fail to inspire the expected awe. For Longinus, though, they fully illustrate the sublime.

The neglect of the literary sublime may be partly due to the fact that Longinus seems in difficulty to define the notion.[40] Despite his criticism of Caecilius for failing to define his subject properly (1.1), Longinus himself does not give a clear definition but seeks to describe its effects and illustrate it with examples (particularly in 1.3–4 and 7.2–4).[41] Longinus does

---

39. For the second person, see *Subl.* 26.2 quoting Herodotus, *Hist.* 2.29: "You will sail up from the city of Elephantine and there come to a smooth plain. And when you have passed through that place." For the vivid present, see *Subl.* 25 quoting Xenophon, *Cyr.* 7.1.37: "Someone has fallen under Cyrus' horse and, as he is trodden under foot, is striking the horse's belly with his dagger. The horse, rearing, throws Cyrus, and he falls." For the use of plurals, see *Subl.* 23.3 quoting an unknown tragic source: "Forth came Hectors and Sarpedons too." For asyndeton, see *Subl.* 20.2 quoting Demosthenes, *Mid.* 21.72: "By his manner, his looks, his voice, when he strikes with insult, when he strikes like an enemy, when he strikes with his knuckles, when he strikes you like a slave."

40. Gustave Flaubert satirizes both the popularity and confusion of the sublime in the nineteenth century (*Bouvard et Pécuchet* [Paris: Lemarre, 1881]; see Lacoue-Labarthe, "Sublime."):

They began to discuss the sublime.

"Some objects are sublime in and of themselves, such as the crash of a torrent, deep darkness, a tree beaten by a storm. A character is beautiful when he triumphs, but sublime when he struggles."

"I understand," said Bouvard. "The beautiful is beautiful, but the sublime is very beautiful. How do you tell them apart?"

"By tact," answered Pécuchet.

"And tact, where does it come from?"

"From taste!"

"And what is taste?"

They defined taste as special discernment, quick judgment, the advantage of distinguishing certain relations.

"Well, taste is taste—but that still doesn't tell you how to acquire it."

They became lost in their reasoning, and Bouvard began to believe in aesthetics less and less.

41. This difficulty results in Longinus proposing definitions by what appears to

succeed in giving us a feeling for what the sublime really is, if only a feeling. For though genius is primarily a gift of nature, it must be honed by art (2.1–3).[42] In addition to describing the sources of the sublime, Longinus describes the effect produced:

> The Sublime consists in a consummate excellence and distinction of language, and … this alone gave to the greatest poets and prose writers their preeminence and clothed them with immortal fame. For the effect of genius is not to persuade the audience but rather to transport them out of themselves. Invariably what inspires wonder, with its power of amazing us, always prevails over what is merely convincing and pleasing. For our persuasions are usually under our own control, while these things exercise an irresistible power and mastery, and get the better of every listener.… A well-timed flash of sublimity shatters everything like a bolt of lightning and reveals the full power of the speaker at a single stroke. (*Subl.* 1.3–4)

Rather than seek an absolute definition of the sublime, I approach the question from a different angle. Setting aside preconceptions as to what is *sublime* according to modern usage, I use the numerous examples Longinus himself provides of what is elevated in language to analyze another contemporary text. In the absence of a satisfactory definition of the sublime, it is possible to identify passages that function in a way similar to those selected by Longinus through careful study of the characteristics of the sublime and the figures that create it. Of the many aspects of the sublime described in the treatise, I discuss six in particular that illuminate Paul's rhetoric.

---

be circular reasoning. In 7.1 he states: "nothing is really great which it is a mark of greatness to despise." In other words, "if you have greatness in you, you will instinctively despise what is not great." Again in 7.3: "If, then, a man of sense, well-versed in literature, after hearing a passage several times finds that it does not affect him with a sense of sublimity … then it cannot really be the true sublime." That is to say: "if the educated man who knows what the sublime is does not feel it to be sublime, then it isn't." Longinus's attempt at definition in 1.3 is a good example of his difficulty: "the Sublime consists in a consummate excellence and distinction of language:" This does not advance the reader much further than furnish a sort synonym for the term ὕψος itself.

42. Thus, of the five sources of the sublime that Longinus describes, the first two are (κατὰ τὸ πλέον, "for the most part") natural sources; the following three are produced by art.

Characteristics of the Sublime and Figures That Create It

Of the six characteristics and figures examined here, all are either unique to Longinus or, if they are figures known elsewhere, Longinus's theory contains features entirely absent from other ancient rhetorical theory.[43]

1. Pathos or Emotion

Pathos, or intense emotion, is a key element of the sublime and a central concept throughout Longinus's treatise. It is one of the five sources of the sublime listed in 8.1.[44] Longinus criticizes Caecilius vigorously for having omitted pathos from his treatment of the sublime, accusing him of considering that pathos does not contribute to the sublime.[45] Longinus affirms:

> I would confidently lay it down that nothing makes so much for grandeur as genuine emotion in the right place. It inspires the words as it were with a fine frenzy and fills them with divine spirit. (*Subl.* 8.4)

---

43. In discussing these features, it is important to remember that, for Longinus, the sublime is never the sum of the figures or other features but that *je ne sais quoi* that seems almost intuitive to him ("judgement in literature is the ultimate fruit of ripe experience" [6], after all). His ruthless criticism of passages and authors he considers fall short of the sublime shows this to be the case (3–5). For Longinus, figures do not guarantee that something is sublime; they contribute to sublimity (amplification, e.g., exists without being sublime, 12; as does oath, 16.3). In chs. 33–36 Longinus argues that flawed genius is much superior to impeccable construction, indicating that it is entirely possible to use figures perfectly without achieving sublimity. Unique to Longinus are the links between the sublime and the following: concealment, pathos, disorder, and calculated omission. Longinus's theory of the following figures contains elements absent from other rhetorical theory: change of grammatical person, question-and-answer, asyndeton, anaphora. Their uniqueness is indicated below.

44. The treatise is structured according to these five sources, each discussed in its order. The exception is pathos. Because a full quaternion (eight pages) of the main manuscript is missing at the point where one would expect the discussion of pathos (at 9.4), debate continues about whether it is discussed on the missing pages, or in a separate treatise, as Longinus himself announces (44.12; cf. 3.5).

45. Longinus, in fact, imagines two possibilities for why Caecilius may have neglected the sublime, the other one being that he thought pathos *always* contributed to the sublime, and thus he did not need to address it.

Longinus associates pathos with many of the figures and techniques he recommends, indeed, with all figures generally: "All [figures] serve to lend emotion and excitement to the style. But emotion is as much an element of the sublime, as characterization is of charm" (*Subl.* 29.2).[46]

2. Change of Grammatical Person (*Subl.* 26–27)

"Change of grammatical person," as Longinus describes it, is a sudden "turning away"[47] from the person addressed in order to address another:

> Change of person gives an equally powerful effect, and often makes the audience feel themselves set in the thick of the danger.... All such passages with a direct personal address put the hearer in the presence of the action itself. By appearing to address not the whole audience but a single individual ... you will move him more and make him more attentive and full of active interest, because he is roused by the appeals to him in person. (*Subl.* 26.1–2)

> The change of construction has suddenly run ahead of the change of speaker. So this figure is useful, when a sudden crisis will not let the writer wait, and forces him to change at once from one character to another. (*Subl.* 27.2)

> Leaving his sense incomplete he has made a sudden change and in his indignation almost a split a single phrase between two persons ... and appearing to abandon the jury, he has yet by means of the emotion made his appeal to them much more intense. (*Subl.* 27.3)

Listeners become concerned personally with what is said, seeing themselves on the scene of events, and are thus more easily affected by them. The author moves from one person to the other suddenly and without

---

46. Longinus associates pathos with selection of ideas (10.3), amplification (11.2), vivid descriptions (φαντασίαι, 15.1 and 15.9), oath (ἀποστροφή, 16.2), concealment (17.2), question-and-answer (18.2), disorder (20.2; 21.2), hyperbaton (22.1), "polyptota" (23.1; 24.2), vivid second person (26.3; 27.1, 3), metaphors (32.4), hyperbole (38.5–6), and word arrangement (39.1; 41.2). Another illustration of the central place pathos holds in Longinus's theory of the sublime is the number of occasions where the two words are paired, often as if they were synonyms: 16.2 (ὕψος καὶ πάθος); 17.2, 3; 23.1; 32.4; see also 2.2 (paired with διηρμένος) and 39.1 (paired with μεγαληγορία).

47. The etymological meaning of ἀποστροφή.

warning, explains Longinus, the words running on ahead of him in his spate of emotion. In the sudden crisis of the author's thoughts, he leaves his sense incomplete. But the effect is powerful, for by appearing to abandon those he was addressing, he, in fact, has made his appeal to them much more intense (26.1–27.3).[48] As seen in the examples that Longinus gives, change of person can involve the author suddenly speaking in the voice of one of his characters, the switch happening suddenly with no indication of the change of speaker.[49]

3. Question and Answer (*Subl.* 18)

Rhetorical questions are treated in Graeco-Roman rhetorical theory, but these usually involve one or a series of questions unaccompanied by the answer.[50] In Longinus's method:

> The inspiration and quick play of the question and answer, and his way of confronting his own words as if they were someone else's, make the passage, through his use of the figure, not only loftier but also more convincing. For emotion is always more telling when it seems not to be premeditated by the speaker but to be born of the moment; and this way of questioning and answering one's self counterfeits spontaneous emotion. (*Subl.* 18.1–2)

Two things are worthy of note in Longinus's treatment of question-and-answer: the fact that it is a series of questions followed by answers given

---

48. This picture of "change of person" is somewhat different from that of the rhetorical handbooks in that these tend to present ἀποστροφή (or *exclamatio*) as the turning from the judges to address the accused and relate specifically to judicial contexts (Rhet. Her. 4.22; Quintilian, *Inst.* 4.1.63–69; 9.2.38–39; Pseudo-Hermogenes, *De inventione* 4.3.6; Hermogenes, *De ideis* 2.1.6; Tiberius, *De figuris Demosthenicis* 7 [Leonard Spengel, ed., *Rhetores Graeci*, 3 vols. (Leipzig: Teubner, 1894), 3:61.28]).

49. This last aspect of "change of person" is unique to Longinus in rhetorical theory, as are the following features: the change without warning, the incompleteness of meaning, and the more powerful message sent while seeming to address someone else.

50. See Aristotle, *Rhet.* 3.18 [1419a], 3.19 [1419b]; Anaximenes, *Rhet. Alex.* 20.5 [1434a]; 36.43–44 [1444b]; Demetrius, *Eloc.* 279; Rhet. Her. 4.22–23, 33–34, Cicero, *De or.* 3.203 [3.53]; Quintilian, *Inst.* 5.11.5, 9.2.6–16, Dionysius of Halicarnassus, *Dem.* 54.5, Theon, *Prog.* 97.23–98.20 (Spengel 3); Ps.-Hermogenes, *De ideis* 1.7.16; 1.11.26; Ps-Hermogenes, *De methodo gravitatis* 10; Apsines, *Rhet.* 10.13.

by the speaker himself and, once again, the importance of pathos for creating conviction.

4. Asyndeton and Anaphora (*Subl.* 19–21)

Longinus treats anaphora and asyndeton together and argues they produce powerful effects when combined.[51] According to his theory, leading elements of these figures are speed and momentum.

> The phrases tumble out unconnected in a sort of spate, almost too quick for the speaker himself.... The phrases being disconnected, and yet none the less rapid, give the idea of an agitation which both checks the utterance and at the same time drives it on. (*Subl.* 19)
>
> Then to prevent the speech coming to a halt by running over the same ground—for immobility expresses inertia, while emotion, being a violent movement of the soul, demands disorder—he leaps at once into further asyndeta and anaphoras.... His very order is disordered and equally his disorder involves a certain element of order. (*Subl.* 20.2–3)
>
> Insert the connecting particles, if you care to do so.... If you thus paraphrase it sentence by sentence you will see that the rush and ruggedness of the emotion is leveled and smoothed out by the use of connecting particles, it loses its sting and its fire is quickly put out. For just as you deprive runners of their speed if you bind them up, emotion equally resents being hampered by connecting particles and other appendages. It loses its freedom of motion and the sense of being, as it were, catapulted out. (*Subl.* 21.1–2)

The elements essential to Longinus's theory of asyndeton and anaphora are original and are not found in other treatises that describe these figures.[52] These elements are speed and momentum, disorder, and the link to pathos. Speed and momentum are created through the asyndetons as the words seem to get ahead of the speaker, thus giving free rein to the expression of emotion. Disorder is also a characteristic of asyndeton, necessary for

---

51. On asyndeton and Paul, see Eberhard Güting and David L. Mealand, *Asyndeton in Paul: A Text-Critical and Statistical Enquiry into Pauline Style* (Lewiston, NY: Mellen, 1998).

52. They are not found in Aristotle, Demetrius, Cicero, Rutilius Lupus, Alexander Numeniu, Dionysius of Halicarnassus, Quintilian, or Ps.-Hermogenes.

the expression of emotion. The link with pathos is also unique to Longinus as seen in relation to momentum and disorder. Emotion is leveled out through the presence of connecting particles.

5. Disorder (*Subl.* 19, 22)

A surprising quality of the sublime according to Longinus is its characteristic disorder: "immobility expresses inertia, while emotion, being a violent movement of the soul, demands disorder" (19.2). The relationship is complex, for the good author's "very order is disordered and equally his disorder involves a certain element of order." (19.3). This disorder is powerful because it gives the impression of natural pathos, or emotion:

> Just as people who are really angry or frightened or indignant, or are carried away by jealousy or some other feeling ... often put forward one point and then spring off to another with various illogical interpolations, and then wheel round again to their original position, while, under the stress of their excitement, like a ship before a veering wind, they lay their words and thoughts first on one tack then another, and keep altering the natural order of sequence into innumerable variations. (*Subl.* 22.1)

Here we see that people who are really under the effect of emotion present one argument only to spring to another one without logical connection. This has the powerful effect of creating the sublime, if it appears natural.

6. Concealment and Calculated Omission

For Longinus, the best figures are those produced without being revealed to the audience.

> For art is only perfect when it looks like nature and Nature succeeds only when she conceals latent art. (*Subl.* 22.1)

> There is an inevitable suspicion attaching to the sophisticated use of figures. It gives a suggestion of treachery, craft, fallacy, especially when your speech is addressed to a judge with absolute authority, or still more to a despot, a king, or a ruler in high place. He is promptly indignant that he is being treated like a silly child and outwitted by the figures of a skilled speaker. Construing the fallacy as a personal affront, he sometimes turns downright savage; and even if he controls his feelings, he

becomes conditioned against being persuaded by the speech. So we find that a figure is always most effective when it conceals the very fact of its being a figure. Sublimity and emotional intensity are a wonderfully helpful antidote against the suspicion that accompanies the use of figures. (*Subl.* 17.1–2)

The sublime thus produces acquiescence unconsciously through grandeur, surprise, stupefaction. The sublime, says Longinus, is not necessarily hidden, but its effect is greater if it is.[53] A further possible technique of the sublime involves carefully avoiding naming uncomfortable issues, and quickly passing on to another subject. This aspect is illustrated by Demosthenes who, in the face of objections, "cunningly avoids naming the result … before his hearers can raise the objection he promptly goes on" (*Subl.* 16.4).

The Offensive Message Delivered through Subliminal Sublime

Having examined six features that contribute to Longinus's sublime, we return to Rom 3. How does Paul deliver a subtle but offensive message? Comparing the rhetoric of Rom 2–3 with the characteristics and figures Longinus illustrates shows that these describe extremely well the mechanisms at work in these chapters. In this passage, we can see at work twelve of the techniques and figures Longinus describes as contributing to the sublime. Of these, the six characteristics and figures we have just examined are those I have chosen to illustrate.[54]

---

53. See also allusions in 32.2; 38.3. The hidden nature of the art of rhetoric is a common theme throughout ancient Greco-Roman theory. See, e.g., Aristotle, *Rhet.* 3.2 (1404b), Quintilian, *Inst.* 8.4.8; Rhet. Her. 1.17; 2.47; 4.10 (and Harry Caplan, [*Cicero*] *Rhetorica ad Herennium*, LCL [Cambridge: Harvard University Press, 1954], 250 n. a). See also Laurent Pernot, *La Rhétorique dans l'Antiquité* (Paris: Librairie Générale Française, 2000), 219. For an interesting example of the same principle in modern argumentation with no allusion to ancient rhetoric, see Thomas F. Mader, "On Presence in Rhetoric," *College Composition and Communication* 24 (1973): 375–81.

54. In addition to the six treated here, other features of the sublime that are also present in Rom 2–3 are (7) universality (*Subl.* 7.3–4): Romans generally has greatly influenced Western thought; (8) hyperbole (*Subl.* 38): Rom 2:17–29; (9) amplification (*Subl.* 11–12): Rom 2:17–24; 3:13–15; (10) selection of ideas (*Subl.* 10): construction of the catena in Rom 3:9–18; (11) complicity with the reader (*Subl.* 7.2): Rom 3:1–9.

1. Pathos or Emotion

Pathos is a central element of Paul's rhetoric in Romans, particularly in chapters 2 and 3.[55] Characteristics such as asyndeton and disorder in this passage contribute to the sublime effect that sweeps listeners off their feet. They also clearly indicate the emotional nature of Paul's subject-matter and contribute to the pathos of the passage. Questions, which Paul also uses throughout this passage, also create pathos, according to Longinus, by creating the feeling that the speaker's words are not premeditated (*Subl.* 18.1–2).

2. Change of Grammatical Person

Longinus described how authors speak suddenly in the voice of one of their characters when they change grammatical person.[56] This is illustrated in the diatribe of Rom 3. Paul made a fierce attack on the hypocritical Jew or Jewish sympathizer at 2:17–29, an attack that he may very well have felt went too far.[57] A Jewish listener would be uncomfortable hearing the litany of criticism Paul pours out and, being offended, would be in danger of becoming closed to Paul's arguments. In a sudden change, Paul now speaks in the voice of the Jew he had been criticizing (3:1). The tables are turned dramatically in Paul's surprise statement that the advantages of Jews are great.[58] Exactly as Longinus specified for this technique, Paul's sudden crisis does not let him wait: driven by his indignation and leaving his meaning incomplete, he changes from one character to another without indication that he is doing so.

---

55. Pathos has been amply studied in relation to New Testament rhetoric. On Paul specifically, see Thomas H. Olbricht and Jerry L. Sumney, eds., *Paul and Pathos*, SymS 16 (Atlanta: Society of Biblical Literature, 2001), particularly Leander E. Keck's contribution: "*Pathos* in Romans? Mostly Preliminary Remarks," 71–96.

56. An additional change Longinus describes is the sudden use of the second person. In Rom 2:1 Paul suddenly and ferociously addresses his hearers in the second-person singular. For Longinus, appearing to address not the whole audience but a single individual has the effect of moving the person to be more attentive and engaged in action.

57. Whether 2:17–29 describes a Jew or a gentile proselyte to Judaism (as Thiessen, Rodríguez, or Thorsteinsson argue) makes no difference to how insulting this hyperbolic image would be to a Jew or even sympathizer with Judaism.

58. See Dodd, *Romans*, 43.

3. Question and Answer

Longinus's description of the question and answer also describes well what we see in Rom 3:1–9. The "quick play of question and answer," says Longinus, "make the passage loftier and more convincing." This figure also lends credence to Paul's emotion, which appears unplanned. In fact, Paul is not trying to convince his hearers through logic but to elicit agreement *despite the logical inconsistency* of his argument. The rapid exchange of questions and answers carries the listener along with the debate, without noticing that Paul has neglected to explain the advantages of Jews. The fact that Paul himself is the one proposing the challenges to his argument enables him to appear objective while avoiding questions he may not wish to answer.[59] Paul's affirmations of Jewish advantages allow him to avoid the indignation of his Jewish audience without modifying his position on the unimportance of the law.

4. Asyndeton and Anaphora

It is the speed and momentum of the exchange that enable Paul to get away with such a faulty argument.[60] This speed is produced by question and answer, as Longinus states, but also by a powerful combination of asyndeton and anaphora. In this passage, the questions tumble out with no connecting particles. The momentum of the passage is created by the anaphora of the repeated οὐκ ἔστιν in the catena (3:10–12).[61] The elements original to Longinus's theory of asyndeton and anaphora are visible in Paul's passage: momentum; emotional expression; disorder.

---

59. This is the same technique used in Plato's Socratic dialogue: any number of objections come to mind reading the responses of Socrates's docile interlocutors; none of these objections can be posed, of course, since we are mere readers of a set text before us and have no ability to interact with the original writer. Plato was well aware of this feature of writing (*Phaedr.* 275d).

60. On the rhetoric of crisis that urges hearers to act quickly, including use of rhetorical questions and exaggeration, see Nina E. Livesey, *Galatians and the Rhetoric of Crisis: Paul—Demosthenes—Cicero* (Salem, OR: Polebridge, 2016), 17–18, 36.

61. A further anaphora appears in the repetition of ὁ in 2:21–23 and serves to emphasize the hyperbole of the hypocritical Jew, building indignation and preparing Paul's sudden reversal of argument in 3:2.

5. Disorder

The disorder of the passage is its lack of coherent logic, as we have noted. "Emotion demands disorder," says Longinus, and causes a speaker to "put forward one point and then spring off to another with various illogical interpolations." But in a way Paul's "disorder involves a certain element of order" (19.3), for his rapid answers to his own questions seem at first hearing to be consistent (and the listener has no time to doubt them).

6. Concealment and Calculated Omission

Calculated omission, according to Longinus, involves avoiding naming uncomfortable issues. As we have seen throughout the discussion of Rom 3, this is exactly what Paul is doing when he avoids continuing his discussion of Jews' advantages. The omission of these important and expected elements, though done so naturally that it does not surprise his audience, is nevertheless a subtle invitation to them to reconsider their own situation, and wonder: "If even Paul cannot think of the advantages that are supposedly so sure, perhaps we also should give them a second thought."

We have seen that there are several conflicting messages at work in this passage. Paul's overt position is that of *equality* between Jew and gentile. But he also affirms that the *advantages* of Jews are great. Nevertheless, the subtle ironies in the passage hint that Jews are, in fact, at a *disadvantage*, as indeed several passages in Romans imply.[62] This message remains implicit because Paul does not want to alienate the Jewish members of his audience who would be offended by an open affirmation that Jewish law is actually unnecessary for obtaining righteousness. Paul appears to emphasize the importance of Jewish heritage, only to question it subtly in a way that causes his listeners to reassess their own opinion. Paul seeks persuasion by circumventing logical reasoning through overwhelming the audience by seemingly divine pathos and other striking effects unique to Longinus. These effects communicate in a covert manner the offensive message Paul seeks to convey.

---

62. Are they disadvantaged or just disobedient and unfaithful, one may ask. It would appear to me that anyone who had advantages but lost access to them through disobedience and unfaithfulness, would be disadvantaged. For passages in Romans, see above n. 17.

Sublime and subliminal?[63] Paul's message is subliminal because it is transferred subconsciously, hidden below the storm of emotion, concealed, just as Longinus suggests. As we have seen, Paul's rhetoric matches many of the features that create the ancient literary sublime and so points us in the direction of describing this passage as a rhetoric of the sublime and the subliminal. How does a passage such as Rom 2–3 achieve sufficient rhetorical force to be among the most studied and influential passages of ancient literature? An analysis using Longinus's theory of the literary sublime aids us in understanding the power of this passage by comparing the rhetorical features present with Longinus's description of their persuasive effects.

The Sublime, Romans, and Sociorhetorical Interpretation

Where does this fit into sociorhetorical interpretation? The sublime is more experience than persuasion, touching the emotions more than it does the reasoning intellect. I suggest that the process through which the sublime brings readers to acquiescence operates primarily through sensory and aesthetic mechanisms. The abrupt change of person, as we have seen, is effective because the persons suddenly addressed see themselves in the action, feel the danger, and identify with the situation being described to them.[64] In fact, emotion, which is essential to sensory-aesthetic perception, is the mechanism that operates in almost every instance of the sublime. The figures of question and answer, asyndeton and anaphora create speed, momentum, and disorder, directly touching the emotional experience of audiences and creating a veil that hides the illogicality of what appears to be logical argument. It is this concealment, in turn, this subliminal communication, that enables the sublime to function. If audiences were to analyze why they have been convinced and were to determine that it was nothing more than being impressed with elevated language, it is likely they would doubt the validity of their conviction. If the sublime's effect remains subliminal, working beneath the fully conscious, the conviction remains.

---

63. "Subliminal" (from Lat. *sub limen*, "below the threshold") is, of course, etymologically unrelated to "sublime" (from Lat. *sublimis*, "elevated").

64. The complicity with the audience creates reassurance and confidence in the speaker, working on the feeling of belonging and understanding.

Divine Speech, Hebrews, and Sublime Rhetoric

Christopher T. Holmes

The treatise *On the Sublime* describes the nature and intended effects of the rhetoric of the sublime or what I call *sublime rhetoric*.[1] Sublime rhetoric moves beyond persuasion, the topic, and assumed goal of much of ancient rhetorical theory. As the treatise explains in the first chapter, sublime rhetoric is characterized by its nonrational or suprarational effects. Couched in language drawn from religious experience, magic, and military conquest, sublime rhetoric has the capacity to lead audiences into ecstasy, to cast a spell on them, and to assert an "irresistible power of mastery" over them (*Subl.* 1.4).[2] The treatise elaborates on the nature and function of sublime rhetoric with examples drawn from a variety of ancient authors. One of the surprising details in *On the Sublime* is its allusion to the creation story in the book of Genesis as an example of sublime rhetoric (*Subl.* 9.9).

This essay takes as its point of departure the author's reflection on this allusion to Genesis. It considers the reasons why the author identifies Genesis as an example of sublime rhetoric and how it relates to the intended effects of sublime rhetoric as they are described elsewhere in the treatise. With this example in mind, the essay explores the theme of God's speech as a way to account for sublime rhetoric in the Letter to the Hebrews. It highlights how the references to God's speech in Hebrews tap into what Yun Lee Too calls the "spatialized and moved language" of sublime rhetoric.[3] According to Too,

---

1. For justification of this translation, see Christopher T. Holmes, *The Function of Sublime Rhetoric in Hebrews: A Study in Hebrews 12:18–29*, WUNT 2/465 (Tübingen: Mohr Siebeck, 2018), 40–41.

2. Unless otherwise noted, Greek text and translations of *On the Sublime* are from Longinus, *On the Sublime*, trans. W. H. Fyfe, rev. Donald Russell, LCL (Cambridge: Harvard University Press, 1995).

3. Yun Lee Too, *The Idea of Ancient Literary Criticism* (Oxford: Clarendon, 1998), 194.

sublime rhetoric displaces audiences by uplifting, transporting, and resituating them. The theme of God's speech demonstrates one facet of how sublime rhetoric in Hebrews is intended to dislocate audience members from their empirical life situation so that they perceive the situation in a new way.

This essay has three parts. First, I provide an orientation to the treatise *On the Sublime*. This part considers both the treatise's central term, ὕψος, and the five sources of sublime rhetoric. The second part analyzes the treatise's reference to the Genesis creation story and the surrounding context. Using the second part as an analytical framework, the third part of the essay considers the nature of God's speech in Hebrews. The essay shows the close connection between sublime rhetoric and religious rhetoric. It also explores the capacity of sublime rhetoric to move its hearers, an important function of the sublime in Hebrews.

An Orientation to *On the Sublime*

The anonymous treatise *On the Sublime*, long attributed to Longinus, most likely dates to the late first or early second century CE, though it is difficult to know for certain when it was written.[4] Most of the treatise is devoted to discussion of ὕψος. Despite this, the treatise lacks a clear definition of the term. The author assumes that the treatise's intended recipient, Terentianus, is aware of previous definitions or discussions of ὕψος (*Subl.* 1.4), so does not revisit them.[5] The Greek word ὕψος and the related term τὸ ὑψηλόν originally denoted a spatial quality of height or high status.[6] The treatise plays on this basic connotation but moves away from a literal understanding of the term. As James Hill has argued, two central images related to ὕψος—height and light—lose all material and figural sense in the treatise. Rather, Hill calls attention to how ὕψος describes a metaphysical category that relates to divine realities and presences.[7]

---

4. For a discussion of the authorship and date of the treatise, see Holmes, *Function of Sublime Rhetoric*, 29–33.

5. For a discussion of Terentianus and his relationship to the author of *On the Sublime*, see Holmes, *Function of Sublime Rhetoric*, 33–34.

6. See, e.g., BDAG, s.v. "ὕψος."

7. James Hill, "The Aesthetic Principles of the *Peri Hupsous*," *JHI* 27 (1966): 265–74.

Despite the absence of a precise definition, the treatise is filled with descriptions of ὕψος and its intended effects.[8] The first eight chapters of the treatise introduce the discussion of ὕψος, including failed attempts to achieve the characteristics of ὕψος in *Subl.* 3–7. The first chapter provides what many interpreters regard as a programmatic statement about sublime rhetoric:

> Further, writing for a man of such learning and culture as yourself, dear friend, I almost feel freed from the need of a lengthy preface showing how the Sublime consists in a consummate excellence and distinction of language, and that this alone gave to the greatest poets and historians their pre-eminence and clothed them with immortal fame. For the effect of genius is not to persuade the audience but rather to transport them out of themselves. Invariably what inspires wonder casts a spell upon us and is always superior to what is merely convincing and pleasing. For our convictions are usually under our own control, while such passages exercise an irresistible power of mastery and get the upper hand with every member of the audience. (*Subl.* 1.3–4)

As this passage makes clear, ὕψος is not so much a matter of style as a matter of effect.[9] As the treatise's discussion elsewhere indicates, sublime rhetoric overpowers and entrances, dominates and inspires, shocks and transports.[10] In *Subl.* 8, the author identifies five sources of sublime rhetoric: (1) the power of conceiving impressive ideas; (2) vehement and inspired emotion; (3) the proper construction of figures of thought and speech; (4) nobility of diction; and (5) superior sentence composition. The

---

8. For an overview, see Donald A. Russell, *"Longinus" On The Sublime: Introduction and Commentary* (Oxford: Oxford University Press, 1964), xxx–xlii. See also F. R. B. Godolphin, "The Basic Critical Doctrine of 'Longinus,' On the Sublime," *TAPA* 68 (1937): 172–83; G. M. A. Grube, "Notes on the ΠΕΡΙ ΥΨΟΥΣ," *AJP* 18 (1957): 355–74; Doreen C. Innes, "Longinus and Caecilius: Models of the Sublime," *Mnemosyne* 4th series 55 (2002): 259–84; Malcolm Heath, "Longinus and the Ancient Sublime," in *The Sublime: From Antiquity to the Present*, ed. Timothy M. Costelloe (Cambridge: Cambridge University Press, 2012), 11–23; Robert Doran, *The Theory of the Sublime from Longinus to Kant* (Cambridge: Cambridge University Press, 2015), 27–81.

9. See Holmes, *Function of Sublime Rhetoric*, esp. 81–102. Cf. Russell, *"Longinus" On The Sublime*, xliii.

10. See Holmes, *Function of Sublime Rhetoric*, 78.

rest of the treatise, with the exception of a few digressions, discusses each of the five sources.[11]

On the Sublime demonstrates significant overlap with other ancient handbooks of rhetoric. It lacks the comprehensive, systematic approach of Quintilian's *Institutes*, the focused and thoroughgoing comparison of Dionysius of Halicarnassus's *On the Orators*, and even the explicit focus on oratory as in Aristotle's *Rhetoric*. However, it certainly overlaps with these in important ways. *On the Sublime* participates in the broader analysis of different types of rhetorical style. While the works of Demetrius, Dionysius, and Cicero discuss several types of style, *On the Sublime* focuses entirely on sublime rhetoric. On the whole, Longinus's sublime rhetoric aligns with the "grand style" of Cicero or the "mixed style" of Dionysius of Halicarnassus, though it differs from both in important ways.

It would be wrong to think of sublime rhetoric only in terms of the ancient analysis of style.[12] Rather, the treatise should be understood within a broader ancient discussion on the power and effects of language. Some authors, like Aristotle in the *Poetics*, attribute to this powerful capacity of language a beneficial, even moral value. Other authors, like Plutarch in *How the Young Man Should Study Poetry*, insist this power must be limited or controlled through reason and a reasoned reading of ancient writings. Like Dionysius of Halicarnassus and Philo of Alexandria, *On the Sublime* links the powerful capacity of language to religious experience and encounters with divine realities.[13]

The Dislocating Effects of Sublime Rhetoric

Sublime rhetoric is characterized chiefly by its intended effects on readers and hearers. As the programmatic statement from *Subl.* 1.3–4 indicates, sublime rhetoric leads to ἔκστασις (εἰς ἔκστασιν ἄγει), to lead audiences outside of themselves. In her discussion of *On the Sublime*, Too refers to

---

11. The treatise's discussion of each is, on the whole, straightforward: chs. 9–15 discuss impressive thoughts, chs. 16–29 concern the use of figures, chs. 30–38 analyze word choice, and chs. 39–43 evaluate sentence structure.

12. For a brief overview, see Russell, *"Longinus" On the Sublime*, xxxii–xl; Holmes, *Function of Sublime Rhetoric*, 41. I have discussed the place of *On the Sublime* within ancient discussion of style more extensively in Holmes, *Function of Sublime Rhetoric*, 81–102.

13. See Holmes, *Function of Sublime Rhetoric*, 102–16.

Divine Speech, Hebrews, and Sublime Rhetoric 69

this effect or capacity of sublime rhetoric to lead audiences into ἔκστασις as "dislocation:"

> But where [Longinus] is concerned, the sublime seeks furthermore to move the reading subject, both in the sense of persuading him or her but also in the sense of transporting this individual to an entirely different "place," as literally and metaphorically understood.... The sublime assumes a parallel between linguistic dislocation and cultural dislocation and reinstitution.[14]

Too describes the capacity of sublime rhetoric to dislocate its hearers (or readers) in a variety of ways. She calls attention to the "spatialized and moved language" of sublime rhetoric that displaces, uplifts, transports, and resituates hearers.[15]

Too suggests that this capacity of language derives from the parallel between *linguistic dislocation* and *cultural dislocation*. On the one hand, linguistic dislocation calls attention to the flexibility or mobility of language itself, seen most clearly in the arrangement of words and the way meaning is made using metaphor. Unlike a statue that is static and unmoving, language is mobile, active, and flexible.[16] On the other hand, cultural dislocation refers to the capacity of sublime rhetoric to distance hearers from their immediate life setting. Sublime rhetoric moves hearers from (ἐκ) one position or place (στάσις) to another. Too explains that this movement has both temporal and spatial dynamics, both of which are activated by the imagination. Ultimately, sublime rhetoric amounts to a "radical transport of the reading subject from his or her present situation."[17] While the effects of sublime rhetoric are transient, they are also transformational. Sublime rhetoric moves hearers out of their immediate situation so that

---

14. Too, *Idea of Ancient Literary Criticism*, 195. This quotation from Too reflects two differences between her understanding of *On the Sublime* and mine. First, she refers to the subject of the treatise as *sublime* whereas I have opted for the phrase *sublime rhetoric*. Second, she links sublime rhetoric with persuasion more closely than I do. Despite this, her discussion of dislocation helps understand *On the Sublime* and the function of sublime rhetoric in Hebrews.

15. Too, *Idea of Ancient Literary Criticism*, 193.

16. Too, *Idea of Ancient Literary Criticism*, 193. Too draws on ancient distinctions between verbal representation and representation in visual art. See, e.g., Alcidamus, *On the Sophists* 27; Isocrates, *Evag.* 75; Apuleius, *Apol.* 14.

17. Too, *Idea of Ancient Literary Criticism*, 210.

they might reenter that situation in a new and more effective way. Each of the examples in *Subl.* 9 serves to re-present the actions described, moving the audience to the scene described.

What is the significance or purpose of the dislocating effects of sublime rhetoric? What long-term effect does this "spatialized and moved" language have? This is the implicit question behind the conversation between Longinus and an unnamed philosopher in *Subl.* 44. The conversation is significant because of how it relates to the dating of the treatise. But it is important to consider that conversation more fully, since it provides insight into how the treatise understands sublime rhetoric, its effects, and its overall purpose.

The explicit topic of conversation concerns the cultural decline in their generation and what the philosopher takes to be the absence of literary genius among their contemporaries.[18] This is how the philosopher evaluates the situation:

> "It surprises me," he said, "as it doubtless surprises many others too, how it is that in this age of ours we find natures that are supremely persuasive and suited for public life, shrewd and versatile and especially rich in literary charm, yet really sublime and transcendent natures are no longer, or only very rarely, now produced. Such a world-wide dearth of literature besets our times." (*Subl.* 44.1)

The philosopher's perspective reflects the distinction between persuasion (or persuasive rhetoric) and sublime rhetoric assumed elsewhere in the treatise. Attention to the spoken and written word, it seems, is limited to those who are "suited for public life." Such people are "supremely persuasive" and "rich in literary charm," but they do not measure up to those with "sublime and transcendent natures." Seen in light of the emphases elsewhere in the treatise, the philosopher acknowledges that there are orators who are charming and persuasive, but there are few in his generation who can move audiences *beyond* persuasion.

Not only does the philosopher diagnose the nature of cultural decline in his generation, he makes a suggestion about its cause. Writing in the age of the empire rather than the republic, the philosopher connects the

---

18. For a similar sentiment, see Tacitus, *Dial.* 1. For a broader discussion of this period in ancient literature, see E. R. Dodds, *The Greeks and the Irrational* (Berkeley: University of California Press, 1951), 236–69.

dearth of great literature with the loss of democracy. He notes the view that "democracy is the kindly nurse of genius" and that "great men of letters flourished only with democracy and perished with it" (*Subl.* 44.2). Democracy and the freedom it affords has "the power to foster noble minds" stirred on by competition, rivalry, and the pursuit of public office (44.2–3). All varieties of oratory flourish in these sorts of environments. According to the philosopher, though, he and his generation no longer have access to those environments; they are cut off from the "fairest and most fertile source of literature, which is freedom" (44.3). Instead, his generation is enslaved, shaped "in servile ways and practices" (44.3) because of the absence of democratic freedom.

After the philosopher presents his understanding of his cultural moment, Longinus responds. He accepts, it appears, the philosopher's diagnosis of cultural decline. He does not disagree about the general dearth in great literature among his contemporaries. He also does not fully disagree with the philosopher's suggestion about the cause of this decline, the loss of freedom. He differs, however, in his understanding of both freedom and domination. According to Longinus, his generation's decline is a consequence of the soul's imprisonment, not the loss of social or political freedom. It is the "endless warfare" of passions that enslave the human soul. Human genius is not stifled by the rise of imperial rule but by the enervating effects of moral vice. In his catalogue of vicious dispositions and behaviors, Longinus emphasizes the degenerative quality of vice. Misdirected love (love of money; love of pleasure; avarice) weigh the person down, sinking their "lives, soul and all, into the depths" (*Subl.* 44.6). The other vices enumerated carry with them a spatial overtone. Vices like immense and licentious wealth, arrogance, and shamelessness keep people from looking *upward* and cause them to forget their "good name" (44.7). Echoing a Platonic perspective, vice shifts the gaze downward, toward earth and earthly things, toward pleasure and power and possessions: "Step by step the ruin of their lives is complete, their greatness of soul wastes away from inanition and is no longer their ideal, since they value [ἐκθαυμάζω] that part of them which is mortal and consumes away, and neglect the development of their immortal souls" (44.8). To bring out the force of the verb, ἐκθαυμάζω more fully, we might say that people in Longinus's generation found wonder in the mortal rather than the immortal; they were amazed by the ordinary rather than the extraordinary.

Longinus ends his assessment by saying that apathy (ῥᾳθυμία) is responsible for "spend[ing] the spirit of the present generation" (*Subl.*

44.11).[19] The use of ῥᾳθυμία in *Subl.* 44.11 aligns most closely with moral connotations of the word. It has to do with irresponsible or intentional laziness, neglect, or inattention. Many writers connect apathy with other vices like carousing and drunkenness, since inactivity or inattention makes slipping into these vices easier. It is particularly relevant for the conversation in chapter 44 that several sources insist that apathy distorts and distracts. It fixates one's attention on the pedestrian matters of wealth, glory, and pleasure while neglecting more important things like progress in virtue and connection with the ideal world.

The conversation in the final chapter of *On the Sublime*, and especially Longinus's words about wonder and apathy, shed new light on sublime rhetoric and its intended effect. Much of the treatise offers readers and hearers the opportunity to wonder in the extraordinary, to be impressed and swept away by the brilliance of earlier writers. Moreover, the effects of sublime rhetoric become, as it were, an antidote to vice. Where vice lowers the mind's gaze and sinks the soul, sublime rhetoric raises the eyes and uplifts the soul. By nature, humans have an innate desire for what is "great and more divine" than itself (35.2), but they tend to fixate on the base things that are immediately before them, things like pleasure, money, and fame. Sublime rhetoric inspires wonder (1.4), not only for a fleeting moment of literary escape, but so that it might reorient audiences to what really matters.

Ultimately, the dislocating effects of sublime rhetoric serve a greater moral or even religious function in the perspective of *On the Sublime*. The treatise relies on certain philosophical and religious assumptions to explore these effects: The good is found in the ideal world; vice is found in the world of perception and its enslaving distractions. The really real is found outside of earthly and human reality, and it is accessed through contemplation and moral formation. By dislocating hearers from their immediate situation, sublime rhetoric makes it possible for them to connect with deeper realities. Through the imagination, sublime rhetoric moves hearers to the place where gods speak and act and dwell. The powerful effects of sublime rhetoric shake them from their stupor, jostling them from apathy, so that they can live more effectively in their world.

---

19. I have analyzed the connotations of the word ῥᾳθυμία among writers from antiquity in Holmes, *Function of Sublime Rhetoric*, 57–60.

The Allusion to Genesis in *On the Sublime* 9.9

With this orientation to *On the Sublime* in mind, I turn now to the allusion to Gen 1 in Longinus's discussion of impressive ideas (*Subl.* 9.1–15.12), the first of the five sources of sublime rhetoric. While transitioning from his discussion of impressive ideas to a discussion of figures, Longinus provides a helpful summary of his understanding of sublime ideas: "This must suffice for our treatment of sublimity in ideas [περὶ τῶν κατὰ τὰς νοήσεις ὑψηλῶν], as produced by nobility of mind [μεγαλοφροσύνη] or imitation [μίμησις] or imagination [φαντασία]" (15.12). The allusion to Genesis occurs in Longinus's presentation of nobility or greatness of mind (9.1–13.1). Although he emphasizes the connection between "nobility of mind" and "natural genius" with sublime rhetoric, he says very little about the disposition or intellectual abilities of persons conceiving those ideas. Instead, the focus is on the nature and function of the ideas themselves.

The authors and sources discussed in this section of the treatise are, for the most part, unsurprising. He evaluates the "literary greats" of ages past such as Homer, Hesiod, and Demosthenes. The inclusion of the "lawgiver of the Jews" (9.9) among eminent figures such as these is, to say the least, unexpected. This inclusion is so surprising, in fact, that earlier scholarship assumed that the reference to Moses was a later Jewish or Christian interpolation.[20] As John Gager notes, however, the question of interpolation was "thoroughly examined and rejected by H[ermann] Mutschmann in 1917, and since his time the question has hardly been raised again."[21] More recent scholarship tends to accept the allusion as original, a conclusion supported by its alignment with its literary context.

---

20. On this question, see Holmes, *Function of Sublime Rhetoric*, 44 n. 44. The discussion by John G. Gager is very helpful. Gager, *Moses in Greco-Roman Paganism* (Nashville: Abingdon, 1972), 58–62. See also W. Rhys Roberts, "The Quotation from Genesis in the *De Sublimitate* (IX.9)," *CR* 9 (1897): 431–36; K. Ziegler, "Das Genesiscitat in der Schrift ΠΕΡΙ ΥΨΟΥΣ," *Hermes* 50 (1915): 572–603; H. Mutschmann, "Das Genesiscitat in der Schrift ΠΕΡΙ ΥΨΟΥΣ," *Hermes* 52 (1917): 161–200; Eduard Norden, *Das Genesiszitat in der Schrift vom "Erhabenen"* (Berlin: Akademie, 1955); Grube, "Notes on the ΠΕΡΙ ΥΨΟΥΣ," 355–74.

21. Gager, *Moses in Greco-Roman Paganism*, 58.

Confident of the authenticity of this example from Moses, it is necessary to say more about the allusion itself. The reference to the creation story in Genesis reads: "So, too, the lawgiver of the Jews, no ordinary man, having formed a worthy conception of divine power and given expression to it, writes at the very beginning of his Laws: 'God said'—what? 'Let there be light,' and there was light, 'Let there be earth,' and there was earth" (*Subl.* 9.9). The reference to the creation story in *On the Sublime* and the text from the Greek translation of Genesis are reproduced in this table:

	Genesis 1:3, 9–10	On the Sublime 9.9
Creation of Light	καὶ εἶπεν ὁ θεός Γενηθήτω φῶς. καὶ ἐγένετο φῶς	εἶπεν ὁ θεός, φησί· τί; γενέσθω φῶς, καὶ ἐγένετο
Creation of Earth	Καὶ εἶπεν ὁ θεός Συναχθήτω τὸ ὕδωρ τὸ ὑποκάτω τοῦ οὐρανοῦ εἰς συναγωγὴν μίαν, καὶ ὀφθήτω ἡ ξηρά. καὶ ἐγένετο οὕτως. καὶ συνήχθη τὸ ὕδωρ τὸ ὑποκάτω τοῦ οὐρανοῦ εἰς τὰς συναγωγὰς αὐτῶν, καὶ ὤφθη ἡ ξηρά. καὶ ἐκάλεσεν ὁ θεὸς τὴν ξηρὰν γῆν καὶ τὰ συστήματα τῶν ὑδάτων ἐκάλεσεν θαλάσσας.	γενέσθω γῆ, καὶ ἐγένετο

The reference to Genesis recalls two moments: the creation of light and the creation of earth. The reference to the creation of light is nearly identical to the Greek version of Gen 1:3, as the table above shows; the only difference is that the version in *On the Sublime* removes φῶς after καὶ ἐγένετο. The reference to the creation of earth, however, amounts to a reconfiguration of Gen 1:9–10 rather than a quotation. It simplifies the version found in Genesis, bringing it closer to the basic structure of Gen 1:3. In Genesis, God's speech first draws the waters into one gathering so that the dry land can be seen. In Gen 1:10, God names the dry land *earth*, and the gathering of water God names *sea*. The shorter version in *On the Sublime* is more dramatic. God speaks, and suddenly earth appears without the intermediate step of gathering the water to reveal dry land. As Gager notes, Longinus's allusion amounts to a "careful rephrasing of the Genesis material." Longinus's treatment of Genesis resembles his practice with other ancient writers: "Just as he regularly rephrased and conflated passages from Homer and Plato, so he also altered the verses from Genesis to suit his own stylistic purposes."[22] In addition to creating a clearer parallel with Gen 1:3, the creation of earth as it appears in *On the Sublime* intensifies the emphasis on the powerful effects of God's speech.

The reference to the Genesis creation story in *On the Sublime* is perhaps the clearest indicator that, whatever else sublime rhetoric may be, it cannot be reduced to fine or excellent style. Compared to the characteristics of the great or elevated styles in the descriptions of Demetrius or Quintilian, the Genesis allusion simply does not measure up. As Casper de Jonge notes, there is in the allusion to Genesis "no bombastic language…, but we are impressed by a simple repetition of ordinary words."[23]

What, then, qualifies the Genesis creation story as an example of sublime rhetoric? Attention to the larger literary context provides important clues. The allusion to Gen 1 occurs in the section devoted to "greatness of thought," the first and most important source of sublime rhetoric. Most examples of greatness of thought that the treatise identifies are, to use the language of de Jonge, "descriptions of impressive divinities."[24] Greatness of thought seems to be primarily religious in nature. In chapter 9, Longinus references four passages from Homer before discussing the paraphrase of the Genesis creation story:

Subl. 9.4: Eris is said to fill the distance between earth and heaven (*Il.* 4.442);

Subl. 9.5: The "horses of heaven" jump as far as the human eye can see (*Il.* 5.770–772);

Subl. 9.6: Homer captures the terror and power of the "battle of the gods" (likely a conflation of *Il.* 21.388 and 20.61–65);

Subl. 9.8: Poseidon parts the sea on his chariot (likely a conflation of *Il.* 13.18; 20.60; 13.19, 27–29).

After the allusion to Genesis, he provides two more examples of greatness of thought:

---

22. Gager, *Moses in Greco-Roman Paganism*, 59.
23. Casper De Jonge, "Dionysius and Longinus on the Sublime: Rhetoric and Religious Language," *AJP* 133 (2012): 297.
24. De Jonge, "Dionysius and Longinus," 277.

Subl. 9.10: Ajax's prayer to Zeus (see *Il.* 17.645–647);

Subl. 9.11: Homer is likened to the war god (see *Il.* 15.605).

It is noteworthy that each example from Homer relates to divine beings or divine power. The other examples discussed in *Subl.* 9 suggest the close connection between divinity and great ideas as Longinus conceives them. De Jonge explains the significance of the Homeric texts for understanding the Genesis paraphrase and the nature of sublime rhetoric more generally:

> Central ideas of these texts are of course immensity, great distances, and unexpectedness.... There is an obvious connection between these sublime effects and the divinities that are portrayed in these lines.... It is the enormous power of gods that is responsible for the sublime as it appears in these examples. In other words, although the sublime can of course occur in narrative passages without gods, Longinus does suggest that there is (at the very least for Homer) a special relationship between divinity and sublimity.[25]

In an article exploring the series of quotations in chapter 9 of *On the Sublime*, M. D. Usher goes further. Expanding on an earlier article by M. L. West, Usher asserts that what binds the quotations in *Subl.* 9 together is "their common origin in Greek and Near Eastern myths of theomachy and creation."[26] He suggests that all of the quotations, in one way or another, call attention to the "cosmic repercussions brought about when gods make war."[27] He stretches the evidence too far in an attempt to make them all about the war of the gods. It is better to think of them more generally as epiphanies of the divine or intrusions of divine beings and divine realities into the earthly realm. His note about the "cosmic repercussions" of such activity is valid nonetheless.

The two references that immediately precede the allusion to Gen 1 demonstrate these cosmic repercussions. First, Longinus explains the lit-

---

25. De Jonge, "Dionysius and Longinus," 278.

26. M. D. Usher, "Theomachy, Creation, and the Poetics of Quotation in Longinus Chapter 9," *CP* 102 (2007): 293. See M. L. West, "Longinus and the Grandeur of God," in *Ethics and Rhetoric: Classical Essays for Donald Russell on His Seventy-Fifth Birthday*, ed. Doreen Innes, Harry M. Hine, and Christopher Pelling (Oxford: Oxford University Press, 1995), 335–42.

27. Usher, "Theomachy, Creation," 295.

erary effects of Homer's theomachy scene in what amounts to a conflation of *Il.* 21.388 and 20.61–65:

> You see, friend, how the earth is split to its foundations, hell itself laid bare, the whole universe sundered and turned upside down; and meanwhile everything, heaven and hell, mortal and immortal alike, shares in the conflict and danger of that battle. (*Subl.* 9.6–7)

It is not the battle itself that seems to interest Longinus so much as it is the effects of the battle in the cosmic realm—the earth is split open, the whole universe is turned upside down, and a pervasive fear comes over all things, material and immaterial. Similarly, the next example, describing Poseidon, derived from portions of *Il.* 13, captures the effects of Poseidon's epiphany:

> Then were the woods and the long-lying ranges a-tremble,
> Aye, and the peaks and the city of Troy and the ships of Achaia
> Neath the immortal feet and the oncoming march of Poseidon.
> He set him to drive o'er the swell of the sea, and the whales at his coming
> Capering leapt from the deep and greeted the voice of their master.
> Then the sea parted her waves for joy, and they flew on the journey.
> (*Subl.* 9.8)

The reference to Poseidon connects with Genesis in two important ways. First, the reference to the "voice of their master" connects with God's powerful speech in Gen 1. Second, but less directly, the parting of the sea recalls God's parting of the water from the land in the fuller Genesis creation narrative. Like Poseidon's voice and presence, God's voice in Genesis transforms the cosmic realm, as light and land are created.

In summary, Longinus finds in the creation account of Genesis an example of an impressive idea that characterizes sublime rhetoric. His allusion to the creation account calls attention to the power of God's speech and how that speech effects the created order.[28] Longinus's allusion occurs in a chapter of references that are related, in various ways, to divine beings entering into the earthly realm. The example of Poseidon immediately preceding the allusion to Gen 1 also calls attention to

---

28. Gager comes to a similar conclusion: "In line with his theory that great style necessarily presupposes great ideas, especially in matters concerning the gods, 'Longinus' praises the deity as one whose power was so great that his word alone was sufficient for creation" (*Moses in Greco-Roman Paganism*, 59).

the power of divine speech. Far from a later interpolation, the allusion is embedded in Longinus's discussion of impressive ideas. With the preceding discussion of *On the Sublime* and the references to Homer and Moses in its ninth chapter in mind, we turn our attention now to the theme of God's speech in Hebrews.

God's Speech in Hebrews

It is not an overstatement to say that Hebrews is filled with references to God's speaking activity and that it is, in its own way, filled with God's speech itself. The poetic prologue to Hebrews highlights two moments in God's speaking activity. God spoke long ago through the prophets, but God has spoken in the last days through the Son (Heb 1:1–2). In the comparison between angels and the Son that follows, Heb 1:5–14 performs God's speech to the Son. Stringing together several citations from the Psalms, the author introduces each with a reference to God's speech, indicated by the repetition of λέγω. As Joshua Jipp argues, one effect of this purposeful resourcing of the Psalms citations is that it reproduces God's enthronement speech in the presence of the hearers.[29] In other words, the series of quotations moves listeners to the place where they overhear God's speech to the Son.

Similarly, the warning passage in Heb 3:7–4:13 moves hearers to the place where God speaks. Again, the author of Hebrews draws on the Psalms to bring about this effect. Throughout this passage, the author contemporizes the "today" of Ps 95. As a result, the passage dislocates hearers from their immediate situation and moves them into the wilderness where they once again experience God's speech. The wilderness denotes the place where the people of God hear and respond to God's voice, and the author warns them against an inadequate response, signaled by a "hard heart" (see Heb 3:8, 12, 15; 4:7). Failure to respond properly to God's voice is tantamount to turning away from the presence of the "living God" (3:12).

Elsewhere in Hebrews God's speech is characterized by its immediacy and effectiveness even as it is mediated through Israel's sacred writings. As we see in Heb 1:5–14, God's speech is also effective. God's speech appoints Jesus as high priest (5:5–6; cf. 7:17–22), and God's promise of the new cov-

---

29. Joshua Jipp, "The Son's Entrance into the Heavenly World: The Soteriological Necessity of the Scriptural Catena in Hebrews 1.5–14," *NTS* 56 (2010): 557–75.

enant makes the old covenant obsolete (8:8–13). In Heb 11:3, the author notes that the "worlds were prepared by the word of God," a sentiment that recalls both Gen 1 and Longinus's allusion to it in *Subl.* 9. Likewise, God's speech moves characters in Israel's history to action: God warns Noah about the flood (Heb 11:7), God calls Abraham (11:8), and God makes promises to Abraham (6:13–14, 17–18; 11:11). Because of God's speech in the past and in the present, it also assures the audience about the future; God promises to act for vengeance (10:30) and never to leave or forsake the audience members (13:5).

It is in Heb 12:18–29 that we most clearly see the immediacy and effectiveness of God's speech as well as its power. It is also the place in Hebrews where we see a description of God's speech that most closely aligns with Longinus's characterization of the nature and effects of sublime rhetoric in *Subl.* 9. It is to this passage that I now turn.[30]

God's Speech in Hebrews 12:18–29

Many interpreters highlight the central significance of Heb 12:18–29. Barnabas Lindars identifies the passage as the "grand finale," while Craig Koester calls it the climax to the author's argument.[31] Kiwoong Son goes so far as to identify Heb 12:18–29 as the hermeneutical key for understanding the whole composition.[32] Tom Long helpfully describes the passage as a "travelogue," calling attention to the author's use of descriptive language and appeal to the imagination.[33] The theme of God's speech is prominent: Hebrews 12:18–24 compares God's speaking presence from two locations, 12:25 compares the hearers' response to that speech, and 12:26–29 highlight the effects of God's speech.

The first location of God's speech, described in 12:18–21, recalls traditions related to Mount Horeb and Mount Sinai in Exodus and Deuteronomy:

---

30. What follows is based in part on the longer discussion in Holmes, *Function of Sublime Rhetoric*, 119–60.

31. Barnabas Lindars, "The Rhetorical Structure of Hebrews," *NTS* 35 (1989): 401; Craig R. Koester, *Hebrews: A New Translation with Introduction and Commentary*, AB 36 (New York: Doubleday, 2001), 548.

32. Kiwoong Son, *Zion Symbolism in Hebrews: Hebrews 12:18–23 as a Hermeneutical Key to the Epistle*, Paternoster Biblical Monographs (Milton Keynes: Paternoster, 2005).

33. Tom Long, *Hebrews*, IBC (Louisville: John Knox, 1997), 137.

> You have not come to something that can be touched, a blazing fire, and darkness, and gloom, and a tempest, and the sound of a trumpet, and a voice whose words made the hearers beg that not another word be spoken to them. (For they could not endure the order that was given, "If even an animal touches the mountain, it shall be stoned to death." Indeed, so terrifying was the sight that Moses said, "I tremble with fear"). (Heb 12:18–21)[34]

Combining imagery from Deut 4 and Exod 19, the author calls attention to the sensible manifestations of God's speaking presence: fire, darkness, a storm, and the sound of a trumpet. The construction of this scene draws the audience members into it, albeit imaginatively, even while insisting that the audience members have not come to such a place (Heb 12:18). The response of the hearers at the first location of God's speaking presence underscores its terrible power. They beg for the cessation of God's speech (12:19), and even Moses trembles with fear (12:21).

The second location of God's speaking presence is described in Heb 12:22–24. The author insists that *this* is the location to which the hearers have come:

> But you have come to Mount Zion and to the city of the living God, the heavenly Jerusalem, and to innumerable angels in festal gathering, and to the assembly of the firstborn who are enrolled in heaven, and to God the judge of all, and to the spirits of the righteous made perfect, and to Jesus, the mediator of a new covenant, and to the sprinkled blood that speaks a better word than the blood of Abel. (Heb 12:22–24)

Speaking more evocatively of a scene filled with otherworldly beings, the author says that hearers have come to the heavenly Jerusalem, the city of the living God. As Jipp notes, it is from this place that the audience overhears God's enthronement speech to the Son in 1:5–14.[35] Although downplayed by many interpreters, the fear and awe associated with God's speech remains, although it is implicit. Given the presence of angels in other biblical and early Jewish texts, the mention of "innumerable angels" gives the scene a solemn, even awe-inspiring sense. Likewise, God appears as the "judge of all," a moniker that recalls references to God's throne in apocalyptic literature. Though it lacks sensible manifestations like fire and

---

34. Unless otherwise indicated, English translations of Hebrews are from the NRSV.
35. Jipp, "Son's Entrance into the Heavenly World."

wind, the second location of God's speech is no less awesome. Drawing near to God's speaking presence remains a serious undertaking. Even if the audience can draw near to God's presence with confidence (4:16), no amount of confidence can eliminate fully the awesome prospect of approaching the living God (see 10:31).

Having described the two locations of God's speech, the one from the sensible mountain and the other from the heavenly Jerusalem, Heb 12:25 describes the responses to God's speech at each location:

> See that you do not refuse the one who is speaking; for if they did not escape when they refused the one who warned them on earth, how much less will we escape if we reject the one who warns from heaven! (Heb 12:25)

The author characterizes the response at the first location as one of insubordination. "Those" hearers refused or rejected God's speech. The hearers at the second location, the audience members addressed by Hebrews and by God's speech, are encouraged to avoid such a response.[36]

God's speech in Heb 12 leads to the transformation of the created order. Hebrews 12:26–27 reads as follows:

> At that time his voice shook the earth; but now he has promised, "Yet once more I will shake not only the earth but also the heaven." This phrase, "Yet once more," indicates the removal of what is shaken—that is, created things—so that what cannot be shaken may remain. (Heb 12:26–27)

Here the author draws again on the contrast between sensible manifestations of God's speech and more intangible ones. The manifestation of God's speech in the first instance recalls traditions related to Horeb and Sinai. Whereas the accounts in Judg 5:4–5 and Exod 19:18 connect the earth's shaking with God's presence, Heb 12:26 connects this more explicitly with God's speech. God's voice shook the earth (ἡ φωνὴ τὴν γῆν ἐσάλευσεν). The manifestation of God's speech in the second instance is less tangible, since it refers to the effects of God's speech that will occur

---

36. For a survey of scholarship related to Heb 12:25, see Gene Smillie, "'The One Who Is Speaking' in Hebrews 12:25," *TynBul* 55 (2004): 275–94. For a broader discussion of God's speech in Hebrews, see Jonathan I. Griffiths, *Hebrews and Divine Speech*, LNTS 507 (London: Bloomsbury T&T Clark, 2014).

at some point in the future. The second instance intensifies the powerful nature of God's speech, however. Quoting Hag 2:6, the author says that God's promised speech will shake not only the earth but also heaven (ἐγὼ σείσω οὐ μόνον τὴν γῆν ἀλλὰ καὶ τὸν οὐρανόν). The author adds that this promise indicates that God's speech "yet once more" will result in the removal (μετάθεσις) of all that has been made so that which cannot be shaken will remain.

There are important connections between this depiction of God's speech in Heb 12 and the examples of the "cosmic repercussions" of God's speech that Longinus catalogues in *Subl.* 9. The first thing to note is the theophanic quality of the scenes described. Whether through the mention of wind and fire or heavenly beings, the passage signals God's awesome presence. What is more, the passage moves the hearers into this presence through descriptive language and its appeal to the imagination. Second, the sheer power of God's speech, especially the emphasis on the removal of all created things, recalls Longinus's comments on Homer's theomachia. It is not a stretch to say that Heb 12:27, like the theomachia, imagines "the whole universe sundered and turned upside down" (*Subl.* 9.6) by God's speech. Third, the connection between divine speech and the shaking of the created order resembles the description of Poseidon's voice and the parting the sea in *Subl.* 9.8. Finally, God's speech in Heb 12:27 aligns with Longinus's allusion to the creation account in Genesis. Of course, Hebrews says that God's speech results in the *removal* of the created order, while Longinus connects God's speech with its *creation*. Still, both accounts emphasize the power of God's speech to alter the cosmic realm fundamentally. Moreover, the shaking that comes with God's speech in Heb 12:27 can also be understood as an act of creation. God's speech results in the removal of all things *so that* those things that cannot be shaken will remain. What remains after God's promised powerful speech can be understood as the creation, or at least the unveiling, of something new.

Hebrews 12:18–29 focuses the attention of the hearers on God's powerful speaking presence. God's speech is powerful, creative, and piercing. The author of Hebrews does not speak about God's speech in a distant, uninvolved manner. Rather, the author insists that the hearers have come to the place where God speaks, to the location where God warns them, much like God spoke to the people of Israel from the earthly mountain. In bringing them to this place, the author's description emphasizes the cosmic repercussions of God's speaking presence.

Reconsidering the Place of God's Speech in Hebrews

The emphasis on God's speech in Hebrews relates to the dislocating effects of sublime rhetoric. In various ways, Hebrews moves hearers to the place where God speaks. As noted above, this includes God's enthronement speech to the Son (Heb 1:5–14), God's piercing speech in the wilderness (Heb 3–4), and God's powerful speech that will shake the whole created order (Heb 12:25–29). By moving the hearers into the place where God speaks, Hebrews dislocates the hearers from their immediate life situation.

Hebrews contains important clues about this life situation. The hearers are apparently second-generation Christians, having received the message from those who first heard it through the Lord (2:3). According to the author, though, they are at risk of drifting away from that message (2:1). In addition, the author is concerned that the hearers might move away from the gathered community by forsaking their gatherings together (10:25). The reasons for their potential drift are apparent as well. The hearers' commitment to the gathered community, both in the past and in the present, has required a break with their surrounding community, and this break has been costly.[37] It has forced the hearers to endure a "hard struggle with sufferings," including public abuse, persecution, imprisonment, and the loss of possessions (10:32–34). It is important to remember that the first recipients of Hebrews likely heard it read in the very gathering that had come to cost them so much. Through its appeal to divine speech, and the intended effects of sublime rhetoric more generally, Hebrews transports the hearers from this place of reviling and persecution into the place where God speaks.

Ultimately, the dislocation caused by sublime rhetoric enables the hearers to reenter their life situation more effectively. First, the textual journey of Hebrews invites the hearers to perceive their gathering together

---

37. For an overview and discussion of the hearers' experience of persecution, see Craig R. Koester, "Conversion, Persecution, and Malaise: Life in the Community for Which Hebrews Was Written," *HvTSt* 61 (2005): 231–51; James A. Kelhoffer, "Persecution, Perseverance, and Perfection in Hebrews," in *Persecution, Persuasion, and Power: Readiness to Withstand Hardship as a Corroboration of Legitimacy in the New Testament*, WUNT 1/270 (Tübingen: Mohr Siebeck, 2010), 127–42. A fuller discussion, including a more nuanced discussion of the methodology required for reading Hebrews with an eye to the social context in which and for which it was written, can be found in Bryan R. Dyer, *Suffering in the Face of Death: The Epistle to the Hebrews in Its Context of Situation*, LNTS 568 (London: Bloomsbury T&T Clark, 2017).

in new light. Far more than a merely human gathering or a source of shame and struggle, their gatherings together are the place where they encounter God. God's speech addresses them. Through the intercession of the Son and heavenly high priest, Jesus, God's forgiveness is experienced (4:14–16). They enter through the "way of Jesus" into the holy of holies (10:20). Second, and as a consequence of the first, the presence of sublime rhetoric in Hebrews is intended to help the hearers endure the persecution that they are currently facing or will face in the near future. It provides them the wherewithal to run with endurance the race that is set before them (12:1–2), to lift drooping hands and to strengthen weak knees (12:12). The new understanding of their gathering as the place where God speaks makes it all the more necessary to protect the integrity of that place through practices of love, hospitality, and sympathy for those who are imprisoned (13:1–3).

Conclusion

Sublime rhetoric is particularly well-suited to conveying the rhetoric of religion. The significance of divine beings and divine realities in the discussion of sublime rhetoric in *On the Sublime* cannot be ignored. Of course, not all of Longinus's examples nor all the components of sublime rhetoric relate directly to religion or religious ideas. Still, Longinus gives significant attention to the depiction of divinities, their activities, and their dwelling places. This is especially true in the section of the treatise devoted to great ideas.

Divine speech, in the view of Longinus, stands out among other great ideas. Longinus finds in Homer and in the "lawgiver of the Jews" powerful examples of the cosmic repercussions of divine speech. God's speech creates and disrupts earthly structures, it shakes the ground and parts the sea. Divine speech is, perhaps preeminently, an example of a sublime idea. But divine speech also shares the moving and dislocating effects of sublime rhetoric. The scenes describing God's speech are awesome, even terrifying, portraits of the raw power of divinity. The scenes move hearers to inhabit the places where God speaks and to share in the emotional and spiritual disposition of those in God's speaking presence. As such, these scenes have the capacity to "lift the eyes of the soul" (see *Subl.* 33–36) so that audiences might contemplate otherworldly realities and move closer to the ideal world.

The perspective of *On the Sublime* provides an important framework for considering God's speech in Hebrews. God's speech plays a prominent role throughout the argument of Hebrews. God's speech is both personal and powerful. Through Israel's sacred texts and through the voice of the community's leaders, God addresses those gathered together in the name of Jesus. God's speech requires the hearers to pay attention to their disposition and to listen carefully. In this way, God's speech is personal. But God's speech is also powerful. God's words spoken to or about the Son are performative; they speak into reality divine purposes and promises. God's speech directs the community's ancestors in the faith to move from one place to another. Finally, as evidenced by Heb 12:18–29, God's speech manifests itself in the same sort of cosmic repercussions that are described in *On the Sublime*. Hebrews 12:18–29 moves the hearers to fear or awe in the presence of divine power, and it transports them to the scenes it represents. One function of this emphasis on divine speech in Hebrews is that it locates God's speech within and among the gathered community. In their gathering together, the community overhears God's speech to the Son, learns of God's speech in the past, and experiences God's speech in the present.

Rhetorical Criticism of the Sublime

Thomas H. Olbricht†

I first became acquainted with different rhetorical styles in a speech course at Northern Illinois University in 1949 taught by Paul Crawford, who had a PhD in speech from Northwestern University, Evanston, Illinois. For the text we purchased William Norwood Brigance's *Speech Composition*.[1] I don't recall that we paid much attention to the sublime style, but we talked of "purple patches," which are also designated "purple passages." These are sections in a discourse that are flowery and ornate and often stand out from the rest of the speech. I recall locating such patches in orations of Robert Ingersoll and sermons of Henry Ward Beecher.[2] From Northern Illinois I entered a graduate program in speech at the University of Iowa. In a course on the history of rhetoric taught by Professor Orville Hitchcock, we read selections from Longinus's *Rhetoric of the Sublime* but didn't spend much time on the sublime style.[3] We focused on the three ancient styles heralded by the Greek and Roman rhetoricians: (1) low or plain style; (2) middle style; and (3) high or grand style.[4] The sublime, when mentioned, was related to the grand style.

---

1. William Norwood Brigance, *Speech Composition* (New York: Crofts, 1937).

2. Robert Ingersoll, *The Works of Robert Green Ingersoll*, 12 vols. (New York: Dresden Publishing, 1900). Henry Ward Beecher, *Lectures to Young Men: On Various Important Subjects; New Edition with Additional Lectures* (Boston: Ticknor & Fields, 1868).

3. Lester Thonssen, *Selected Readings in Rhetoric and Public Speaking with Introductory Comments* (New York: Wilson, 1942). We also read Thonssen and A. Craig Baird, *Speech Criticism, the Development of Standards for Rhetorical Appraisal* (New York: Ronald Press, 1948).

4. Donald A. Russell, *Criticism in Antiquity* (Berkeley: University of California Press, 1981).

After the 1950s, I did not give much attention to the sublime, though in a course at Harvard Divinity School with the dean, Samuel Miller, we read and discussed Rudolf Otto's *The Idea of the Holy*, and I thought at some length then and since about numinous experiences.[5] In the middle 1960s, I taught a humanities course at Pennsylvania State University in which, among several other documents, we read William Wordsworth's "Lines Composed a Few Miles above Tintern Abbey." I was impressed especially with how Wordsworth envisioned the innate or Platonic sense of beauty and moments of sublime experiences. I also in that time frame read the works and important interpreters of the eighteenth-century Scottish rhetoricians.[6] I spent some time with Hugh Blair and his reflections on the sublime. All of this background was brought to bear when I read Wilhelm Wuellner's problematic essay on the sublime and tried to make sense of it.[7]

In this essay I will probe the views of the sublime in Blair, Wordsworth, and Wuellner. With their insights as a backdrop, I will construct a tentative proposal in regard to rhetorical criticism of the sublime and set out concrete principles for rhetorical analysis of the sublime in the Ephesian epistle.

Hugh Blair

Hugh Blair (1718–1800), along with George Campbell (1719–1796) and Richard Whately (1787–1863), was one of the major book-publishing

---

5. Rudolf Otto, *The Idea of the Holy: An Inquiry into the Non-rational Factor in the Idea of the Divine and Its Relation to the Rational* (Oxford: Oxford University Press, 1959).

6. Michael Moran, ed., *Eighteenth Century British and American Rhetorics and Rhetoricians: Critical Studies and Sources* (Westport, CT: Greenwood, 1994); Wilbur Samuel Howell, *Eighteenth Century British Logic and Rhetoric* (Princeton: Princeton University Press, 1971); Howell, *Logic and Rhetoric in England, 1500–1700* (Princeton: Princeton University Press, 1956); James L. Golden, and Edward P. J. Corbett, *The Rhetoric of Blair, Campbell, and Whately* (Carbondale: Southern Illinois University Press, 1990); George Campbell, *Philosophy of Rhetoric*, ed. with an introduction by Lloyd Bitzer (Carbondale: Southern Illinois University Press, 1988).

7. Wilhelm Wuellner, "Reconceiving a Rhetoric of Religion: A Rhetorics of Power and the Power of the Sublime," in *Rhetorics and Hermeneutics: Wilhelm Wuellner and His Influence*, ed. James D. Hester and J. David Hester, ESEC 9 (London: T&T Clark International, 2004), 23–77.

eighteenth-century Scottish Enlightenment rhetoricians.[8] Of the three, Blair commented most on the sublime. The backdrop for Blair's observations on the sublime is laid in his Lecture II on taste. In Lecture III he discussed sublimity in nature and persons, and in Lecture IV "The Sublime in Writing." The whole of the first volume is essentially dedicated to style. Rosaleen Greene-Smith Keefe aptly stated,

> Throughout the 48 lectures, he stresses the importance of a thorough knowledge of one's subject. He makes it clear that a stylistically deficient text reflects a writer who doesn't know what he thinks; anything less than a clear conception of one's subject guarantees defective work, "so close is the connection between thoughts and the words in which they are clothed" (I, 7).... In sum, Blair equates taste with the delighted perception of wholeness and posits such delight as a psychological given.[9]

In regard to Wuellner's capstone focus upon the sublime, David Hester too hastily asserts that

> The transformation of a rhetoric of the Bible to a rhetoric of power as a rhetoric of the sublime represents a watershed event in the field. It is the only sustained (if not complete) attempt since Longinus to return rhetoric to the sublime. It represents an important synthesis and gives a new direction to a myriad of issues and concerns Wilhelm has voiced in previous articles.[10]

This declaration betrays the lacuna similarly endemic in Wuellner's history of rhetoric that essentially ignores the important contributions of Scottish, British, and American rhetoricians. I offer as a case in point Blair, who in his acclaimed *Lectures on Rhetoric and Belles Lettres* discusses the

---

8. Hugh Blair, *Lectures on Rhetoric and Belle Lettres*, 2 vols. (London: Strahan & Cadell; Edinburgh: Creech, 1783). George Campbell, *The Philosophy of Rhetoric*, new ed., 2 vols. (Edinburgh: Creech, 1808); Richard Whately, *Elements of Rhetoric* (London: Parker, 1851).

9. Rosaleen Greene-Smith Keefe, "'A Peculiar Power of Perception': Scottish Enlightenment Rhetoric and the New Aesthetic of Language" (PhD diss., University of Rhode Island, 2016), xi.

10. David Hester, "The Wuellnerian Sublime: Rhetorics, Power, and the Ethics of Commun(icat)ion," in Hester and Hester, *Rhetorics and Hermeneutics*, 5.

sublime at some length.[11] Admittedly, Blair does not attempt a systems synthesis of the sort proposed by Wuellner. But he does build on Longinus and advances beyond him as it pertains to Christian rhetoric.

Blair was born in Edinburgh in 1718. He was awarded an MA from the University of Edinburgh in 1739. He was notable for his sermons, several of which were published, and his belles lettres lectures. He commenced lecturing on composition at the university in 1759 and was appointed Regius Professor of Belles Lettres in 1762, which he continued until his retirement in 1783.[12]

In the first place, Blair believed that rhetorical sublimity must be related to objects or beings that are sublime. The ultimate sublimity therefore pertains to God.

> No ideas, it is plain, are so sublime as those taken from the Supreme Being; the most unknown, but the greatest of all objects; the infinity of whose nature, and the eternity of whose duration, joined with the omnipotence of his power, though they surpass our conceptions, yet exalt them to the highest. In general, all objects that are greatly raised above us, or far removed from us, either in space or in time, are apt to strike us as great. Our viewing them, as through the mist of distance or antiquity, is favourable to the impressions of their sublimity.[13]

The discourse that poses the greatest prospect for the sublime is therefore religious discourse. Blair argued that, in fact, the rhetoric of the pulpit did not match any of the ancient genres and was so distinct as to require a separate genre.

> It will, however, suit our purpose better, and be found, I imagine, more useful to follow that division which the train of modern speaking naturally points out to us, taken from the three great scenes of eloquence, popular assemblies, the bar, and the pulpit; each of which has a distinct character that particularly suits it. This division coincides in part with the ancient one. The eloquence of the bar is precisely the same with what

---

11. Blair, *Lectures on Rhetoric and Belles Lettres*. I will refer to Blair's section on the sublime in Golden and Corbett, *Rhetoric of Blair*, 37–87.

12. John Hill, *An Account of the Life and Writings of Hugh Blair* (Edinburgh: Ballantyne, 1807). See also Lois Agnew, "The Civil Formation of Taste: A Re-assessment of Hugh Blair's Rhetorical Theory," *RSQ* 28 (1998): 25–36.

13. Golden and Corbett, *Rhetoric of Blair*, 54–55.

the ancients called the judicial. The eloquence of popular assemblies, though mostly of what they term the deliberative species, yet admits also of the demonstrative. The eloquence of the pulpit is altogether of a distinct nature, and cannot be properly reduced under any of the heads of the ancient rhetoricians.[14]

One of the chief ways in which Blair perceived pulpit oratory as different was in regard to the sublime.

Blair introduced the sublime in setting forth his outlooks on taste in the second lecture. He believed that taste was acquired in stages, the first focusing upon the simplest and plainest but moving upward toward the intricate and compounded.[15] This does not mean, however, that the capacity for the grander style is acquired. "Taste, as I before explained it, is ultimately founded on an internal sense of beauty, which is natural to men, and which, in its application to particular objects, is capable of being guided and enlightened by reason."[16] He believed that learning the rules are of help but that some persons of genius know them apart from education. Blair argued that one of the features of sublimity is that it brings pleasure to the beholder. The sublime is discovered both in objects and through their description in discourse or writing.[17] Much grandeur is to be discovered in natural phenomena with nothing being "more sublime than mighty power and strength."[18] That which borders on the terrible likewise assists the sublime such as darkness, solitude, and silence. Sublimity also is enhanced by obscurity.

> Thus we see that almost all the descriptions given us of the appearances of supernatural beings, carry some sublimity, though the conceptions which they afford us be confused and indistinct. Their sublimity arises from the ideas, which they always convey, of superior power and might, joined with an awful obscurity.[19]

Human actions and traits also exhibit the sublime, in like manner as nature through heroism. High virtue is a source of moral sublimity.[20]

---

14. Golden and Corbett, *Rhetoric of Blair*, 99.
15. Golden and Corbett, *Rhetoric of Blair*, 39.
16. Golden and Corbett, *Rhetoric of Blair*, 44.
17. Golden and Corbett, *Rhetoric of Blair*, 52.
18. Golden and Corbett, *Rhetoric of Blair*, 53.
19. Golden and Corbett, *Rhetoric of Blair*, 54.
20. Golden and Corbett, *Rhetoric of Blair*, 55–56.

In Lecture IV Blair discussed the nature of the sublime in writing. He takes up the views of Longinus on the sublime but declared that Longinus often confused elevated conceptions with what pleases. Longinus pointed out five sources of the sublime: (1) grandeur of thoughts; (2) the pathetic; (3) application of figures; (4) the use of tropes and beautiful expressions; and (5) musical structure and arrangements of words.[21] Blair declared the first two are pertinent to the sublime in discourse. The sublime must begin with the sublime object.

> In the next place, the object must not only, in itself, be sublime, but it must be set before us in such a light as is most proper to give us a clear and full impression of it; it must be described with strength, with conciseness, and simplicity.[22]

In poetry he extolled simplicity and conciseness and eschewed rhyming. "The boldness, freedom, and variety of our blank verse, is infinitely more favourable than rhyme, to all kinds of sublime poetry. The circumstances must themselves be grand such as the flaring up of a tempest, and emotion laden."[23] Faults of style opposite to the sublime are the frigid and the bombast.[24] It is clear therefore that by the sublime Blair had in mind the grandeur of objects and persons that the rhetor in turn depicted in a sublime rhetorical style.

On the contribution of the Scottish common sense rhetoric Keefe concluded,

> Far from following basic Enlightenment philosophy of mind but inserting a Common Sense epistemology to the detriment of any substantial rhetorical renovation, I put forward that Campbell and Blair, and the Common Sense school of which they are a part, create an insightfully inventive theory of language and its use. This new Common Sense philosophy of language reunites Logic and Rhetoric, which had been separated in Protestant teaching since the work of Petrus Ramus. They do this via a rhetorical theorization of Common Sense philosophy's realism in conjunction with Hume's philosophy of mind. The realist vision of language that emerges from the rhetorics of George Campbell, Hugh

---

21. Golden and Corbett, *Rhetoric of Blair*, 58.
22. Golden and Corbett, *Rhetoric of Blair*, 59.
23. Golden and Corbett, *Rhetoric of Blair*, 62.
24. Golden and Corbett, *Rhetoric of Blair*, 65.

Blair, and, later, Alexander Bain, presents an understanding of language in which verbal communication—by virtue of its unique place in human reasoning—is recursive, and therefore progressive; relational, therefore social in its inception and product; natural, thus subject to universal laws; and finally, perhaps most importantly of all, is inherently a method, or praxis of inquiry and knowing.[25]

The attention to eloquence and taste provides access to universal love for the good and beautiful. The power of rhetoric lies in its raison d'être as an ethical project that draws upon universal standards, yet negotiates with individual outlooks to foster a moral life.

William Wordsworth

William Wordsworth (1770–1850) is a noted poet and with Samuel Taylor Coleridge designated the founder of Romantic sublime in the English-speaking world.[26] He declared that the mind sought to grasp the sublime but in the process lost consciousness, and thereby the spirit was momentarily able to embrace the sublime. In these ecstatic moments, life's loads of care are detached, enlightenment achieved, and wholeness attained. Wordsworth finds both awe and terror in the sublime moment. Humans apprehend beauty in innate nature forms through which they experience wholeness.[27]

Wordsworth was born in the Lake District of Cumberland (now part of the county of Cumbria) of northwestern England. His early education was in mediocre schools, but he entered Oxford University and obtained the BA in 1791.[28] He was famous for long walks through woodlands, hills, and lofty mountains with his sister Dorothy and later with friends. In 1790 he went on a walking tour of Europe. He was particularly impressed with natural beauty. From the aesthetic majesty of surrounding nature, he created poetry and reflected on the Romantic perception of the sublime. He was widely acclaimed in his own lifetime, and on him were conferred

---

25. Keefe, "Peculiar Power," 67–68.
26. Klaus P. Mortensen, *The Time of Unrememberable Being: Wordsworth and The Sublime, 1787–1805*, trans. W. Glyn Jones (Copenhagen: Museum Tusculanum, 1998).
27. William Wordsworth, *Our English Lakes, Mountains, and Waterfalls as Seen by William Wordsworth 1770–1850* (London: Bennett, 1864).
28. John Worthen, *The Life of William Wordsworth: A Critical Biography*, Blackwell Critical Biographies (Chichester: Wiley Blackwell, 2014).

honorary doctorates from the universities of Durham (1838) and Oxford (1839). He was declared poet laureate in 1843.

Philip Shaw, in an online British Library essay "Wordsworth and the Sublime," expands on Wordsworth's sense of the sublime.[29] Shaw quotes, in his observations, Wordsworth's autobiography, *The Prelude*:

> The poet's failure to locate the sublime in nature is countered, however, by a rousing hymn to the imagination. In lines that affirm the superiority of mind over nature, Wordsworth writes of how imagination reveals the "invisible world" where "greatness" lives (line 536). "Our destiny, our nature, and our home", he continues:
>
>   Is with infinitude, and only there;
>   With hope it is, hope that can never die,
>   Effort, and expectation, and desire,
>   And something evermore about to be. (*1805 Prelude*, lines 538–42)
>
> At this point in the poem imagination, revealed as infinite in power and scope, appears triumphant over "the light of sense" (line 534), a synonym for the time-bound world of nature. But this image of the mind's transcendence of matter is matched by a terrifying sequence of lines in which the "blasts of waterfalls," "thwarting winds" and the noise of a "raving stream" become "Characters of the great apocalypse, / The types and symbols of eternity, / Of first, and last, and midst, and without end" (lines 558–72; passim). With echoes of the *Book of Revelation* and of *Paradise Lost* the mode of sublimity that wins out in these lines is not the sublimity of nature or of mind, but of God.[30]

Much like Blair, Wordsworth connects the sublime with God or the transcendent one. We will return to the sublime as consummated in the transcendent as we reflect on Wuellner's essay.

We now turn to Wordsworth's poem regarding his hikes in the area north of Tintern Abbey.[31] During the fall of 1990, I taught in Pepperdine University's London international program. One of my courses was the history of the Anglican Church. I decided that I wanted to see Tintern Abbey,

---

29. Philip Shaw, "Wordsworth and the Sublime" (British Library, 2014), https://tinyurl.com/SBL4831b.

30. Harold Bloom, ed., *William Wordsworth's, "The Prelude,"* Modern Critical Interpretations (New York: Chelsea House, 1986).

31. William Wordsworth, *Lines Composed a Few Miles above Tintern Abbey on Revisiting the Banks of the Wye during a Tour, July 13, 1798*, https://tinyurl.com/SBL4831d.

so Dorothy and I took a train from Paddington Station to Chepstow, Wales. From Chepstow it was necessary to secure a taxi to the abbey. The drive in the Welsh hills gave some hint of the isolated beauty where Wordsworth struggled through increasingly rugged terrain. I was intrigued by the abbey. The monastery was permanently closed during the reign of Henry VIII, the lead subroof removed and reconstituted into bullets for Henry's war with Spain. Over the centuries the timbers decayed and the slated roofs fell to the ground. Much of the rubble was removed and the grounds carefully manicured. The sky glowered a light gray the day we were there. Centuries of blackened, weathered stonework rose in bold relief against the autumn sky. The setting and ghost-like structures instigated a numinous interlude. My thoughts inexplicably conjured up the arrival of Saint Augustine and his monks, sixth-century apostles to the English. Overlaying the vision of the crumbling foundations of Saint Augustine's Abbey in Canterbury were the pervasive rugged hills provoking the realization that Wordsworth walked this way almost two hundred years before. The fallout from my conflicts with Pepperdine students and my quarrel with the taxi driver over his adamant insistence that we visit Chepstow Castle faded into nothingness. The sublime moment generated peace, fulfillment, and wholeness.

Wordsworth's *Tintern Abbey* was written after a second walking tour of the region. His memory encompassed the sensations of the previous hike. The first occasion remained but blended in with those of the new walk, expanded and deepened.

> Five years have past; five summers, with the length
> Of five long winters! and again I hear
> These waters, rolling from their mountain-springs
> With a soft inland murmur.—Once again
> Do I behold these steep and lofty cliffs,
> That on a wild secluded scene impress
> Thoughts of more deep seclusion; and connect
> The landscape with the quiet of the sky. (lines 1–8)

In the second stanza Wordsworth professes that true reality lies not in the objects themselves, but in pleasant images resulting in reminiscence upon friends and their acts of kindness and love. The consequence is affirmation and the goodness of humankind.

> As is a landscape to a blind man's eye:
> But oft, in lonely rooms, and 'mid the din

> Of towns and cities, I have owed to them,
> In hours of weariness, sensations sweet,
> Felt in the blood, and felt along the heart;
> And passing even into my purer mind
> With tranquil restoration:—feelings too
> Of unremembered pleasure: such, perhaps,
> As have no slight or trivial influence
> On that best portion of a good man's life,
> His little, nameless, unremembered, acts
> Of kindness and of love.

Even more sublime, however, is the manner in which the suprasensible reality surpasses and assimilates that which is flesh and blood. The sublime creates wholeness at a transcendental level in a living soul resulting in harmony and joy. It enables the pulling back of the curtains of the sensible so as to comprehend that which gives life to being.

> To them I may have owed another gift,
> Of aspect more sublime; that blessed mood,
> In which the burthen of the mystery,
> In which the heavy and the weary weight
> Of all this unintelligible world,
> Is lightened:—that serene and blessed mood,
> In which the affections gently lead us on,—
> Until, the breath of this corporeal frame
> And even the motion of our human blood
> Almost suspended, we are laid asleep
> In body, and become a living soul:
> While with an eye made quiet by the power
> Of harmony, and the deep power of joy,
> We see into the life of things.

The germinating force of the sublime may commence in nature's concretion. But the sublime power of the moment is to apprehend nature anew from the transcendent aspect.

> For I have learned
> To look on nature, not as in the hour
> Of thoughtless youth; but hearing oftentimes
> The still sad music of humanity,
> Nor harsh nor grating, though of ample power
> To chasten and subdue.—And I have felt

> A presence that disturbs me with the joy
> Of elevated thoughts; a sense sublime
> Of something far more deeply interfused,
> Whose dwelling is the light of setting suns,
> And the round ocean and the living air,
> And the blue sky, and in the mind of man:
> A motion and a spirit, that impels
> All thinking things, all objects of all thought,
> And rolls through all things.

The mind beginning from these rudimentary experiences can become a reservoir for lovely forms, melodies, and harmonies. These are healing noetic modes that result in wholeness and joy. The vision is Platonic. True existence transcends the mundane. Earthly realities palely reflect the primal forms breaking in from the transcendent realm. The sublime occurs in the natural world when the invisible intellectual forms penetrate the realm of sense.

> When these wild ecstasies shall be matured
> Into a sober pleasure; when thy mind
> Shall be a mansion for all lovely forms,
> Thy memory be as a dwelling-place
> For all sweet sounds and harmonies; oh! then,
> If solitude, or fear, or pain, or grief,
> Should be thy portion, with what healing thoughts
> Of tender joy wilt thou remember me,

We now see from Wordsworth's experiences how nature impacted his memory and intellect. He was led from the sense world into a comprehension of the emotive and intellectual forms that underpin all of reality. The result is a sublime apprehension of love, acceptance, harmony, wholeness, joy, and health. We understand further that Wordsworth believed that the sublime can be conveyed to others, however inadequately, through poetry, discourse, art, and music. While perhaps it is incorrect to declare that he created a rhetoric of the sublime, nevertheless he set out the foundations upon which a rhetoric of the sublime can be constructed.

Wilhelm Wuellner

Wilhelm Wuellner (1927–2004), with a PhD from the University of Chicago and later connected with the Graduate Theological Union in Berkeley, California, was a major contributor to the global flowering of rhetorical analysis of Scripture during the latter part of the twentieth century. His contributions have been appropriately heralded by James D. Hester, J. David Hester, Vernon K. Robbins, Lauri Thurén, and myself.[32] Wuellner researched a broad sweep of methods and understandings that provided an insightful perspective on the power of biblical texts. In this regard, toward the end of his life he investigated the rhetoric of the sublime and published a prolegomenon to the significance of sublime rhetoric.

Wuellner was attracted to the importance of rhetoric for biblical interpretation in the late 1960s. He met James Muilenberg and members of the rhetoric department at the University of California, Berkeley. He launched a serious scrutiny of rhetoric at the beginning of the next decade. He wrote:

> I spent most of my first sabbatical leave (1970/71) at the Dölger Institute for Antiquity and Christianity in Bonn (the godfather of the Claremont Institute) in the study of this conflict between rhetorical traditions. Another first contact with a rhetorician during 1970/71 was with Joachim Dyck (then a young professor at Freiburg, a student of Walter Jens) whose work on the critical reception of biblical rhetoric in the 17th century attracted my attention.

He further elaborates,

---

32. Hester and Hester, *Rhetorics and Hermeneutics*; Hester and Hester, "The Contribution of Wilhelm Wuellner to New Testament Rhetorical Criticism," in *Genealogies of New Testament Rhetorical Criticism*, ed. Troy W. Martin (Minneapolis: Fortress, 2014), 93–126; Vernon K. Robbins, "Where Is Wuellner's Anti-Hermeneutical Hermeneutics Taking Us?," in Hester and Hester, *Rhetorics and Hermeneutics*, 105–25 (I concur with Robbins and his cohort in their efforts to approach documents utilizing analytical methods compatible with the discourses' unique features rather than superimposing a Procrustes-like schemata, most likely a prefabricated classical rhetoric, upon multiple types of communication); Lauri Thurén, "Where Is Rhetorical Criticism Taking Us Now?," in *Voces Clamantium in Deserto—Essays in Honor of Kari Syreeni*, ed. Sven-Olav Back and Matti Kankaanniemi, Studier i exegetik och judaistik utgivna av Teologiska fakulteten vid Åbo Akademi 11 (Åbo: Åbo Akademi University, 2012), 333–50; Thomas H. Olbricht, "The Flowering of Rhetorical Criticism in America," in *The Rhetorical Analysis of Scripture: Essays from the 1995 London Conference*, ed. Stanley E. Porter and Thomas H. Olbricht, JSNTSup 146 (Sheffield: Sheffield Academic, 1997), 79–102; Olbricht, "Wilhelm Wuellner and the Promise of Rhetoric," in Hester and Hester, *Rhetorics and Hermeneutics*, 78–104; Olbricht, "Response to James D. Hester and J. David Hester: A Personal Reflection," in Martin, *Genealogies*, 127–31.

> Another influence on me was my personal acquaintance with James Muilenburg as a colleague in biblical studies at the graduate Theological Union in Berkeley. I discussed with him, and with his doctoral students, his 1968 SBL Presidential address advocating his version of rhetorical criticism. Some of Muilenburg's students took courses at UC-Berkeley's rhetoric department; it was through them that I met William Brandt, then chairman of the department and consultant on several Ph.D. dissertations at the GTU.[33]

While Wuellner did not publish a major work on rhetoric for all the New Testament documents, he did produce several individual essays on Luke, John, Romans, 1 Corinthians, and 1 Thessalonians.

We are chiefly interested in Wuellner's proposals that led to an appreciation of his views on the rhetoric of the sublime.[34] We need to note, however, that for Wilhelm analysis of the sublime was the capstone that followed conventional analysis. Wuellner set forth his vision of the stages on the way to the rhetoric of the sublime. First, analysis builds on the insights of classical rhetoric as set forth by George Kennedy, then modified by the work of Chaim Perelman. It would take into account continental literary rhetoric as well as American social science hermeneutics. The areas that must be addressed are the rhetorical situation of the text, the text's argumentation, the text's intentionality, the text's activity and power, the social, cultural and ideological values, and the stylistic techniques.[35] Furthermore, attention must be given to modern and postmodern approaches to rhetoric.

Regarding what Wuellner proposed in respect to the rhetoric of the sublime, the Hesters aptly stated, "For Wuellner the goal of rhetorical criticism is not the depiction of aesthetics of a text but a description of its pragmatic and ethical implications, which he understood as more than is conventionally the case."[36] The power of rhetoric is in a total bodily ecstatic movement in which delivery and message are conflated. Wuellner incorporated much from Longinus. According to the Hesters, the goal of persuasion "is to inspire wonder and 'cast a spell' on the hearer or reader. This spell is evidence of the truly sublime, which 'pleases all people at all

---

33. Quoted from a letter to me and published in Olbricht, "Flowering," 95.
34. Wuellner, "Reconceiving a Rhetoric of Religion."
35. Olbricht, "Wilhelm Wuellner and the Promise of Rhetoric."
36. Hester and Hester, "Contribution of Wilhelm Wuellner," 116.

times.'"[37] Wuellner aspired to more than redirecting historical criticism of the Scriptures. He yearned to exhibit the power of the biblical discourses in their efforts to effect ethics and action, power and sublimity. Ultimately, the attainment of the spiritual is the fundamental purpose for communicating and involves that "holy moment" when Yahweh declares, "Come let us argue it out."[38]

I will cast Wuellner's vision in bolder relief by comparing his outlooks with those of Blair. I am first struck by the somewhat different nuance Wuellner brings to bear by focusing on the power of the sublime. Blair gives attention to the sublime's power, but more in the sense of aesthetic appreciation, though also in regard to the power of the numinous. Wuellner, however, is more interested in the aspect that transforms lives. Furthermore, he gives more emphasis to the manner in which the sublime encapsulates the total person:

> mindful that we, as rhetoricians of the sublime, i.e., as "stewards of the mysteries of God" (1 Cor 4:1) ... cannot escape the incarnational, i.e., fully human reality of "having this [sublime] treasure in earthen vessels"—a "treasure" in our hearts, i.e., at the center of our physical, emotional and spiritual humanity. Out of this we are empowered to give, i.e., to share in speaking and acting, "the light of the knowledge of the glory of God in the face of Christ" (2 Cor 4:7). Paul adds, as a constant reminder to us that our empowerment by the sublime is of spiritual origin and not of human cultural origin. In other words, the power of the sublime integrates the esoteric with the exoteric, with the spiritual component empowering us for an integrating balance, a "harmony" of "treasure" and "vessel." Through the sublime, "the Logos becomes flesh," thereby enabling and empowering a union, a communion, of "the inner human being with the outer human being" and vice versa.[39]

Wuellner, as Blair, is interested in the dark side of the sublime. In the case of Blair, the terror generated by the dark side intensifies the power of the sublime, but not so much as a threat to one's existence. Wuellner, however, focuses on the dark side as life-threatening, having to do with sickness, cancerous, lifeless, distorted, restrained, or perverted.[40] But the divine

---

37. Hester and Hester, "Contribution of Wilhelm Wuellner," 122.
38. Hester and Hester, "Contribution of Wilhelm Wuellner," 120–22.
39. Wuellner, "Reconceiving a Rhetoric of Religion," 35–36.
40. Wuellner, "Reconceiving a Rhetoric of Religion," 70–72.

also has an integrative power respecting thinking and imagination, feeling and intuition, willing and inspiration, plus the three language levels of the physical, the emotional, and the spiritual. Wuellner further wrote of the metaphoric and tropic nature of human language that has special bearing on discourse respecting the divine. Blair gave little attention to the analogical character of language respecting deity, and Wuellner likewise in his essay did little to elaborate on the power, character, and significance of the metaphorical. He does, however, look in greater detail at various ways in which the figurative nature of human language manifests itself.[41]

Wuellner spoke, as did Blair, of the relation between the grandeur in nature and that found in the human language of the rhetor. He also includes the audience and is more interested in the empowering side, not just the descriptive as is essentially true of Blair. As Wuellner moves to the sublime in human language he emphasizes its contribution to thinking, feeling, and willing, bringing to bear considerably more concretion from scripture than Blair. He likewise is much more specific in regard to the bodily, emotive, and spiritual aspects.[42] He is appreciably attuned to internal appearances rather than to natural settings.

In my concluding remarks in response to the Hesters I wrote,

> Wilhelm envisioned an existential, ontological significance to rhetoric. Sublime words have to do with wholeness and health. They contribute to well-being and healing and impact mundane regular occurrences in life. In a chain of transcending dimensions, however, they extend into the beyond. Wilhelm had in mind a rapprochement between "heaven and earth," for which words are somehow a means...... Anyway for Wilhelm, rhetoric and being interact.[43]

Commonalities

We are now in a position to reflect on the commonalties of the views of Blair, Wordsworth, and Wuellner on the sublime. Along with Longinus, all three held that humans experience stand-apart or ecstatic moments not only in viewing nature, but also in art, music, and discourse. It is in such ecstatic intervals that words or rhetorics have power. They are the occa-

---

41. Wuellner, "Reconceiving a Rhetoric of Religion," 35–46, 46–61.
42. Wuellner, "Reconceiving a Rhetoric of Religion," 46–50, 57–61, 73–74.
43. Olbricht, "Response to Hester and Hester," 131.

sions in which readers or auditors are elevated from their commonplace existence to a transcendental, mystical reality. Blair especially stressed that the source of the sublime is the highest existing being, that is, God. For him, preaching or God discourse is different in that the rhetoric of the sublime employs words about God. Wordsworth gave more attention to the sublime extrapolated from observing nature, but the sublime ascended to surpass nature situated in a Platonic suprasensible reality in which humans receive sublime forms from the invisible realm, which in turn impacts the invisible soul. The God Wuellner heralds is biblically conceived and seeks dialogue with humankind made in his image.[44]

The sublime also presents moments in which the dark side or terror impacts the recipient. Both Blair and Wordsworth acknowledge the numinous that strongly afflicts the unwary and depresses them, positioning them beyond the present in a countermystical exposure. Wuellner especially depicts the horrors of disaster and disease that rob those impacted of their immediate setting. But for all three, powerful words of the sublime retrieve the beneficent moment, destroying and healing nature's torments.

Though to some degree both Longinus and Blair reflect upon the aesthetic emphasizing stylistics in regard to the sublime, Wordsworth and Wuellner especially are much more focused on the manner in which the sublime enhances health, wholeness, and healing. For Wordsworth, words or poems depicting nature properly refined and executed lift the reader or auditor to a new level of reality, creating germinating beds for love, friendship, acceptance, and health. Wuellner likewise is of the disposition, despite major afflictions, to think that sublime rhetoric created by dialogue of humans with the divine will restore, heal, and bring joy to the recipients. The ends of rhetoric are therefore love, justice, and wholesomeness. To paraphrase Quintilian, a good communicator is an ethical, compassionate person speaking well. Inadequate communication occurs through special pleading on behalf of a few. Wuellner quotes Perelman, who declared that justice has widespread appeal and commands a uni-

---

44. For the reflections of a rhetorician on divine-human dialogue, see David Frank, "Engaging a Rhetorical God: Developing the Capacities of Mercy and Justice," in *Responding to the Sacred: An Inquiry into the Limits of Rhetoric*, ed. Michael Bernard-Donals and Kyle Jensen (University Park: Pennsylvania State University Press, 2021); Frank, "Arguing with God, Talmudic Discourse, and the Jewish Countermodel: Implications for the Study of Argumentation," *Argumentation and Advocacy* 41 (2004): 71–86.

versal audience.⁴⁵ Actually, Wuellner spends little time depicting and denouncing poor or pejorative rhetoric. He is engrossed in advancing honorific communicative acts.

The Sublime and Rhetorical Criticism

Based on my research for this essay, I have constructed a critical method for the rhetoric of the sublime. I will employ the new procedure in a perusal of the Ephesian epistle. I submit the following steps.⁴⁶

1. Assessment of the rhetorical situation
2. Assessment of the aims of the discourse
3. The main arrangement of the discourse
4. The transcendental intentions of the discourse
5. The macrocosm sublime aspects of the discourse
6. The sublime moments of the discourse
7. The experience of sublime terror
8. The effects of the sublime discourse

An Analysis of Ephesians from the Standpoint of Sublime Rhetoric Criticism

From ancient times readers have noted divergences in Ephesians concepts and style from other New Testament epistles. These differences have been

---

45. Chaim Perelman and Lucie Olbrechts-Tyteca, *The New Rhetoric: A Treatise on Argumentation*, trans. John Wilkinson and Purcell Weaver (Notre Dame: University of Notre Dame Press, 1969).

46. With Blair, I propose a method of rhetorical criticism that is consonant with the document under consideration. The classical rhetoricians were not cognizant of Jewish and Christian discourses. See Thomas H. Olbricht, "The Foundations of Ethos in Paul and in the Classical Rhetoricians," in *Rhetoric, Ethic and Moral Persuasion in Biblical Discourse*, ed. Thomas H. Olbricht and Anders Eriksson, ESEC 11 (New York: T&T Clark, 2005), 138–59. Hester and Hester, "Contribution of Wilhelm Wuellner," 122, wrote: "More directly related to New Testament criticism, use of Wuellner's special theory of rhetoric might help critics develop a more robust understanding and definition of what Thomas Olbricht calls 'Christian' or 'church' rhetoric found in the literature of the early church." For additional Olbricht comments, see Lauri Thurèn, ed., *Rhetoric and Scripture: Collected Essays of Thomas H. Olbricht*, ESEC 23 (Atlanta: SBL Press, 2021).

attributed to audience, intent, and situation.[47] We are able to account for many distinctive characteristics of Ephesians by perceiving the epistle as an exemplar of the rhetoric of the sublime.

1. Assessment of the Rhetorical Situation

The rhetorical situation of Ephesians is nonspecific.[48] Many scholars argue that the document is more a sermon than an epistle, but not a sermon for a specified audience. The context geographically is not identified. It has been assumed that the readers are situated in a region in Asia Minor. According to Edgar Goodspeed, the discourse was aimed at the larger Christian world as a cover letter for the Pauline corpus. Goodspeed's suggestion, though entertained, has attained little scholarly consensus.[49] Both Jewish and gentile readers are projected, especially the latter. It is this context in early Christianity that provides a situational milieu. Though Paul the apostle spent many months in Ephesus, even those who affirm Pauline authorship doubt that the words "in Ephesus" (1:1) pinpoint the rhetorical situation. The discourse setting is therefore a more universal audience. The nature of the situation makes possible a wide-ranging rhetoric of the sublime.

2. Assessment of the Aims of the Discourse

The aim of Ephesians is affirmation. The document has two major sections. The first section, Eph 1–3, affirms a Christian worldview, the second,

---

47. A limited list of books on Ephesians is Charles H. Talbert, *Ephesians and Colossians*, Paideia (Grand Rapids: Baker Academic, 2007); Markus Barth, *Ephesians*, 2 vols., AB 34, 34A (Garden City, NY: Doubleday, 1974); Roy R. Jeal, *Integrating Theology and Ethics in Ephesians: The Ethos of Communication*, Studies in the Bible and Early Christianity 43 (Lewiston, NY: Mellen, 2000); Lynn H. Cohick, *Ephesians: A New Covenant Commentary* (Cambridge: Lutterworth, 2013); Frank Thielman, *Ephesians*, BECNT (Grand Rapids: Baker Academic, 2007); and Timothy O. Gombis, *The Drama of Ephesians: Participating in the Triumph of God* (Downers Grove: IVP Academic, 2010).

48. Lloyd Bitzer, my fellow University of Iowa graduate student in rhetoric, popularized the notion of "the rhetorical situation." See Bitzer, "The Rhetorical Situation," *Philosophy and Rhetoric* 1 (1968): 1–14.

49. Edgar Goodspeed, *The Meaning of Ephesians* (Chicago: University of Chicago Press, 1933).

Eph 4–6, affirms a Christian lifestyle. These observations are more helpful in identifying the rhetoric than the classical genres: deliberative, forensic, and epideictic. I offer two observations from the Scottish rhetoricians. First, as Blair argued, the context for Christian rhetoric is the pulpit, which necessitates its own parameters. Second, the Scots classified speech types, not according to settings, but according to the goals of the speaker, whether to persuade, convince, or inform. In a sense *persuade* and *convince* overlap, but *persuade* results in action and *convince* in noetic acceptance.[50] The first part of Ephesians elicits conviction; the second part action. In both parts of Ephesians the outcome has to do with the rapprochement of the divine and the human. These provide rich opportunities for sublime rhetoric. The discourse will enable the readers to appreciate Paul's contact with the sublime one and discern the implications.

> for surely you have already heard of the commission of God's grace that was given me for you, and how the mystery was made known to me by revelation, as I wrote above in a few words, a reading of which will enable you to perceive my understanding of the mystery of Christ. (Eph 3:2–4)[51]

3. The Main Arrangement of the Discourse

The arrangement of Ephesians is not that of a speech or even an abstract treatise. It is clearly the normal organizational structure for ancient correspondence. It commences by identifying the author, specifying the recipients, and pronouncing a greeting. The greeting "grace and peace" opens the door for the rhetoric sublime that follows. This raises the question of the style of Ephesians. It is wordy; sentences in the original are

---

50. John Hagaman, "On Campbell's 'Philosophy of Rhetoric' and Its Relevance to Contemporary Invention," *RSQ* 3 (1981): 145–54. Aristotle's *Rhetoric* focused on persuasion. New Testament documents feature persuasion. Not all communication, however, is persuasion, despite Kennedy and other writers on rhetoric. Forms of rhetoric that are to persuade, convince, and inform are pedagogically meaningful even if persuade, convince, and inform may be found in the same discourse. See Thomas H. Olbricht, *Informative Speaking* (Glenview IL: Scott-Foresman, 1968). I have found George Campbell's delineation very helpful in teaching speech, which I did at the University of Dubuque and Pennsylvania State University for nine years. To declare that all discourse is persuasion is the same as declaring all animal husbandry identical despite the difference in caring for alpacas, mustangs, and zebras.

51. All biblical quotations are from the New Revised Standard Version.

long; the vocabulary is more generalized and elevated. Various scholars have dated the letter to the late first or early second century CE. They contend that the style is that of the Second Sophistic rather than that of the usual Koine Greek. Another possibility, however, is that the style is that of rhetoric sublime. The body of the letter reflects the comingling of heaven and earth in the terrestrial sphere. The conclusion highlights the blessings of the Father and the Lord Jesus Christ for the believers. The sublime words "peace," "whole community," "grace," and "love" regale the reader.

> Peace be to the whole community, and love with faith, from God the Father and the Lord Jesus Christ. Grace be with all who have an undying love for our Lord Jesus Christ. (Eph 6:23–24)

4. The Transcendental Intentions of the Discourse

Ephesians placards God the Father, who has broken into human history, and the Lord Jesus Christ. As Blair asserted, sublime vocabulary depicts the greatest being in the universe. In Ephesians the focus is on the everlasting God who blessed humankind from before the foundation of the world (Eph 1:4) and on the Lord Jesus Christ raised by God from the dead (1:20). Christ gave himself up as a sacrifice for the believers (5:2), who are redeemed and forgiven through his blood (1:7) so that they received salvation and, though dead, were made alive (2:5). The Christian narrative encompasses the whole of reality from before the beginning and extends "forever and ever" (Eph. 3:21). The Father and the Lord Jesus Christ dwell in the heavenly places: "God put this power to work in Christ when he raised him from the dead and seated him at his right hand in the heavenly places" (ἐπουράνιος, Eph 1:20). Believers are raised to the same heavenly place (Eph 2: 6). Additionally, the dark forces run rampant in the same realm (Eph 6:12). Although they are surrounded by "the cosmic powers of this present darkness" (6:12), God has provisioned the faithful with substantial spiritual weapons in order that they may withstand the onslaught of the "spiritual forces of evil" (6:12). Those in Christ occupy a spiritual region that transcends commonplace empirical existence. This is a sublime reality beyond as held by Wordsworth, but without certainty of his Platonic features. The author of Ephesians obviously set out to convince his readers of the sublimity of the Christian worldview by highlighting the Christian story of history and life. Based on the acceptance of that worldview, he proceeded in the last half of the letter to depict the lifestyle consonant with the sublime narrative.

Wuellner earmarked the power of a discourse as the means by which to apprehend its intended impact. The power of Ephesians may be accessed in the mystery of Christ (3:4). Paul declared the mystery as the focal point of his letter (3:9, also 1:9; 3:3, 4; 5:32; 6:19). The message highlighted the mystery of the gospel (6:12). The mystery was the Christian story presented above. God and the Lord Jesus Christ by their power initiated the story (1:9). Their sovereignty overwhelmed the dark forces at work in the disobedient (2:2). God conferred the power for proclaiming the Christian narrative on Paul (3:7). The authenticity of the story lives in the being of those convicted (3:20). Ephesians is focused on the sublime—on God and the Lord Jesus Christ. The message likewise specified the lifestyle of those who, because of their convictions, dwelt in the heavenly realm with deity. The language of power and mystery reflect concepts and vocabulary highlighting the sublime as pinpointed by Blair, Wordsworth, and Wuellner.[52]

5. The Macrocosm Sublime Aspects of the Discourse

Wuellner avowed that a rhetoric of the sublime nurtured health, wholeness, friendship, equity, and peace. Those engaged in such exchange brought universal benefits to all humans. Paul contended that many favorable traits accrued from the sublime rhetoric of the Ephesians correspondence. The

---

52. Hester and Hester make an important observation: "Olbricht expressed appreciation for Wuellner's wide ranging reading in secondary literature but argues that he did not delve deeply enough in 'fundamental research' that might have provided bases for theorizing. See Olbricht, 'Wuellner and the Promise of Rhetoric,' 104. Given his agenda it is unlikely that Wuellner shared Olbricht's concept of what might constitute 'fundamental' research" ("Contribution of Wilhelm Wuellner," 98, n. 8). I envision the discrepancy alleged as the status of the matter. It has frequently been observed that, e.g., Demosthenes did not conform to the so-called rules of classical rhetoric. The alleged assured results from rhetorical analysis employing classical rhetoric are therefore constructed on tenuous grounds. Wuellner did not make a study of actual discourses through two millennia, he read authorities who generalized about the characteristics of the discourses. I am not of the opinion that no insight is obtained that way, but most disciplines valorize studies that keep rechecking the interpreters against original concrete documents and artifacts. It is on these bases that I justify an original sublime rhetorical analysis of Ephesians. I still am indebted to Wuellner for observations leading to this effort.

advantageous specifics located in the conviction section (Eph 1–3) are: peace and grace (1:2, 6, 7; 3:7, 13); spiritual blessings (1:3); being chosen, holy, and blameless in love (1:4); adoption (1:5); redemption (1:14); inheritance (1:14, 18); the promised Holy Spirit (1:13; 2:3; 3:5); love for all the saints (1:15); kindness (2:7); being brought near (2:14); peace (2:14, 15, 17); one new humanity (2:15); reconciliation (2:16); being members of the household and family (2:19; 3:15); and being built together spiritually (2:22). These traits depict a renewed, universal, improved reality that achieved Wuellner's goal for rhetoric sublime.

In Eph 4–6, many of the same traits characterize the believers who now occupy the heavenly places. They are loving and patient (4:2; 5:1–2), unified (4:3, 4, 15), full of grace (4:7), and mature (4:13); they manifest truth and love (4:15), are godlike (4:24), and are loving servants as husbands, wives, children, and slaves (5:21–6:9). They have been raised up to a new sublime reality and are characterized by sublime discourse.

6. The Sublime Moments of the Discourse

While the whole of Ephesians to a greater or lesser extent displays sublime style, I will highlight two especially elegant and elevated passages. The first is Eph 1:20–23 and the second 3:18–21. Ephesians 1:20–23 is God-focused and envisions Christ elevated above normal earthly terrain. He exists apart from (ἔκστασις) pedestrian physical surroundings. The powers are universal, Christ rules them all and their divine action is on behalf of the church, which is his body and that encompasses complete reality.

> God put this power to work in Christ when he raised him from the dead and seated him at his right hand in the heavenly places, far above all rule and authority and power and dominion, and above every name that is named, not only in this age but also in the age to come. And he has put all things under his feet and has made him the head over all things for the church, which is his body, the fullness of him who fills all in all. (1:20–23)

This pericope obviously employs words heralding transcendence: "raised from the dead," "heavenly places," "far above," and "head over all things." It highlights words that have universal implications: "all rule and authority and power and dominion," "every name," "all things under," "head over all things," and "the fullness." Some phrases adumbrate ubiquity:

"this age and the age to come," "head over all things," and "the fullness of him who fills all in all." These concepts and phrases characterize sublime being and action.

The second section, 3:18–21, exhibits even increased sublimity. Paul placards "all the saints." He affirms the outer limits of breadth, length, height, and depth. He extols an elevated love that "surpasses knowledge." The experience is superior and fulfilling. Paul further declared that the action of God supplies an abundance that is even beyond imagination. These magnificent gifts are received in the church and are without limits. One is reminded of Wordsworth's Romantic version of the sublime. The eloquent and sublime prayer has captured Christian admiration down through the centuries.

> I pray that you may have the power to comprehend, with all the saints, what is the breadth and length and height and depth, and to know the love of Christ that surpasses knowledge, so that you may be filled with all the fullness of God. Now to him who by the power at work within us is able to accomplish abundantly far more than all we can ask or imagine, to him be glory in the church and in Christ Jesus to all generations, forever and ever. Amen. (3:18–21)

7. The Experience of Sublime Terror

The first hint of the dark side in the Christian story is the declaration that God, after Christ's resurrection, placed him over all authority, power, and dominion (1:21). The opponent is "the ruler of the power of the air, the spirit that is now at work among those who are disobedient" (2:2). The believers' skirmishes with the dark forces are genuine because the devil and the cosmic powers also inhabit the heavenly places (6:12). These sublime terrorists likewise operate in the terrestrial realm (2:1–4; 4:17–20) where the gentile believers were attacked and subdued prior to their acceptance of Christ. These sinister rulers and authorities are endemically an attribute of the divine narrative (6:11–12). The redeemed, however, are no longer intimidated by the evil sublimity of these spiritual, cosmic powers. Christ has outfitted the saints with the spiritual accoutrements of truth, righteousness, peace, faith, salvation, and the Spirit (6:14–17). Divine sublimity in Ephesians assures victory over the dark powers. Blair, Wordsworth, and Wuellner acknowledged the dark side of the sublime.

8. The Effects of the Sublime Discourse

The classical rhetoricians insisted that speaking excellence produced beneficial results for humankind. A good speech was determined by the favorable results it produced. Perelman insisted that global good was ascertained by a universal audience. Wuellner avowed that the product of sublime communication was health, wholeness, and peace along with other nurturing characteristics. He projected the well-being of humankind as the goal of sublime rhetoric. Ephesians qualifies as sublime rhetoric because the letter's content and style are transcendent, ubiquitous, inclusive, redeeming, and healing.

This essay is my attempt to meet Wuellner's challenge of demonstrating a rhetorical sublime analysis.

Coleridge's Sublime and Rhetorical Interpretation of New Testament Texts

Murray J. Evans

Studies of the sublime show no prospect of decline in recent years, judging from the number of monographs and anthologies of select readings and essays that continue to appear.[1] These publications address not only the history of the sublime, from Longinus through Edmund Burke and Immanuel Kant to the present. They also discuss many sublimes: feminist, ecological, architectural, postmodern, and so on. The sublime may not be a grand theory, meant to organize all other knowledge, but it continues to attract attention in the current broad aesthetic/hermeneutic landscape.[2] As a scholar in English literary studies, my work as a medievalist has focused on the relationship between the religious and (roughly speaking) the secular in medieval texts and manuscript collections.[3] As a Romanti-

---

1. Examples include Mark Canuel, *Justice, Dissent, and the Sublime* (Baltimore: Johns Hopkins University Press, 2012); Timothy M. Costelloe, ed., *The Sublime: From Antiquity to the Present* (New York: Cambridge University Press, 2012); Emily Brady, *The Sublime in Modern Philosophy: Aesthetics, Ethics, and Nature* (Cambridge: Cambridge University Press, 2013); Philip Shaw, *The Sublime*, 2nd ed., New Critical Idiom (London: Routledge, 2017); Robert R. Clewis, ed., *The Sublime Reader* (London: Bloomsbury Academic, 2019).

2. The term *grand theory* is from Quentin Skinner, "Introduction: The Return of Grand Theory," in *The Return of Grand Theory in the Human Sciences*, ed. Quentin Skinner (Cambridge: Cambridge University Press, 1991), 3.

3. Murray J. Evans, *Rereading Middle English Romance: Manuscript Layout, Decoration, and the Rhetoric of Composite Structure* (Kingston: McGill-Queen's University Press, 1995). My strong interest and reading in theology has been informed over the years by Larry Hurtado (late Emeritus Professor in the School of Divinity, New College, University of Edinburgh) and Roy Jeal (Professor Emeritus, Booth University College, Winnipeg).

cist, I have specialized in the philosophical religion of English Romantic poet and thinker Samuel Taylor Coleridge (1772–1834)—most recently on the interrelations of religion/theology, literature, aesthetics, and politics in his later prose.[4] Finally, my work has been grounded in rhetoric: from the primary classical Latin texts, through the indelibly rhetorical texts of Chaucer, Langland, and Malory, and finally to Coleridge's prose, where the eighteenth century inheritance of classical rhetoric meets the Romantic imagination and sublime. I will begin by touching on Coleridge's biography and two of his major influential ideas, before defining his version of the sublime. Next, a discussion of some hermeneutical concerns in bringing Coleridge's sublime to ancient texts follows. I then discuss some ideological implications of paradigms for sublime rhetoric as they relate to theology and issues of power. Finally, regarding focus on specific traditional rhetorical figures or modern adaptations of them, I provide a case study of one of Coleridge's devices of sublime rhetoric.

Coleridge is popularly known as author of the poems "The Rime of the Ancient Mariner" and "Kubla Khan." He was also notorious in his time as an opium addict (in a century when there were many) and as a plagiarist.[5] His tumultuous youth was marked by the early death of his father, his dropping out of Cambridge University, abortive plans to cofound a radical community in America, and an unhappy marriage in 1795. His friendship with fellow poet William Wordsworth eventuated in their publication of the *Lyrical Ballads* in 1798—often regarded as a manifesto of the Romantic period. They also visited Germany, Coleridge for almost a year, where he learned German and attended lectures. Coleridge thus launched his lifelong interest in German theology, philosophy, and science, which "made him the most influential English interpreter of German Romanticism in

---

4. My recently published book project, Murray J. Evans, *Coleridge's Sublime Later Prose and Recent Theory: Kristeva, Adorno, Rancière* (Palgrave Macmillan, 2023), puts Coleridge in dialogue with the sublime in modern theorists Julia Kristeva, Theodor Adorno, and Jacques Rancière.

5. Richard Holmes presents a thorough and judicious view of Coleridge's plagiarisms: "Where he stole ... he also transformed, clarified and made resonant. He brought ideas to life" poetically in a way that has "no equivalent in his German sources.... To sum up: one can say that Coleridge plagiarized, but that no one plagiarized like Coleridge." See Holmes, *Coleridge: Darker Reflections* (London: Harper Collins, 1998), 280–81 n. *. I highly recommend this second volume of Coleridge's biography along with the first: Holmes, *Coleridge: Early Visions, 1772–1804* (London: Penguin, 1990).

his generation."⁶ The first decade or so of the 1800s saw the eventual breakdown of his friendship with Wordsworth, his deepening opium addiction, a stint as a journalist, and several series as a popular lecturer (famously on Shakespeare). After a deep crisis of depression in the early 1810s, he emerged with a flurry of publications, including his famous *Biographia Literaria* (1817) and two books of poetry (1816, 1817). The 1820s and early 1830s before his death saw work on his unfinished magnum opus, his widespread influence on younger authors (including Thomas Carlyle, John Keats, and Ralph Waldo Emerson), and the publication of two important later works. The first was *Aids to Reflection* (1825), a collection of aphorisms with Coleridge's commentaries, largely drawn from the seventeenth-century works of Anglican Archbishop Robert Leighton. The *Aids* "had a powerful influence" on "the Broad Church movement, and the reforming zeal of the Christian Socialists—John Sterling, Julius Hare, F. D. Maurice."⁷ His final major prose publication, *On the Constitution of the Church and State* (1829), advocated for a "clerisy" or diverse intelligentsia to counterbalance the politics of expediency, a vision that has haunted political and cultural thought to the present. One author influenced by Coleridge's clerisy was John Stuart Mill, who less than a decade after Coleridge's death published essays on Jeremy Bentham and Samuel Taylor Coleridge, whom he regarded as the two seminal thinkers of their times. Adding to these aspects of Coleridge's fame, his coinages are legion, including the ubiquitous phrase the "willing suspension of disbelief."⁸

Two of Coleridge's ideas have long stood out in understandings of his contributions to literary studies. Both have ties to theology. The first is his presentation of definitions of the imagination and the fancy in chapter 13 of *Biographia Literaria*.⁹ First, he distinguishes between *primary* and *secondary* imagination. The first he calls "the living Power and prime Agent of all human Perception." Thus primary imagination is "the most

---

6. Richard Holmes, *Coleridge* (Oxford: Oxford University Press, 1982), 15. I am indebted to Holmes's biographical chapter (2–46) for many details presented in this paragraph.

7. Holmes, *Coleridge*, 43.

8. Samuel Taylor Coleridge, *The Collected Works of Samuel Taylor Coleridge: Biographia Literaria*, ed. James Engell and W. Jackson Bate, Bollingen Series 75.7, 2 vols. (Princeton: Princeton University Press, 1983), 2:6.

9. Coleridge, *Biographia*, 1:304–5. All references to the *Biographia* in this paragraph are to these pages; 304 n. 4 and 305 n. 1 provide Coleridge's sources for his formulations of imagination and fancy.

vital and primary mental activity in the *human* mind," enabling "the world of minds and nature, of thoughts and things, of self and others to rise up around us and become rich with meaning."[10] Coleridge's comparison of primary imagination to God's act of creation emphasizes this agency: primary imagination is "a repetition in the finite mind of the eternal act of creation in the infinite I AM." Coleridge's secondary imagination has the same "*kind* of ... agency" as the primary but differs "in *degree*" and "*mode*." For the secondary imagination "dissolves, diffuses, dissipates" the "fixed" objects of experience "in order to recreate" them—or at least "struggles to idealize and to unify" them. This, for example, is the imagination of authors of fairy stories, who, to adapt J. R. R. Tolkien, take the "frogs" and "men" of the world of our senses and by combining them, imagine "frog-kings."[11] Second, and in contrast with the imagination(s), the fancy as "a mode of Memory" can only dispose those same "dead" objects of experience, "ready made," without creatively changing them. Such a mental faculty is at play in an observer's recounting the various marching bands in a parade, simply in sequence without any additional highlights or rearrangement: "and then ... and then."[12] These Coleridgean definitions of imagination and fancy have been central to much literary criticism from his own time through to the mid-twentieth century.

His other idea with a long reach—the symbol—finds one of its most memorable formulations in Coleridge's *Statesman's Manual* (1816), written to commend the Old Testament to the upper classes as a guide to

---

10. Kathleen Wheeler, "Imaginative Perception in Coleridge's *Biographia Literaria*," *The Coleridge Bulletin* NS 38 (2011): 16, emphasis original.

11. J. R. R. Tolkien, "On Fairy-Stories," in *Essays Presented to Charles Williams*, ed. C. S. Lewis (Grand Rapids: Eerdmans, 1973), 72: "If men really could not distinguish between frogs and men, fairy-stories about frog-kings would not have arisen." In adapting Tolkien, I do not mean to imply that his definition of imagination is the same as Coleridge's. Coleridge's *imagination*, moreover, is very different from some other notions: of the imagination as "running wild" (particularly in children) or as the faculty of *receiving* images.

12. My example of the parade is a paraphrase inspired by Owen Barfield, *What Coleridge Thought* (London: Oxford University Press, 1972), 16–17 on "attending and thinking," and by a related passage in Samuel Taylor Coleridge concerning "an habitual submission of the understanding to mere events and images as such, and independent of any power in the mind to classify or appropriate them." See Coleridge, *The Collected Works of Samuel Taylor Coleridge: The Friend*, ed. Barbara E. Rooke, Bollingen Series 75.4, 2 vols. (Princeton: Princeton University Press, 1969), 1:451.

political thought and action. Here Coleridge characterizes symbol "above all by the translucence of the Eternal through and in the Temporal." Symbol is that which "abides itself as a living part of that Unity, of which it is the representative."[13] Another formulation is more explicitly theological in his allusion to John 3:3, 7. Here symbol or analogy is where being "born again" spiritually is "expressed by the same thing" but "in a lower but more known form," that is, by being born naturally.[14] Much of Coleridge's writing draws on such a symbolic or, as many have argued, sacramental worldview.

In recent decades, however, Coleridge scholarship suggests that these two ideas are more representative of his earlier career than his later. While Coleridge never abandoned his sense of the importance of imagination, his later work is preoccupied with other matters.[15] In his *Coleridge's Later Poetry*, moreover, Morton Paley establishes that Coleridge's poetic practice departed, as early as 1807, from the "oracular" and "'high' Romantic mode" of his earlier famous poems. In the later poetry, "the appropriate tropes are ... simile rather than metaphor, personification rather than synecdoche; the mode of signification is typically allegory *rather than symbolism*."[16] Furthermore, just two decades ago editions appeared of Coleridge's last notebooks, final volumes of marginalia, and collected fragments of his magnum opus, the *Opus Maximum*.[17] These editions

---

13. Samuel Taylor Coleridge, *The Collected Works of Samuel Taylor Coleridge: Lay Sermons*, ed. R. J. White, Bollingen Series 75.6 (Princeton: Princeton University Press, 1972), 30.

14. Samuel Taylor Coleridge, *The Collected Works of Samuel Taylor Coleridge: Aids to Reflection*, ed. John Beer, Bollingen Series 75.9 (Princeton: Princeton University Press, 1993), 205.

15. Alan Gregory, "Philosophy and Religion," in *Romanticism: An Oxford Guide*, ed. Nicholas Roe (Oxford: Oxford University Press, 2005), 107–8.

16. Morton D. Paley, *Coleridge's Later Poetry* (Oxford: Clarendon, 1996), 40, emphasis added. The date of 1807 is given for the notebook verse fragment that Paley is discussing by Nicholas Halmi, Paul Magnuson, and Raimonda Modiano, eds., *Coleridge's Poetry and Prose: Authoritative Texts, Criticism*, Norton Critical Edition (New York: Norton, 2004), 231.

17. Samuel Taylor Coleridge, *The Notebooks of Samuel Taylor Coleridge, Vol. 5: 1827–1834*, ed. Kathleen Coburn and Anthony John Harding, Bollingen Series 50 (Princeton: Princeton University Press, 2002); Coleridge, *The Collected Works of Samuel Taylor Coleridge: Marginalia*, ed. H. J. Jackson and George Whalley, Bollingen Series 75.12, vols. 4–6 (Princeton: Princeton University Press, 1998–2001); Coleridge, *The Collected Works of Samuel Taylor Coleridge: Opus Maximum*, ed. Thomas McFar-

have made later Coleridge texts, written after his *Biographia Literaria* (1817), readily accessible in modern critical editions. Accordingly, Coleridge scholars have been busy revising and sophisticating previously received knowledge of Coleridge.[18] One such topic is his theology and literary theory, where his earlier symbolic/sacramental worldview is no longer the whole picture.[19]

What, then, does Coleridge mean by the sublime? In an important passage on the topic, he distinguishes, first, between the sublime and the grand in a "passage in Milton":

> *—Onward he moved*
> *And thousands of his saints around.*

This is grandeur, but it is grandeur without completeness: but he adds—

> *Far off their coming shone;*

which is the highest sublime. There is *total* completeness.

So I would say that the Saviour praying on the Mountain, the Desert on the one hand, the Sea on the other, the City at an immense distance below, was sublime. But I should say of the Saviour looking towards the City, his countenance full of pity, that ... the situation ... was grand.

He then contrasts the beautiful and the sublime:

---

land, with the assistance of Nicholas Halmi, Bollingen Series 75.15 (Princeton: Princeton University Press, 2002).

18. These publications include Jeffrey W. Barbeau, ed., *Coleridge's Assertion of Religion: Essays on the "Opus Maximum,"* StPT 33 (Leuven: Peeters, 2006); Murray J. Evans, *Sublime Coleridge: The "Opus Maximum"* (New York: Palgrave Macmillan, 2012); Alan P. R. Gregory, *Coleridge and the Conservative Imagination* (Macon, GA: Mercer University Press, 2003); Nicholas Reid, *Coleridge, Form and Symbol: Or the Ascertaining Vision* (London: Ashgate, 2005); Suzanne E. Webster, *Body and Soul in Coleridge's Notebooks, 1827–1834: "What Is Life?"* (New York: Palgrave Macmillan, 2010).

19. I pursue this issue in my recent monograph, Murray J. Evans, *Coleridge's Sublime Later Prose*. Nicholas Halmi provides a useful summary of "Coleridge's Early Symbolist Theory." Halmi, "Coleridge on Allegory and Symbol," in *The Oxford Handbook of Samuel Taylor Coleridge*, ed. Frederick Burwick (Oxford: Oxford University Press, 2009), 347–51.

> When the whole and the parts [here, of a passage of writing] are seen at once, as mutually producing and explaining each other, as unity in multeity ... combined with pleasurableness in the sensations ... there results the beautiful....
>   Where neither whole nor parts, but unity, as boundless or endless *allness*—the Sublime."[20]

Raimonda Modiano helpfully summarizes a double aspect of Coleridge's sublime evident in this quotation. First, his sublime involves a "unity of an indeterminate character, which cannot be localized in physical forms, yet is hazily apprehended through them."[21] Second, and ironically, Coleridge's sublime discourse involves "an intense engagement with the objects of sense."[22] Concerning another of Coleridge's examples of the sublime, a mountain obscured by cloud, Modiano states:

> What makes the clouded mountain sublime is not just the fact that its boundaries are obscured, but that by virtue of this obscurity it is "*seemingly* blended with the sky." The union of the mountain with the sky is merely guessed at, not seen, since the combined effect of mists and clouds makes it impossible to perceive an outline of harmonious shape.[23]

Here again, being able to "perceive an outline of harmonious shape" would have been "beautiful" rather than "sublime." Thus a "hazy apprehension" of "boundless or endless *allness*" is a portable watchword for Coleridge's sublime.

Besides the grand, beautiful, and sublime, Coleridge's taxonomy of figures for the passage from *Paradise Lost* includes the majestic, shapely, delightful, formal, and picturesque—all these in terms of the relationship of wholes and parts. Although his sublime conveys *allness*, its hazy and

---

20. Samuel Taylor Coleridge, *The Collected Works of Samuel Taylor Coleridge: Table Talk, Recorded by Henry Nelson Coleridge (and John Taylor Coleridge)*, ed. Carl Woodring, Bollingen Series 75.14 (Princeton: Princeton University Press, 1990), 2:370–71. Note 42 indicates that Coleridge cites from *Paradise Lost* 6.767–768.

21. Raimonda Modiano, *Coleridge and the Concept of Nature* (Tallahassee: Florida State University Press, 1985), 115.

22. Raimonda Modiano, "Coleridge and the Sublime: A Response to Thomas Weiskel's *The Romantic Sublime*," *Wordsworth Circle* 9 (1978): 117.

23. Modiano cites Coleridge's marginalium to Herder's *Kalligione*, excerpted in J. Shawcross, "Coleridge Marginalia," *Notes & Queries* 4 (1905): 342 (Modian, *Coleridge and Nature*, 115–16, emphasis added).

vast presentation through indistinct particulars sounds quite different from his early sense of symbol as a "translucent eternal" shining through a sacramental "temporal"—as when the figure of being born in this world embodies a spiritual being "born again." Readers may not sign on to all Coleridge's figural distinctions, but his careful distinguishing of the sublime from other figures remains good guidance for avoiding a vague paradigm of the sublime, already challenging for even Coleridge himself to define! A case in point is Roy Jeal's "The Rhetoric of the Sublime in the Narrative of Mary the Mother of Jesus (Luke 1–2)," in part 1 of this volume, which takes care with this issue. At one point in relation to the sublime, Jeal concludes that "texts can communicate beyond themselves." But he does not mean that all rhetorical figures are sublime or that the sublime is identical with the aesthetic. Instead, he specifies that in the parlance of sociorhetorical interpretation, the sublime is a *texture* of the Gospel of Luke. He memorably characterizes sublime rhetoric in Luke as "rhetoric on the edge" of "comprehension and belief," a major approach in his close reading of the Lucan infancy narrative. This approach combines well with his other tag for the sublime—"a rhetoric of the moment"—that purveys tacit knowledge without clear understanding.

Coleridge's definition implies some additional parameters for discussing his and others' sublimes. Emily Brady makes three helpful distinctions for framing the sublime.[24] The first kind is "phenomenological experience of the sublime," say, Coleridge's "actual experience" of the sublime in nature. Readers, of course, have no direct experience of Coleridge's own experience except through his reports, an example of Brady's second kind of sublime: "sublime discourse … expressive of such experiences." A specific example of this second kind is in Coleridge's description while walking on a "Mountain Ridge, which looks over the blue Sea-lake to Africa."[25] He remarks that none of the surrounding mountains had "shapes" that were "striking": they were not, in his own terms, beautiful. But "the sea was so

---

24. Emily Brady, "The Environmental Sublime," in Costelloe, *Sublime*, 172–73. The examples from Coleridge are mine. Brady adds that the "three categories" she defines "tend to run together in practice."

25. David Vallins cites British Library Add. MS 47512, ff. 12v–15, corresponding to Samuel Taylor Coleridge, *The Notebooks of Samuel Taylor Coleridge*, ed. Kathleen Coburn, 3 vols. (London: Routledge & Kegan Paul, 1962), 2:2045. See Vallins, *Coleridge's Writings Volume 5: On the Sublime* (New York: Palgrave Macmillan, 2003), 75.

blue, calm, & sunny," that where not "enshored by Mountains," it had "its indefiniteness the more felt from those huge Mountain Boundaries, which yet by their greatness prepared the mind for the sublimity of unbounded Ocean." Finally, Brady's third category is "reflective or analytic discourse" on the sublime.[26] Coleridge's discussion of the grand, the beautiful, and the sublime above is a good example.

Brady's three distinctions imply that similar traits of the sublime appear in different contexts as well as in the three kinds of phenomenological experience, literary discourse, and philosophy. In this light, the sublime in nature, religion, love, and so on manifest shared characteristics of the sublime—for example, indeterminate vastness. Coleridge believes that these different domains of the sublime are analogous: in his examples above, he conceives of the sublime as a quality of literary texts (Milton) and of nature (a mountain partly covered by cloud). A reason for this is that, in general, he thinks that different discourses partake of the same intrinsic pattern. For example, in his *Opus Maximum*, he draws on chemistry to discuss different ways that two substances can relate to one another. In the example of water, hydrogen (H) and oxygen (O) combine to make water (H_2O), what Coleridge sometimes calls *synthesis*. Two such substances viewed as opposites, moreover, could also preexist in a state that contains both before they differentiate as distinct entities. Coleridge calls this preexisting, undifferentiated state *prothesis*.[27] He uses synthesis and prothesis along with other related terms to present as analogous the various discourses in *Opus Maximum*—chemical, grammatical, geometrical, theological, and so on.[28] In regard to geometry, for example, he asks readers to imagine a "point" expanding "in opposite directions" to become a line; its "endpoints" are now "opposite poles to one another."[29] Thus "before the point expanded itself into a line, we can 'contemplate' it as having 'two poles, or opposites'

---

26. Guy Sircello, "How Is a Theory of the Sublime Possible?," *Journal of Aesthetics and Art Criticism* 51 (1993): 542, quoted by Brady, "The Environmental Sublime," 173.

27. Evans discusses prothesis and synthesis as two members of Coleridge's pentad, a set of terms that he derives from Pythagoras (*Sublime Coleridge*, 98–101). The other three members are thesis, antithesis, and indifference.

28. Evans, *Sublime Coleridge*, 20–24.

29. Murray J. Evans, "C. S. Lewis and Coleridge, Revisited: *The Abolition of Man*," in *The Inklings and Culture: A Harvest of Scholarship from the Inklings Institute of Canada*, ed. Monika B. Hilder, Sara L. Pearson, and Laura N. Van Dyke (Newcastle upon Tyne: Cambridge Scholars Publishing, 2020), 45; Coleridge, *Opus Maximum*, 188.

tucked inside itself and not yet differentiated."[30] This pattern of prothesis in geometry Coleridge next sees recurring in grammar, in the verb substantive "I am." It can occur as a noun—supremely in the Hebrew name for God, "I AM"—or as a verb expressing an act of being.[31] Coleridge calls this relationship of discourses through a common pattern or dynamic, *coinherence*: the discourses exist together, inside one another.[32] Accordingly, different domains of the sublime—nature, religion, literature, and the rest—share the same dynamics of the sublime. As a result, Coleridge's sublime offers the advantage of using illustrations from other modes of the sublime, say nature, to illuminate sublime rhetoric. Common traits of the sublime exist across the different domains.

For those interested in analyzing sublime rhetoric in New Testament texts, when it comes to choosing whom to use as a paradigm, Longinus has the advantage of hailing from roughly the same period as the biblical texts, the first century CE. Longinus has his deficiencies, however, as contributors to part 1 acknowledge. In his essay, Jonathan Thiessen comments that "Longinus never precisely defines the sublime" and his translator Nicolas Boileau-Despréaux was "forced" to expand on his vagueness.[33] Jeal's paper cites James I. Porter who "offers a 'typology' of 'markers'" of Longinus's views "in order to show a 'logical structure' of the sublime."[34] Another remedy for such problems with Longinus lies in the history of the sublime after him. Boileau-Despréaux's French translation of Longinus in 1674 and William Smith's English one in 1739 inaugurated a major industry on the sublime in subsequent philosophy, literature, art, and religion, surviving and sometimes thriving into our own century. Thomas Olbricht's essay discusses three such inheritors of the eighteenth-century revival of the sublime: Hugh Blair, William Wordsworth, and Wilhelm Wuellner.[35] The sophistication of these and other modern reflections helps address the shortcomings of Longinus.

---

30. Evans, "Lewis and Coleridge," 45; Coleridge, *Opus Maximum*, 188.

31. Coleridge, *Opus Maximum*, 188. Coleridge's paradigm for the prothesis "in its divine dimension" is "Absolute Will," the divine "I AM" (Evans, *Sublime Coleridge*, 24).

32. Coleridge, *Opus Maximum*, 151.

33. See Jonathan Thiessen, "The Sublime and Subliminal in Romans 2–3," in this volume.

34. See Roy R. Jeal, "The Rhetoric of the Sublime in the Narrative of Mary, the Mother of Jesus (Luke 1–2)," in this volume.

35. See Thomas H. Olbricht, "Rhetorical Criticism of the Sublime," in this volume.

Applying modern sublime theory to ancient texts is not without its concerns. Some might have doubts about the hermeneutic validity of the practice. I have found one remedy in "enter[ing] a relationship" between past and present in which "neither ... speaks for the other." Thus the view of each "becomes open, subject to still further change."[36] This issue has come to my mind in relation to Thiessen's essay "The Sublime and Subliminal in Romans 2–3," which brings careful close reading to these chapters in Paul's epistle and to Longinus's discussion of six pertinent rhetorical figures for the sublime. In his conclusion, in pairing the sublime and subliminal, Thiessen writes: "Paul's message is subliminal because it is transferred subconsciously, hidden below the storm of emotion, concealed, just as Longinus suggests," part of "a rhetoric of the sublime and the subliminal."[37] Writing as a classicist and a New Testament scholar, Thiessen in his discourse spans the ancient—in Paul and Longinus—and the modern psychoanalytic "subliminal" and "unconscious." As a scholar of English literature and literary theory, I find the juxtaposition of ancient and modern teasing me to historicize the relationship a bit more.[38] I think of C. S. Lewis's historical tracing of the word *genius*, by Coleridge's time a term for connoisseurs of—among other things—the sublime. According to Lewis, the ancients regard one's genius or "daemon" as "an invisible, personal, and external attendant."[39] Genius in subsequent periods, Lewis continues, then becomes humans' "true self, and then ... cast of mind, and finally (among the Romantics) [their] literary or artistic gifts"—and then,

---

36. Marguerite Waller, "The Empire's New Clothes: Refashioning the Renaissance," in *Seeking the Woman in Late Medieval and Renaissance Writings: Essays in Feminist Contextual Criticism*, ed. Sheila Fisher and Janet E. Halley (Knoxville: University of Tennessee Press, 1989), 163.

37. Thiessen, "Sublime and Subliminal in Romans 2–3."

38. Elsewhere I have written on psychoanalytic theory and the sublime. Murray J. Evans, "Coleridge's Sublime and Langland's Subject in the Pardon Scene of *Piers Plowman*," in *From Arabye to Engelond: Medieval Studies in Honour of Mahmoud Manzalaoui on His Seventy-fifth Birthday*, ed. A. E. Christa Canitz and Gernot R. Wieland (Ottawa: Actexpress; University of Ottawa, 1999), 155–74. Noteworthy psychoanalytic approaches to the sublime include Neil Hertz, ed. *The End of the Line: Essays on Psychoanalysis and the Sublime* (New York: Columbia University Press, 1985); and Thomas Weiskel, *The Romantic Sublime: Studies in the Structure and Psychology of Transcendence* (Baltimore: Johns Hopkins University Press, 1976).

39. C. S. Lewis, *The Discarded Image: An Introduction to Medieval and Renaissance Literature* (Cambridge: Cambridge University Press, 1971), 42.

I might add, the subliminal/unconscious in Freud, Lacan, and the rest.[40] Coleridge himself makes Lewis's point thus. In ancient times, the person of genius was *possessed* by it, but in modern times, the person of genius *possesses* it.[41] Making allowance (in Lewis's words) for this "great movement of internalisation" in Western discourse of the psyche enables us to distinguish ancient and modern receptions of—case in point—Longinus's text. What difference does historical imagination—historicizing these different receptions—make to our analysis? Might we, for example, consider ancient readers' likely experience of sublime discourse as the imperious working of one's "daemon"? How does this relate to a modern experience of sublime discourse as the sublimation of psychic drives à la Freud—or as a Coleridgean apprehension, "feeling and thinking along the edge of what readers can conceive"?[42] In answering this and related questions, I commend to readers the Romantic sublime Coleridge, the first person to use the word *unconscious* in English.[43]

Another fruitful practice in working with sublime rhetoric is using the categories and devices of the long rhetorical tradition—or creative adaptations of them—in analysis of New Testament texts. Specific rhetorical devices not only provide lenses for analysis; they also provide *vehicles* of the sublime for readers' experience. In his essay on the Epistle to the Hebrews in part 1, Christopher Holmes provides an example of this use of specific devices of sublime rhetoric, "scenes" related to God's speeches.[44]

---

40. Julia Kristeva, *This Incredible Need to Believe*, trans. Beverley Bie Brahic (New York: Columbia University Press, 2009), 33–34. I pursue this last development in the work of Julia Kristeva, in Evans, *Coleridge's Sublime Later Prose*.

41. Coleridge, *Biographia*, 2:26–27: "What then shall we say? even this; that Shakspeare [sic], no mere child of nature; no automaton of genius; no passive vehicle of inspiration possessed by the spirit, not possessing it."

42. Evans, *Sublime Coleridge*, 153.

43. *OED* online, s.v. "unconscious," B.n.1. This entry cites the following from Samuel Taylor Coleridge: Coleridge, *Notebooks of Samuel Taylor Coleridge*, 3:4397: "As in every work of Art the Conscious—is so impressed on the Unconscious, as to appear in it.—so is the Man of Genius the Link that combines the two."

44. A likely classical rhetorical tradition for scenes concerns loci (settings, places) in two senses. Paul Piehler discusses setting, including the *locus amoenus*, "the enclosed garden, park or paradise" associated with gods, with sources in the garden of Eden and Ovid (43 BCE–17 CE). See Piehler, *The Visionary Landscape: A Study in Medieval Allegory* (London: Arnold, 1971), 77–78, 81–82. Richard A. Lanham comments on places in a second sense, relating to the "classical doctrine of memory as one of the five parts of rhetoric," which associated "a particular pattern of argument with

Citing Yung Lee Too, Holmes also underlines how the power of its sublime rhetoric "resituates" readers."[45] Holmes speaks of "the moving and dislocating effects of sublime rhetoric" in his text, moving "hearers to inhabit the places where God speaks and to share in the emotional and spiritual disposition of those in God's speaking presence." This is a very fertile insight for the movement of sublime rhetoric itself. There are potential downsides to Longinus's comment that a "well-timed flash of sublimity shatters everything like a bolt of lightning."[46] After all, rhetoric also lives in succession, in the unfolding discourse whose aim is to move and to persuade. Holmes's argument is congenial to Coleridge's concern that sublime rhetoric "move" in the foothills and the plains, as well as the mountaintops of its discourse.[47] Attention to this unfolding "between the mountaintops" is a very important, and sometimes overlooked trait of sublime rhetoric.

Theologians using the sublime for rhetorical analysis may also benefit from considering the fit between a paradigm of the sublime and the models of theology that inform their work. One advantage of Coleridge in this regard is the relative prominence of theology in his paradigm. Alan Gregory states that "conventional accounts of the sublime" in the eighteenth century emphasize the summit of sublime theory in Burke (England) and Kant (Germany). Such emphases "tend to underestimate the importance of theology in the English contribution to this tradition."[48] Indeed, theology of some kind is in the bones of much recent sublime theory, such as

a particular visual scene." See Lanham, *Handlist of Rhetorical Terms: A Guide for Students of English Literature* (Berkeley: University of California Press, 1968), 178–79. A classic discussion of scenes, relating scenes to classical and biblical tradition, rhetoric, and the sublime, appears in Erich Auerbach, *Mimesis: The Representation of Reality in Western Literature*, tr. Willard R. Trask (Princeton: Princeton University Press, 1974), 96–122.

45. See Christopher T. Holmes, "Divine Speech, Hebrews, and Sublime Rhetoric," in this volume.

46. Thiessen, "Sublime and Subliminal in Romans 2–3," citing Longinus, *On the Sublime*, trans. W. H. Fyfe, rev. Donald Russell, LCL 199 (Cambridge: Harvard University Press, 1995), 1.4.

47. My discourse of topography here is an adaptation of Coleridge's from the visual arts in Coleridge, *Biographia*, 2:122–23. Murray J. Evans relates the passage to Coleridge's own sublime discourse in *Aids to Reflection*. See Evans, "Sublime Discourse and Romantic Religion in Coleridge's *Aids to Reflection*," *Wordsworth Circle* 47 (2016): 28.

48. Alan Gregory, "Coleridge's Higher Sublime?," *Coleridge Bulletin* NS 38 (2011): 100.

Theodor Adorno's.[49] Coleridge differs from conventional thinkers on the sublime in his period, for example, because he conceives of the sublime in the context of the incarnation of the Second Person of the Trinity in Jesus Christ as the servant of Isa 50:

> The obedience of the Incarnate Christ, who, as Isaiah's "Servant," gives his "back to the smiters," enacts within the creation, the relationship of willed Being and Divine Willing, the Being given and Being received and returned that constitutes the life of God [in the Trinity].[50]

In all, Coleridge "open[s] up the possibility of developing an account of sublimity from a starting-point in Christian theology."[51] In Coleridge, this relationship neither diminishes the buzz of the sublime nor waters down his sense of the incarnation. For those of us who wish to tap the sophistication and grand conceptual reach of Christian theologies—I do not mean a necessarily confessional use of the tradition—Coleridge's sublime is an attractive candidate.

Decisions about thinkers on the sublime will have other ideological dimensions, of course. For example, the famous "dynamical" sublime of Kant "pertains to observers' fearful sight, when 'in security,' of 'bold, overhanging, and as it were threatening rocks; clouds piled up in the sky, moving with lightning flashes and thunder peals ... the boundless ocean in a state of tumult; the lofty waterfall of a mighty river, and such like.'"[52] Such experiences "raise the energies of the soul above their accustomed height and discover in us a faculty of resistance of a quite different kind, which gives us courage to measure ourselves against the apparent almightiness of nature."[53] In contrast, the Coleridgean sublime lacks a number of features of Kant's

---

49. I pursue this topic for Adorno and other modern theorists of the sublime in Evans, *Coleridge's Sublime Later Prose*.

50. Gregory, "Higher Sublime," 103. Coleridge is also unique among his contemporaries: "With the partial exception of Ussher, the more theologically explicit accounts of the sublime all work with Lockean assumptions, the assumptions Coleridge critiqued so vigorously" (100).

51. Gregory, "Higher Sublime," 104.

52. Evans, *Sublime Coleridge*, 132, citing Immanuel Kant, "B. Of the Dynamically Sublime in Nature, Second Book: *Analytic of the Sublime*; From *Critique of Judgment*," in *The Critical Tradition: Classic Texts and Contemporary Trends*, ed. David H. Richter (New York: St. Martin's Press, 1989), 266.

53. Kant, "B. Of the Dynamically Sublime," 266.

sublime of domination: the "mind's rupture from sensible forms" and "flight into the supersensible realm of ideas"; and the "threat of being engulfed" by a hostile nature. In Coleridge's sublime, there is no preceding "crisis or collapse" in the imagination of the subject, who experiences "neither pain nor bafflement."[54] In contrast with "the rhetoric of power ... prevalent in eighteenth-century treatises on the sublime," Coleridge's kind of "transcendence occurs gradually ... through an intense engagement with the objects of sense."[55] Coleridge's sublime, then, offers a paradigm marked by a gradual sense of transcendence grounded in the material, instead of by psychic violence, collapse, and domination. There is an added political dimension to Coleridge's and other Romantics' presentation of the sublime, as Mark Canuel argues. The "sublime's perspective on justice" highlights "asymmetry, complaint, and disagreement." In this way, the sublime is in stark "contrast to beauty's emphasis on sameness and replication," along with its "controls and limits" on "literary and political theorizing."[56] Romantic sublimes, and Coleridge's in particular, thus offer congenial paradigms for those readers interested in issues of power and open-ended interpretation.

I want to return to the advantage of attending to traditional rhetorical figures—or their modern adaptations—for analyzing sublime discourse. Well aware of rhetorical traditions, Coleridge also adapts traditional devices for his own purposes. His general formula for sublime rhetoric involves the antinomies, the dynamic twists and turns of a *dialectical* sublime rhetoric.[57] One specific figure of such rhetoric appears in his treatment of his first assumption or "postulate" for the whole argument of Opus Maximum: "the actual being of WILL."[58] He approaches his definition of will by using "negative proof."[59] This rhetorical strategy entails the collation of a number

---

54. Modiano, "Coleridge and the Sublime," 116–17.
55. Modiano, *Coleridge and Nature*, 121–22; Modiano, "Coleridge and the Sublime," 117.
56. Canuel, *Justice*, 4, 7. Canuel critiques the views of Elaine Scarry, Wendy Steiner, and Peter DeBolla, which have elevated beauty to become "the most influential aesthetic discourse" in the early 2000s (5). While Canuel uses Kant's sublime "mainly for its philosophical clarity" (9), I find his comments on Coleridge's poetry and other Romantic writers congenial to my own focus on Coleridge's sublime.
57. I discuss these aspects of Coleridge's sublime rhetoric in Evans, *Sublime Coleridge*, 95–153 and passim.
58. Coleridge, *Opus Maximum*, 17–18.
59. Samuel Taylor Coleridge, *The Collected Works of Samuel Taylor Coleridge: Logic*, ed. J. R. de J. Jackson, Bollingen Series 75.13 (Princeton: Princeton University

of negatives, candidate definitions for the will that Coleridge then shows to be faulty. To begin, will cannot be instinct, or an "effect" of a preexisting "cause," or an "appetite" like "hunger." He proposes "the only positive which ... present[s] itself": that will is "the *power* of *originating* a *state*." Coleridge next tests this "verbal definition" of will, through additional negative proof. Will, for example, must be "incapable of explication or explanation" or else it would need an "antecedent"—whereas will as verbally defined cannot follow from something else. Eventually Coleridge "concludes that negative definition of Will leaves [only one] positive," his own definition of will. It has excluded "by default" all "other [proposed] meanings of the word," tested and found wanting.[60] Coleridge will be even more emphatic later in *Opus Maximum* with a particular version of this kind of negative proof. I call this rhetorical device "the absurdity of the contrary."[61] The alternatives to his proposed views are not just faulty. They are absurd.

Coleridge's absurdity of the contrary, and the class of negative proof to which it belongs, have a long rhetorical pedigree. In his *Handlist of Rhetorical Terms* and as a subset of *definitio*, Richard Lanham lists "negative [definition]—defining something by proving what it is not." He also defines *litotes* as "denial of the contrary."[62] Lanham proposes, moreover, a cluster of related devices under *significatio*, "sign" or "emphasis," in its "reverse negative" incarnation: "saying less than you mean, implying more than you say." Such a rhetorical approach requires "the audience to fill it in"—"invites [their] complicitous completion."[63] His precursors for such definitions are, generally, "the many patterns of ambiguity and Irony" in rhetorical tradition and in particular, the pseudo-Ciceronian *Rhetorica ad Herennium* (86–82 BCE) and George Puttenham's *The Arte of English Poesie* (1589).[64]

These traditional rhetorical descriptions bear on Coleridge's absurdity of the contrary as a rhetorical vehicle of the sublime for readers to expe-

---

Press, 1981), 264. I am grateful to the late J. R. de J. Jackson for his having drawn attention to this and related passages in an email of July 10, 1999.

60. Evans, *Sublime Coleridge*, 17, emphasis original.
61. Evans, *Sublime Coleridge*, 113.
62. Lanham, *Handlist*, 47, 184.
63. Lanham, *Handlist*, 138.
64. Lanham, *Handlist*, 139–40; dates are from 197–98. For "the absurdity of the contrary" Coleridge adapts to his own uses Plato, and in his more recent past, Leibniz and Kant (Jackson, pers. comm.).

rience. Certainly the logic of absurdity of the contrary in defeating false alternatives to Coleridge's ideas (as in my example above) helps establish his definition of will. But this is not all, for in Lanham's phrase, the figure implies "more than you can say."[65] Coleridge's version of Lanham's phrase is that if some "positive idea" is not "given previously," it must be "furnished by and, as it were, reflected from the negative positions themselves."[66] For absurdity of the contrary, then, what is this something left over after dismissing the absurd alternatives? The answer must relate to the reader's own feeling of the absurdity of positions contrary to Coleridge's *will*. As his primary assumption or postulate in *Opus Maximum*, the will qualifies, as he writes elsewhere, as one of his "Ideas," including "the Ideas of Being, Form, Life, the Reason, the Law of Conscience, Freedom, Immortality, God!"[67] Such "universal" truths are "immediately insusceptible to the conviction they produced; the moment they were understood they were as certain as they would be after 100 years of attention."[68] Coleridge adds here that such truths bear "in themselves the absurdity of their contrary." Thus, on the one hand, the sense of absurdity marks for readers an abiding certainty about his definition of will: it requires no more "attention"—even one hundred years' worth more would not help. On the other hand, since Coleridge does not directly prove his definition of will, this certainty, while abiding, is not necessarily complete. There remains for readers an accompanying sense of "the penny not yet quite dropping," even after thinking through the false alternatives for will strenuously.[69] As Coleridge states, "we affirm [the principle of the will], not because we comprehend the affirmation, but because we clearly comprehend the absurdity of the denial."[70] How then does this statement qualify the absurdity of the contrary as a figure of *sublime* rhetoric?

---

65. Lanham, *Handlist*, 138.
66. Coleridge, *Opus Maximum*, 254.
67. Coleridge, *Friend*, 1:106.
68. Samuel Taylor Coleridge, *The Collected Works of Samuel Taylor Coleridge: Lectures 1818–1819: On the History of Philosophy*, ed. J. R. de J. Jackson, Bollingen Series 75.8, 2 vols. (Princeton: Princeton University Press, 2000), 2:584–85.
69. Evans, *Sublime Coleridge*, 14. Evans (140) describes another protracted example where Coleridge uses thirty manuscript pages to critique religious views at variance with Christianity (Coleridge, *Opus Maximum*, 273–90). Here he dismisses the absurdity of knowing God "by the sense, God as space, seeing God with our eyes, and the argument from design" (Evans, *Sublime Coleridge*, 140).
70. Coleridge, *Opus Maximum*, 221.

A clue to the answer lies in how this felt sense of the absurdity of the contrary regarding the will also joins with what Coleridge calls the "fact" of "the existence of conscious responsibility."[71] This fact of experience is "the same as" Coleridge's postulate of the will because the postulate can be both a proposition and an intuition: an assumption able to be thought about, and an idea "directly known" by "consciousness":[72]

> Now ... I am conscious of a somewhat within me which peremptorily commands [the Golden Rule], that it is a primary and unconditional injunction ... *a fact* of which I am no less conscious and (though in a different way) no less assured than I am of any appearance presented to my mind by my outward senses.[73]

In this description, the idea of will, what Coleridge also calls "conscience," is no longer merely conceptual.[74] His material rhetoric of the absurdity of the contrary has awakened a felt sense of absurdity, thereby exhibiting one characteristic of Coleridge's sublime: that it involves "an intense engagement with the objects of sense"—here, his rhetorical figure.[75] But Coleridge's universal truths or ideas also bear "*in themselves* the absurdity of their contrary."[76] Thus readers already encounter the "positive idea" of will "reflected from the negative positions" in the absurdity of the contrary.[77] That is, readers are already experiencing—in a negative way—that second characteristic of Coleridge's sublime: "unity of an indeterminate character, which cannot be localized in physical forms, yet is hazily apprehended through them."[78] This unity includes both the sense of absurdity

---

71. Coleridge, *Opus Maximum*, 21.
72. Coleridge, *Opus Maximum*, 11, 21.
73. Coleridge, *Opus Maximum*, 58–59, emphasis original.
74. "But the consciousness of a conscience is itself conscience" (Coleridge, *Opus Maximum*, 21).
75. Modiano, "Coleridge and the Sublime" 117. Elinor Shaffer cites Coleridge's example from the natural sublime, parallel to my rhetorical case. Concerning "a thirsty traveller who hears a sound he imagines to be trickling water," Coleridge "considers that the aesthetic pleasure lies in the power of the mind to be *interested*.... The interest is not in the sensation of thirst, nor yet in interest itself as a sublime state of mind, *but in the object*, in the sound of trickling water" (Shaffer, "Coleridge's Theory of Aesthetic Interest," *Journal of Aesthetics and Art Criticism* 27 [1969]: 404, emphasis added).
76. Coleridge, *Lectures 1818–1819*, 2:585, emphasis added.
77. Coleridge, *Opus Maximum*, 254.
78. Modiano, *Coleridge and Nature*, 115.

and more fully, the intuitive and mysterious experience of the fact of the postulate, of "a somewhat within me."[79] This direct knowledge of "conscious responsibility" is knowledge of Coleridge's big-I idea of will as conscience.[80] Coleridge conveys the "hazy apprehension" of this knowledge in his definition of one kind of manifestation of any "Idea": as "a mere *instinct*, a vague appetency toward something which the mind incessantly hunts for but cannot find, like a name which has escaped our recollection, or the impulse which fills the young poet's eye with tears, he knows not why."[81] Through the rhetoric of the absurdity of the contrary, along with other devices of negative proof in *Opus Maximum*, Coleridge invites readers—where the dismissal of absurd alternatives leaves off—"to participate in a meditative state" at "the sublime limits of conceptual containment"; here, "as Coleridge is fond of reminding us, humans can only 'apprehend' but not 'comprehend.'"[82]

I have argued, then, that Coleridge usefully distinguishes his sublime from other modes of figuration such as the grand and the beautiful, and

---

79. Coleridge, *Opus Maximum*, 58.
80. Coleridge, *Opus Maximum*, 21.
81. Samuel Taylor Coleridge, *The Collected Works of Samuel Taylor Coleridge: Shorter Works and Fragments*, ed. H. J. Jackson and J. R. de J. Jackson, Bollingen Series 75.11, 2 vols. (Princeton: Princeton University Press, 1995), 1:633, emphasis original. I pursue this second sense of idea for Coleridge in Evans, *Sublime Coleridge*, 41, 52–60. His first sense is of idea existing "in a clear, distinct, definite form, as that of a circle in the mind of an accurate geometrician" (Coleridge, *Shorter Works*, 1:633; Evans, *Sublime Coleridge*, 41–52).
82. Evans, *Sublime Coleridge*, 57. Evans cites Coleridge, *Opus Maximum*, 98, 211, 216. Other recurring rhetorical figures of negative proof in *Opus Maximum* are cautionary warnings against the limitations of analogy (Evans, *Sublime Coleridge*, 118–20), and appeals to a meditative state, sometimes presenting as injunctions to contemplate the Idea alone without distraction (*Opus Maximum*, 196–98). Meanwhile, rhetorical devices of positive proof, which build an unfolding system of thought in Coleridge's sublime rhetoric, include the use of best words or the citing of authorities (Evans, *Sublime Coleridge*, 107–8), the necessary falsehood of the contrary (106), and the use of illustrations (121–23). Necessary falsehood of the contrary, a positive counterpart of Coleridge's absurdity of the contrary, is the extrapolation of deductions from a necessary first postulate, in *Opus Maximum* the will. Once having granted this first assumption as tentatively true, no deduction may regress on the initial postulate (Evans, *Sublime Coleridge*, 106). Coleridge's sublime rhetorical devices positive and negative also combine, sometimes blending into one another (95–130). This is the case with my present example where absurdity of the contrary combines with appeal to a meditative state.

treats the sublime as sharing common traits among different discourses and contexts. Readers may recognize an engagement with sensory particulars combining with an indeterminate vastness in the sublime of nature and in the rhetorical sublime, for example. Modern theologians analyzing sublime rhetoric may profit from the use of modern thinkers on the sublime; any fear of anachronism finds remedy in some historicizing of past and present. Use of specific traditional rhetorical devices, or their modern adaptations, enhances persuasive argument. Ideological concerns in analyzing sublime rhetoric include attention to the theological implications of the particular paradigm of the sublime; Kant's sublime, while perhaps the most famous, is also a sublime of domination. Coleridge's theology and sublime of nondomination are both worth consideration in these regards. Finally, my example of Coleridge's "absurdity of the contrary" provides a case in point for the more general concerns of my essay.

New Testament theologians experimenting with Coleridge's sublime may also find an unexpected familiarity with his legacy. His embeddedness in English literary studies from the time of his death until the mid-twentieth century and beyond means that many of our received notions of literary reading bear his stamp. I close with brief mention of two such notions. First, in *Biographia Literaria* Coleridge calls the method he will use in his criticism of Wordsworth's poetry "practical criticism": "how little instructive any criticism can be," he says elsewhere, "which does not enter into minutiae."[83] Coleridge's term became the title of I. A. Richards's *Practical Criticism* (1929).[84] This book was influential in the New Criticism, an approach "which flourished from the 1930s to the 1960s" and "regarded [Coleridge] as one of its presiding deities."[85] Emphasizing reading for symbol, metaphor, irony, ambiguity, and paradox, this approach—both in itself and also nested in subsequent theoretical schools—became a staple of literary reading and criticism. My second mention of Coleridge's legacy still with us has to do with a concept mentioned in this collection of essays and elsewhere, by practitioners of sociorhetorical interpretation. Again in the *Biographia*, Coleridge states that a "poem is that species of composition" that has, "for its *immediate* object pleasure, not truth." It particularly proposes

---

83. Coleridge, *Biographia*, 2:19. Note 1 cites Coleridge, *Notebooks of Samuel Taylor Coleridge*, 3:3970.

84. Richards, *Practical Criticism* (New York: Harcourt, Brace, 1929).

85. Coleridge, *Biographia*, 1:lxxi–lxxii.

"to itself such delight from the *whole*, as is compatible with a distinct gratification from each component *part*."[86] Thus, in the words of the *Biographia* editors, "each 'part' (each phrase, cadence, image, metaphor, episode)" provides "a pleasure in and through itself" besides a "further pleasure … architectonically to the 'whole.'"[87] Coleridge "is speaking, in other words, of what" for some time "we have called 'texture'"—also an analytical term in sociorhetorical interpretation. For many of us, then, considering Coleridge's sublime and its contexts for our work is not so much a strange country somewhere else, but instead, something close by, perhaps next door.

---

86. Coleridge, *Biographia*, 2:13, emphasis original.
87. Coleridge, *Biographia*, 1:cviii.

Part 2
Development: The Terrifying Sublime

Terror and the Logic of the Sublime in Revelation

Christopher T. Holmes

The concept of the sublime attracts interest across scholarly divides from philosophy and theology, to aesthetics and classics. Many, though certainly not all, theories of the sublime relate to the anonymous literary treatise, *On the Sublime*, attributed traditionally to Longinus. As James Porter and others have shown, however, reflection on the sublime in no way starts or ends with this work.[1] Nevertheless, it offers important perspectives on the concept.

On the Sublime has proven a useful and generative resource for interpreting New Testament writings, although interpreters have not given it as much attention as they have to the rhetorical handbooks of Aristotle, Cicero, and Quintilian.[2] This essay draws on the treatise to analyze and assess the nature and function of terror in the Revelation of John. To do so, I first provide an orientation to the treatise and offer a description of

---

1. See James Porter, *The Sublime in Antiquity* (Cambridge: Cambridge University Press, 2016).
2. For an overview of rhetorical critical interpretation of the New Testament, see Vernon K. Robbins and John H. Patton, "Rhetoric and Biblical Criticism," *QJS* 66 (1980): 327–50; Wilhelm Wuellner, "Where Is Rhetorical Criticism Taking Us?," *CBQ* 49 (1987): 448–63; and Wuellner, "Rhetorical Criticism in Biblical Studies," *Jian Dao* 4 (1995): 73–96. In addition, several monographs have been devoted to the topic. See, e.g., George A. Kennedy, *New Testament Interpretation through Rhetorical Criticism* (Chapel Hill: University of North Carolina Press, 1984); Burton L. Mack, *Rhetoric and the New Testament*, GBS (Minneapolis: Fortress, 1990); Duane F. Watson, *The Rhetoric of the New Testament: A Bibliographic Survey*, Tools for Biblical Study 8 (Leiderdorp: Deo, 2006); Ben Witherington III, *The New Testament Rhetoric: An Introductory Guide to the Art of Persuasion in and of the New Testament* (Eugene, OR: Cascade, 2009). See also the essays in Troy W. Martin, ed., *Genealogies of New Testament Rhetorical Criticism* (Minneapolis: Fortress, 2014).

how I use the treatise as a framework for thinking about the sublime and terror in Revelation. Drawing on the view of Porter that *On the Sublime* functions as a "theory of reading," I explore the logic of the sublime in Revelation and discuss several scenes that evoke terror in Revelation: the initial revelation of the heavenly Christ in Rev 1, the worship scene in Rev 4, scenes of God's judgment in Rev 6-16, and the depiction of the beasts in Rev 12-13. The essay shows how terror serves Revelation's hortatory goals, providing audiences with the proper object of fear and religious devotion.

Orientation to *On the Sublime*

Time and space prohibit a full discussion of *On the Sublime* and its traditional author, Longinus. I have discussed both at length in other places, and there are several helpful introductions to the treatise.[3] For my purposes here, a few brief notes are in order. First, the title of the treatise takes its name from its central topic: the Greek word ὕψος, a term that denotes height, loftiness, and might.[4] The treatise, however, moves beyond this basic meaning. In the treatise, ὕψος refers especially to the quality and intended effect of language. As Donald Russell pointed out several decades ago, ὕψος refers primarily "not to a manner of writing but an effect."[5] To capture this sense of the word, I refer to ὕψος as "sublime rhetoric."[6] Still, there are important points of connection with those who

---

3. In addition to the chapters in this volume, see Christopher T. Holmes, *The Function of Sublime Rhetoric in Hebrews: A Study in Hebrews 12:18-29*, WUNT 2/465 (Tübingen: Mohr Siebeck, 2018), esp. 29-63. Additionally, see Holmes, "(Religious) Language and the Decentering Process: McNamara and *De sublimitate* on the Ecstatic Effect of Language," *JCH* 2 (2015): 53-65. For introductions, see, e.g., Robert Doran, *The Theory of the Sublime from Longinus to Kant* (Cambridge: Cambridge University Press, 2015); F. R. B. Godolphin, "The Basic Critical Doctrine of 'Longinus,' *On the Sublime*," *TAPA* 68 (1937): 172-83; Malcolm Heath, "Longinus and the Ancient Sublime," in *The Sublime: From Antiquity to the Present*, ed. Timothy M. Costelloe (Cambridge: Cambridge University Press, 2012), 11-23; Heath, "Longinus, *On Sublimity*," *PCPS* NS 45 (1999): 43-74; Doreen C. Innes, "Longinus and Caecilius: Models of the Sublime," *Mnemosyne* 4th series 55 (2002): 259-84; Porter, *Sublime in Antiquity*; Donald A. Russell, *"Longinus" On the Sublime: Introduction and Commentary* (Oxford: Oxford University Press, 1964), xxx-xl.

4. See LSJ, s.v. ὕψος; cf. Holmes, *Function of Sublime Rhetoric*, 40.

5. Russell, *"Longinus" On The Sublime*, xliii.

6. For a rationale, see Holmes, *Function of Sublime Rhetoric*, 39-41.

think of ὕψος in terms of the sublime generally or of the rhetorical sublime more specifically.[7]

Second, *On the Sublime* enquires how spoken and written language affects and influences people; in this way, it is like other literary and rhetorical treatises from antiquity. In a programmatic statement at the beginning of the treatise (*Subl.* 1.3–4), Longinus states that sublime rhetoric does more than persuade, the assumed goal of ancient oratory and rhetorical theory. Rather than persuade, sublime rhetoric leads to ἔκστασις (εἰς ἔκστασιν ἄγει). Translators of the treatise render this Greek term in a variety of ways, but several emphasize the language of *transport*.[8] In fact, the emphasis on the capacity for language to lead hearers into ἔκστασις is one of the definitive characteristics of the treatise. As the treatise presents it, sublime rhetoric moves its hearers out of themselves in a number of ways: it dislocates them through descriptive language that moves them through the scenes described; it destabilizes hearers by evoking or creating powerful emotions; and it reorients them to what really matters, often through some connection (or at least allusion) to extraworldly realities.

Third, the treatise identifies and discusses five sources that help facilitate the ecstatic effects of sublime rhetoric. The first two sources, "impressive ideas" and "vehement emotion" (*Subl.* 8.1), are particularly relevant for interpreting Revelation. Longinus's discussion of impressive ideas focuses on the nature and function of the ideas themselves, rather than on the mental acuity or intellectual ability of the speakers or writers from whom they originate. In many cases, impressive ideas are associated with divine or superhuman realities or with representations of divine power. Implicit in much of this discussion is the idea that an encounter with divine power or presence is an overwhelming experience. In other words, impressive ideas are themselves associated with

---

7. For alternative understandings, see Godolphin, "Basic Critical Doctrine"; G. M. A. Grube, "Notes on the ΠΕΡΙ ΥΨΟΥΣ," *AJP* 18 (1957): 355–74; James J. Hill, "The Aesthetic Principles of the *Peri Hupsous*," *JHI* 27 (1966): 265–74; Innes, "Longinus and Caecilius"; Charles P. Segal, "ΥΨΟΣ and the Problem of Cultural Decline in the *De Sublimitate*," *HSCP* 64 (1959): 121–46; George B. Walsh, "Sublime Method: Longinus on Language and Imitation," *ClAnt* 7 (1988): 252–69.

8. See Doran, *Theory of the Sublime*, 42 and notes; 62–65. Doran speaks of Longinus's conception of ἔκστασις in terms of transcendence, an experience of the divine that leads to "a momentary transcendence of the human condition" (*Theory of the Sublime*, 43). See also the discussion of *On the Sublime* in Yung Lee Too, *The Idea of Ancient Literary Criticism* (Oxford: Clarendon, 1998).

terror and awe. Two examples from the treatise illustrate this observation. In *Subl.* 9, the author evaluates the quality of impressive ideas in the writings of Hesiod and Homer. He concludes that Homer's description of the "horses of heaven" succeeds where Hesiod fails primarily because Homer adequately represents an experience of terror (δεινός). Similarly, Homer's description of the "battle of the gods" and Moses's creation account qualify as impressive ideas because both demonstrate the authors' adequate representation of divine power. Implicit in both of these examples is the assumption that an overwhelming, awesome experience often accompanies impressive ideas and that many have to do with divine power.

In addition to impressive ideas, Longinus's analysis of emotion, the second source of sublime rhetoric, is significant. References to the emotions indicate that it is both a source of sublime rhetoric and one of its effects. In other words, emotions play a central role in the moving nature of sublime rhetoric. As M. A. Screech notes, this is suggested by the etymology of the Greek work ἔκστασις itself, which "took on the sense of a form of acute distraction, brought on by a strong emotion such as terror or astonishment." The related verb ἐξίστημι eventually "acquired the meaning of 'to astonish' or 'to amaze.'"[9] Both impressive ideas and strong emotion facilitate the effects of sublime rhetoric.

Fourth, the significance of impressive or awe-inspiring ideas and strong emotion in the treatise takes us to the topic of terror. Robert Doran highlights the significant place of terror in sublime rhetoric: "Terror is considered to be the strongest emotion and therefore the emotion that is most associated with a displacement from the mundane condition, such as that which accompanies a divine vision."[10] Doran's analysis of terror in *On the Sublime* indicates that, like the emotions more generally, it is both a source of sublime rhetoric and a characteristic effect. Moreover, terror is "most associated" with the ecstatic, self-displacing effects of sublime rhetoric. Doran's connection of terror and its effects with visions of the divine is very important.

On the Sublime is an important tool for analyzing a New Testament writing like Revelation. It is apparent that Longinus would likely *not* regard Revelation as a source or example of sublime rhetoric. Viewed from the

---

9. M. A. Screech, *Ecstasy and the Praise of Folly* (London: Duckworth, 1980), 48–49; quoted in Doran, *Theory of the Sublime*, 43.

10. Doran, *Theory of the Sublime*, 43.

perspectives of classics like the poetry of Homer or the oratory of Demosthenes, it is doubtful that Revelation would fit within Longinus's socially and culturally conditioned canon of great authors that he and his circle agreed were worthy of consideration and imitation.[11] But even if Longinus would not recognize Revelation as worthy, we can use *On the Sublime* and the concept of the sublime to analyze it. Here the perspective of Porter is particularly helpful.

Porter argues that sublimity has "coordinates that can be mapped out well beyond the lexicon."[12] This is because the sublime in antiquity is "marked thematically as well as lexically" and includes themes or motifs that "provide the best available clue to its nature." As such, the sublime "has a logical structure that is more intricate and diverse than any of its individual lexical markers or five sources."[13] Porter provides an expansive list of elements of this intricate and diverse logical structure.[14] In addition, he offers a more synthetic statement about these elements:

> The features collectively point to an underlying logic of sorts, one that is composed of extremes, contrasts, intensities, and incommensurabilities, of transgressed limits, excesses, collisions, and structures on the edge of collapse or ruin (revealing their fundamental contingency), whether of physical objects or of meanings, though to be sure this logic is not easily stated in a propositional form. The sublime is not so much found in these sorts of causes as it is provoked by them.[15]

---

11. See Porter, *Sublime in Antiquity*, xvii–xx.
12. Porter, *Sublime in Antiquity*, 14.
13. Porter, *Sublime in Antiquity*, 53.
14. Porter, *Sublime in Antiquity*, 51–53. The list includes: immense heights or profound depths; sudden or extreme, often violent, motions or changes; gaps, especially marked by extraordinary heights and depths; limits revealed in their transgression; notions of space or place beyond; unthinkingly large masses and quantities and surfaces (mountains, heavens, celestial bodies, etc.); bold or sudden expansions/compressions; "cosmic magnifications of non-cosmic events" (52); unsurpassed qualities; lasting and everlasting qualities; sharp collisions and contrasts; sharp antagonisms and tensions; uncontainable forces (whirlwinds, thunder, etc.); vivid and terrifying collapse of form and order; indefinability; ephemerality, evanescence, epiphanic appearances/disappearances; blinding moments of pleasure or pain, fear and awe, or vertigo; an overwhelming focus on details; moments of intense and vital danger, risk, and crisis; natural, mythical, divine, or literary phenomena embodying any of the above; forces that work against nature and nature's laws.
15. Porter, *Sublime in Antiquity*, 53.

For Porter, *On the Sublime* points to an underlying logic that is present in the treatise itself but that cannot be fully contained by the treatise. Elements of this logic include excesses and extremes, collisions, and the violation of boundaries. This logic, in other words, stretches perception, meaning, and even the imagination.

Longinus offers what Porter calls a "theory of reading." He explains: "Longinus' theory of the sublime is not, or not only, a theory of how to write, because it is in the first instance a theory of reading, conceived as a prerequisite to knowing how to write but also as a method for analyzing the way writings have been constructed for their readers."[16] Porter confirms the conclusion of Russell noted earlier: *On the Sublime* focuses on the effects of great writing that results from its content and construction. Porter adds that *On the Sublime* functions as a "manual in the art of identifying sublime literature, in reading the signs of sublimity, and in reproducing the effects of sublimity in one's response to the great classics of literature."[17]

In the following discussion of Revelation, I draw on the treatise as a theory of reading for identifying and assessing the sublime and terror in Revelation. I do so with the underlying logic of the ancient sublime in mind as well as elements of *On the Sublime*. Specifically, I consider how impressive ideas, vehement emotion, and vivid description relate to and convey terror in Revelation.

The Logic of the Sublime and Terror in Revelation

Porter's explanation of the underlying logic or coordinates of the ancient sublime provides an entry point for discussing the sublime and terror in Revelation. Several elements from Porter's list of elements in the logic readily apply to Revelation's images and ideas: immense heights and profound depths; notions of space beyond; exceptionally large masses, quantities and surfaces; uncontainable forces like whirlwinds and thunder; vivid and terrifying collapses of form and order. The list could be expanded. At the least, Porter's suggestion that *On the Sublime* provides a theory of reading offers an illuminating framework for approaching Revelation.

---

16. Porter, *Sublime in Antiquity*, 118.
17. Porter, *Sublime in Antiquity*, 123.

Similarly, even a cursory reading of Revelation suggests it is a candidate for considering the relationship between the sublime and terror. It focuses on heavenly realities and extraworldly creatures. It describes sudden and violent disruptions in the heavens and on the earth. It depicts strange hybrid beasts and recounts wars between the armies of God and the armies of Satan. Scenes of God's judgment leave the earth and its inhabitants ravished with streams of flowing blood and human carcasses being consumed by birds. On the surface level, the ideas and imagery in Revelation reflect the experience of terror and evoke it in its audiences. Before considering scenes in Revelation that relate particularly to terror, some additional remarks about the nature of fear and terror in the document are in order.

A Lexicon of Fear in Revelation

One place to begin the discussion of fear or terror in Revelation is to consider relevant Greek words. Louw's and Nida's *Greek-English Lexicon of the New Testament Based on Semantic Domains* groups "Fear, Terror, and Alarm" in subdomain V of words related to attitudes and emotions.[18] As a note about this subdomain indicates, the words related to fear, terror, and alarm focus "upon the fear" and a form of fear that is "significantly more acute" than in other subdomains related to anxiety or apprehension.[19] The lexicon includes eighteen words in the subdomain of "fear, terror, and alarm."[20]

Compared to the range of words identified by Louw and Nida, Revelation's "lexicon of fear" is rather restrained. Revelation includes only three words from the "Fear, Terror, and Alarm" subdomain—φόβος, φοβέομαι, and δειλός—that occur only ten times in total.[21] A survey of these occurrences indicates important details about fear and the role it

---

18. Johannes P. Louw and Eugene A. Nida, eds., *Greek-English Lexicon of the New Testament Based on Semantic Domains*, 2nd ed. (New York: United Bible Societies, 1989), 25.251–69.

19. Louw and Nida, *Greek-English Lexicon*, 316 n. 18.

20. The words are φόβος, φοβέομαι, ἀφόβως, φοβερός, ἔκφοβος/ἔμφοβος, ἐκφοβέω, φόβητρον, τρέμω, φρίσσω, ἔντρομος, θροέομαι, πτύρομαι, πτοέομαι, πτόησις, δειλία, δειλιάω, δειλός, ἀσθένεια.

21. φόβος occurs three times (Rev 11:1; 18:10; 18:15); φοβέομαι occurs six times (Rev 1:17; 2:10; 11:18; 14:7; 15:4; 19:5); δειλός occurs once (Rev 21:8).

plays in the rhetorical and theological project of Revelation. Above all, God and God's agents are presented most frequently as the objects of fear. The exhortation in Rev 14:7 captures this aspect: "Fear God and give him glory, for the hour of his judgment has come; and worship him who made heaven and earth, the sea and the springs of water."[22] In this single verse, important thematic and theological elements emerge. Fear is tied to acts of religious devotion—giving God glory and worshiping the creator of heaven and earth. Likewise, there is a specific object of fear, God, and the fear of God is prompted by the arrival of the hour of judgment. Adding greater significance to the meaning of Rev 14:7, the preceding verse describes the exhortation as an "eternal gospel" for all inhabitants of the earth. Fear in Revelation is particularly religious in nature; it is directed toward God, and it is related to other religious ideas such as human worship and divine judgment.

As the discussion above suggests, Revelation encourages a religious fear in its audiences that is closely connected with God's glory, God's role as creator, and God's coming judgment. These qualities and actions of God are worthy of human fear and the fear indicates devotion. God's servants and faithful ones characteristically "fear and glorify your name" (Rev 15:4; cf. 11:18, 19:5). Those opposed to God, God's people, and God's ways experience fear differently, however. For example, the former business associates of "Babylon," a codeword for Rome, watch in "fear" (φόβος) as God's judgment is inflicted on the city (18:10, 18:15).[23] Their experience of fear is not tied to religious devotion per se. While fear here is related to God's judgment, it stems from the demise of their city and their business interests, not their religious devotion.

---

22. All translations from the New Testament are from the NRSV. Greek texts are from NA^{28}.

23. See discussion in David E. Aune, *Revelation 6–16*, WBC 52B (Dallas: Word, 1998), 829–32. Aune notes the use of Babylon as a symbol for Rome in other apocalyptic literature: "As a cipher for Rome, the term 'Babylon' occurs occasionally in Jewish apocalyptic literature, though the fact that all the references occur in literature that postdates A.D. 70, the year when Jerusalem fell to Titus, has suggested to many scholars that the equation Babylon = Rome was not made until after that date and suggests that Revelation must have been written after that date" (829). Aune notes the equation (Babylon = Rome) in 1 Pet 5:13; 4 Ezra 3.1–2, 28–31; 16.44, 46; 2 Bar. 10.2; 11.1; 67.7; and Sib. Or. 5.143, 159, 434 (830). He also notes other symbolic names used by Jewish writers to refer to Rome.

While God and God's judgment are rightly feared, Revelation insists that other objects are unworthy of human fear. In the first place, suffering is not worthy of fear. Faithful obedience to God and, by extension, resistance to Rome's demand for obedience (1:17), will result in suffering. Revelation admonishes courage, not fear, in the face of suffering. At the end of Revelation, a list of those who are destined for the lake of fire includes the "cowardly" (δειλός) and the "faithless" (ἀπίστοις, 21:8). In addition to the other items in the list, both the "cowardly" and the "faithless" contrast with "the one who conquers" (ὁ νικῶν) in 21:7.[24] Elsewhere in Revelation those who conquer are blessed by God (2:7, 11, 17, 26; 3:5, 12, 21).[25] Revelation 15:2 identifies "those who had conquered the beast and its image and the number of its name." While Revelation does not make light of the real threat of persecution, it relativizes the fear associated with Rome and other human powers. Ultimately, these forces are nothing in comparison to the fear evoked by God and God's coming judgment. Neither suffering nor the agents who inflict persecution on those who remain faithful to God are worthy of fear.

In summary, Revelation contrasts two types of fear: a desirable type related to God and God's judgment, and an undesirable type related to Rome and Rome's machinations. Revelation inspires and instills the first type while preventing or dismissing the second. With this lexicon of fear in Revelation in mind, I now turn to discuss passages that prove particularly illuminating for understanding the nature and function of terror.

An Initial Glimpse at the One Like the Son of Man (Rev 1)

Elements of fear and terror characterize Revelation's description of divinities and the places they inhabit. The opening vision of Jesus (Rev 1:9–20) is

---

24. Cf. David Aune, *Revelation 17–22*, WBC 52C (Dallas: Word, 1998), 1131: "The term 'cowards' here seems to be intentionally used as the antonym of the 'conqueror' in v. 7a." Aune helpfully notes that the two terms, *cowards* and *unbelievers*, in Rev 21:8 do not appear in other vice lists in the New Testament. That cowardice and faithfulness would both be deemed vices, along with more standard and serious offenses such as idolatry, murder, sorcery, and sexual immorality, supports Blount's observation that one of the purposes of Revelation was to stir up a frenzy in the first audiences. Brian K. Blount, *Revelation: A Commentary*, NTL (Louisville: Westminster John Knox, 2009), 13.

25. Aune suggests the likelihood that "conquering" here draws from a military metaphor, rather than an athletic one, because of the possibility of death (*Revelation 1–5*, 151).

a case in point. After a voice commands him to write to the seven churches (1:11), John turns to see the source of the voice:

> Then I turned to see whose voice it was that spoke to me, and on turning I saw seven golden lampstands, and in the midst of the lampstands I saw one like the Son of Man, clothed with a long robe and with a golden sash across his chest. His head and his hair were white as white wool, white as snow; his eyes were like a flame of fire, his feet were like burnished bronze, refined as in a furnace, and his voice was like the sound of many waters. In his right hand he held seven stars, and from his mouth came a sharp, two-edged sword, and his face was like the sun shining with full force. (Rev 1:12–16)

These verses invite readers to identify the figure described with the raised Jesus.[26] The imagery, much of which derives from Israel's prophetic tradition, is powerful: eyes like flaming fire; a voice like rushing water; a hand holding seven stars; a sword extending out of a mouth; and a face with the force of the shining sun. The imagery recalls the mysterious "Son of Man" figure from Dan 7 and draws important connections between this Son of Man and depictions of the God of Israel in the Hebrew Bible, including the "Ancient of Days" (Dan 7:9, 13, 22). As Eugene Boring notes, John's combination of language describing the Son of Man, the Ancient of Days, and heavenly messengers serves "to express the transcendent glory of the exalted Christ," without the need for metaphysical precision.[27] The wording also recalls Porter's description of the logic of the sublime. The repetitive use of simile emphasizes the incommensurability of the figure John sees: eyes like a flaming fire and a face like the sun. Massive, nearly limitless objects are somehow contained in this single image of Jesus.

John's response to this vision of the exalted Christ underscores its powerful, terrifying nature. On seeing Jesus, John falls at his feet "as though dead" (1:17). David Aune says that this is a stereotypical response common in vision reports (e.g., Isa 6:5, Ezek 1:28; Dan 8:17).[28] In the vision reports,

---

26. "Though the identity of Daniel's messianic figure was uncertain (the people of Israel? the archangel Michael, who represents Israel? a human individual?), for John he is certainly the faithful witness, Jesus Christ" (Blount, *Revelation*, 44).

27. Eugene Boring, *Revelation*, IBC (Louisville: Westminster John Knox, 1989), 83.

28. "The stereotypical responses of recipients of visions upon the appearance of supernatural revealers constitute recurring literary themes in revelatory literature" (David Aune, *Revelation 1–5*, WBC 52A [Dallas: Word, 1998], 99). He notes Bauckham's

the act of bowing or falling down is often motivated by a sense of fear or awe in the presence of the divine. Consequently, Jesus's reassuring words address John's fear: "Do not be afraid; I am the first and the last and the living one. I was dead, and see, I am alive forever and ever; and I have the keys of Death and of Hades" (1:17).

What is the nature of the fear John experiences and the exalted Jesus seeks to dispel? First, there is the fear caused by witnessing the awesome presence of Jesus. The scene itself is awe-inspiring and terrifying. Second, we can think of the fear here in connection with the fear associated with John's commissioning as a prophet. In this way, the command, "Do not fear," evokes God's words of assurance to Israel's leaders and prophets of old.[29] Finally, Jesus's long self-description suggests another function of the command not to fear: Jesus relativizes other potential sources of fear. The description emphasizes Jesus's permanence ("I am alive forever and ever") and his power ("I have the keys of Death and of Hades"). Blount explains the significance of this description: "Knowing Christ's status should relieve John's fears about Roman claims to ultimate lordship and Rome's oppressive enforcement of those claims…. Rome should not be feared, because Christ is the true Lord."[30] The opening vision is rightly characterized as terrifying, and the description of the enthroned Jesus contains elements of the underlying logic of the sublime. John's response models the intended effect of the vision: it too should lead hearers or readers to recognize the awesome presence of the risen Jesus that minimizes the fear of other powers.

Terror and Awe in God's Presence (Rev 4)

Revelation employs stereotypical images associated with God's presence that evoke the emotion of terror. The narrative makes frequent reference to lightning and thunder, smoke and fire, earthquakes and other disruptions

---

identification of two main types of this stereotypical response. In one, the seer becomes extremely frightened and involuntarily falls prostrate. In the other, the act of prostration is the result of "reverential awe" (99). Aune likens John's response in Rev 1:17 to the first type. Cf. Richard Bauckham, "The Worship of Jesus in Apocalyptic Christianity," *NTS* 27 (1981): 322–41.

29. See, e.g., God's command to Abraham (Gen 15:1), Hagar (Gen 21:17), Isaac (Gen 26:24), Jacob (Gen 46:3), Moses (Num 21:34), Joshua (Josh 11:6), Elijah (2 Kgs 1:15), Ezekiel (Ezek 2:6), and the whole people of Israel (Isa 10:24; 37:6; 41:10; 44:8; Jer 1:8; 10:5; 30:10; 42:11; Zech 8:13, 15).

30. Blount, *Revelation*, 46.

to the cosmic order, phenomena that are associated with the theophany at Mount Sinai (see Exod 19:16–19) and God's presence more generally (see Ps 18:6–16; Isa 29:6).[31] Boring captures the significance of these descriptions: "Though unseen and indescribable, God is certainly and terribly *present*" in Revelation.[32]

There are clear indications of God's terrible presence in Rev 4:1–12. This passage has four major parts:

1. The open door to heaven and the invitation to come up (4:1);
2. The description of the throne, the enthroned one, and those gathered around the throne (4:2–6a);
3. The four living creatures worshiping the enthroned one (4:6b–8);
4. The response of the twenty-four elders (4:9–12).

Two implicit features of the text suggest the solemn nature of the scenes described. First, the vision takes place in the heavenly throne room. Whether one thinks of biblical precedents like Isaiah's vision of the throne of God (Isa 6:1–5) or extrabiblical precedents like Enoch's heavenly journey (1 En. 14), any description of God's heavenly throne carries with it a sense of awe, if not outright danger. As God warned Moses, no one can see God and live (Exod 33:20); how much more threatening for anyone who enters God's presence in heaven! Second, John witnesses heavenly worship led by the four living creatures and the twenty-four elders. The creatures' cry of "Holy, Holy, Holy" recalls Isaiah's vision and the praise of the cherubim around God's throne (Isa 6:3). The scene evokes the solemnity of worship, intensified by its heavenly locale and its supernatural liturgists. The allusions to biblical imagery and stereotypical associations of cultic worship convey the serious, awesome nature of the scene John witnesses in Rev 4.

Details typically associated with theophanies coalesce around the description of the heavenly throne: "Coming from the throne are flashes of

---

31. John's description of the throne of God in Rev 4:5 includes lightning, thunder, and fire. Lightning, thunder, an earthquake, and hail accompany the opening of the God's temple in Rev 11:19. Both Rev 8:5 (lightning, thunder, earthquake) and 16:18 (thunder, lightning, earthquake) associate these phenomena with the final stage in the unfolding of God's judgment of the earth. In this way, they signal both God's judgment and God's presence.

32. Boring, *Revelation*, 104 (emphasis original).

lightning, and rumblings and peals of thunder, and in front of the throne burn seven flaming torches, which are the seven spirits of God; and in front of the throne there is something like a sea of glass, like crystal" (Rev 4:5–6). As Blount notes, the imagery here "builds from a wealth of Hebrew Bible sources" that signal "God's cosmic presence."[33] The imagery appeals to the senses, adding to what Longinus calls "vivid description" (see *Subl.* 15). Through John's vision the readers see flashes of lightning and burning torches, they hear the peals of thunder and feel the rumblings, and they smell the smoke of the burning torches. In front of the throne John sees something like a sea of glass like crystal. Another biblical allusion is the heavenly dome in Ezekiel's vision in Ezek 1:22.[34] The use of simile (ὡς ... ὁμοία) underscores the incomprehensible nature of the scene and the way it presses the limits of language. This "sea of glass" stretches language into paradox, as the image communicates both the vast chaos of the sea and the miraculous calming of its force in the presence of God. The image suggests that God has frozen the sea into place along with the hostility it represents.[35]

The description of the four living beasts also signals the logic of the sublime. Drawing a composite picture of the creatures in Ezek 1:5–25 and Isa 6:1–4, John makes out the nature of the creatures: one like a lion, one like an ox, one like a human being, and one like an eagle (4:7).[36] Even though John differentiates the four living creatures, all of them are covered with eyes, both inside and out (4:8). Each creature has six wings. They all cry out in a language that John can understand, adding to the hybrid and discordant depiction of the creatures. According to Blount, the description indicates the living creatures' mobility and omnipresence.[37] The description registers with elements of Porter's notion of the logic of the sublime. The hybrid, fantastic descriptions of the living creatures evoke forces that work against nature and the orderliness of nature. The countless eyes signal lasting and everlasting qualities. The descriptions border on indefinability, epiphanic appearance, and even the collapse of form and order.[38]

---

33. Blount, *Revelation*, 91.
34. Blount, *Revelation*, 92.
35. Blount, *Revelation*, 92.
36. Blount, *Revelation*, 92.
37. Blount, *Revelation*, 93.
38. These elements are based on the extensive list of elements that make up the logic of the sublime enumerated in Porter, *Sublime in Antiquity*, 51–53. For the full list, see n. 14 above.

Above all, the description of the living creatures, along with the portrait of the throne and the enthroned one, conveys the incommensurability of what John sees. The whole scene is imbued with a sense of terror. Blount captures the significance of description in these verses: "The shock and awe of the throne room theophany add to the splendor that the throne and its room decor already exude."[39] Although there is no mention of John's terror or fear in proximity to the heavenly throne, we can assume the awe-inspiring nature of the imagery and its effects on the audiences of Revelation.

God's Terrifying Judgment (Rev 6–16)

Revelation's description of God's judgment using powerful, even violent imagery again registers terror. A significant portion of Rev 6–16 describes three cycles of seven symbolic actions that relate to God's judgment. Blount captures the function of these three cycles well: "John is the master of a three-ring narrative circus. The seven seals (6:1–8:1), the seven trumpets (8:2–11:18), and the seven bowls (16:1–21) stage the same preparatory build-up to the last judgment. They do so, however, from different perspectives."[40] Each cycle in the series includes elements that convey terror or the terrible. Some of the most powerful images and ideas deserve further comment.

After the opening of the sixth seal, John describes cosmic signs that anticipate the day of the Lord, drawing on images from the prophetic tradition.[41] There is an earthquake, the sun becomes black like a sackcloth, the moon becomes red like blood, stars fall to earth, the sky is rolled up "like a scroll," and mountains and islands are removed from the face of the earth (6:12–14). The logic of the sublime is apparent in the depiction of inconceivably large masses as well as their sudden, epiphanic appearance or disappearance. The response of earth's inhabitants underscores the terrifying nature of these events: from the greatest to the least, those on earth try to hide themselves in caves and among the rocks of the mountains (6:15).[42]

---

39. Blount, *Revelation*, 91.
40. Blount, *Revelation*, 120.
41. For the darkening or disruption of the sun, moon, and stars, see Isa 13:10; Ezek 32:7–8; Joel 2:30–31; Amos 8:9; Zeph 1:15; cf. Matt 24:29. For the image of the sky rolling up, see Isa 34:4; cf. Sib. Orac. 3.82–83, 233.
42. The people's request that the mountains and rocks fall on them may evoke a similar request in Hos 10:8. Aune suggests an allusion to Isa 2:19–21. He explains

The sounding of the first four trumpets in Rev 8:1–12 announces dramatic events that impact one-third of the earth or its inhabitants. Several of these events resemble the plagues described in the exodus tradition. They include terrifying elements described elsewhere: objects falling from the sky, blazing fire, and the darkening of heavenly bodies. The symbolic force of these events is clear: they impact the whole created order. Land, sea, fresh water, and sky experience some form of destruction. Even these cosmological events are not enough: the sounding of the fifth trumpet in Rev 9 unleashes locusts from the "bottomless pit" (9:1) that look like war horses (9:7) and that have a mix of human and animal features (9:7–10). These "demon locusts" are sent out to torture those who do not have the "seal of God on their foreheads" (9:5).[43] With the sounding of the sixth trumpet, four angels and their massive troops are sent out to kill one-third of humankind (9:14–16). As with the locusts, the description of the angels' cavalry is disturbing. The horses are hybrid creatures with lion's heads and tails like snakes (9:17, 19). Fire, smoke, and sulfur emanating from the horses carry out the extinction of one-third of the people (9:18).

When the seventh bowl is poured into the air, a loud voice from God's throne declares, "It is done!" (16:17). Typical signs of God's presence and judgment—lightning, thunder, and an earthquake—follow this declaration (16:18). But this earthquake is definitive in both its strength and the destruction it brings. The narrative indicates that "the great city was split into three parts, and the cities of the nations fell" (16:19). What is more, even the islands "fled away" and the mountains could no longer be found (16:20), details associated with scenes of God's presence and judgment in Israel's sacred texts.[44]

God's judgment manifests itself on earth in powerful and terrifying ways. The effects of God's judgment appear in the sky, in the sea, in rivers and lakes, and throughout the earth. God's judgment terrifies the inhabit-

---

the background of the response: "During times of invasion or siege, residents of cities and towns would often flee to the mountainous regions to hide from their enemies" (David Aune, *Revelation 6–16*, WBC 52B [Dallas: Word, 1998], 419–20). He adds that the primary reason for fleeing from the presence of God in the Old Testament is to "avoid judgment" (420).

43. For the identification of these as "demon locusts," see Blount, *Revelation*, 173. The description of the locusts may draw on both the exodus tradition and Joel 2:1–11, a text related to the feared day of the Lord. Aune observes the comparison of horses to "bristling locusts" in Jer 51:27 (*Revelation 6–16*, 531).

44. See, e.g., Ps 97:5; Isa 40:4; Ezek 38:20.

ants of the earth, so much so that they flee to the mountains in hope of hiding from God's wrath. Revelation insists, though, that terror in and of itself is not an adequate response to God's judgment. The inhabitants of the earth flee in fear, but they refuse to worship God or give God glory. Almost as a refrain, the passage describing the seven bowls repeats three times that the people cursed God, did not repent, and refused to give God glory (see 16:9, 11, 21).[45] Still, the logic of the sublime and the emotion of terror overlap in these scenes depicting God's judgment. Both serve the rhetorical and theological purposes of Revelation, buttressing the audience's perception of God's power and prompting their continued worship of God while effectively eliminating the authority of those who claim power and exert force in the earthly sphere.

The Real but Limited Terror of Satan and the Beasts (Rev 12–13)

Between the second and third cycles of sevens, Revelation describes certain forces opposed to God and God's people in beastly, monstrous ways. Revelation 12 describes Satan as a "great red dragon" while Rev 13 describes two beasts who serve as the dragon's emissaries on earth. The depictions of Satan and the beasts deserve further attention, especially as they relate to the nature of terror in Revelation.

In Rev 12, John sees "a great red dragon, with seven heads and ten horns, and seven diadems on his heads" (12:3). This dragon has vast power. The beast's tail sweeps down one-third of the stars of heaven and throws them down to earth (12:4). This dragon stalks the "woman clothed with the sun" (12:1) so that he can devour her soon-to-be-born son (12:4). But the dragon is spurned by God's intervention that protects both the woman and her child (12:5–6). Even with God's action, the dragon remains a powerful force opposed to God. According to 12:7–9, war breaks out in heaven between the dragon and his emissaries and the angels of God. The dragon is vanquished and cast down to earth, where he once again pursues the woman and the "rest of her children" (12:13–17). Revelation 12 presents a paradoxical image of the dragon. There is no doubt that the dragon has been conquered (12:11), and yet the dragon continues to exercise power

---

45. Cf. Aune, *Revelation 6–16*, 889: "The response of blaspheming or reviling the name of God on the part of the people who have been affected by divine retribution occurs only here and in vv 11 and 21 and forms a distinctive motif in Revelation found only in 16:1–21 (though the beast is said to revile God and his dwelling in 13:6)."

on earth and carries out a campaign of violence against those who "keep the commandments of God and hold the testimony of Jesus" (12:17).

Revelation 13 builds on this description of the dragon, as it presents two additional beasts that are set in opposition to God and the people of God. Revelation 12:18–13:10 describes the first beast that rises out of the sea. In important ways, this first beast resembles the dragon. It too has multiple heads, horns, and diadems (13:1). The beast appears as a combination of different animals: it is like a leopard but has feet like a bear and a mouth like a lion. It is not insignificant that all three animals mentioned—a leopard, a bear, and a lion—are predators and that the description singles out features of their anatomy related to their ability to capture and kill prey. The beast combines the speed of the leopard with the powerful feet of a bear and the ferocious mouth of a lion. The beast appears particularly well equipped to dominate and destroy. According to Rev 13:3, the "whole earth" is amazed (ἐθαυμάσθη), which leads them to ask, "Who is like the beast, and who can fight against it?" (13:5). Like the dragon, the first beast exercises significant power in the earthly sphere, even over God's people (13:7), and it is given authority over every tribe of the earth (13:7). Whether a result of devotion or coercion, all the inhabitants of the earth worship the beast (13:8). The beast's fearsome presence and power prompt the world's worship, resembling the close connection between fear and worship elsewhere in Revelation.

John describes a second beast in Rev 13:11–18. The text provides fewer details about the second beast's physical description, noting only that it had two horns like a lamb and that it spoke like a dragon (13:11). The description focuses instead on how the second beast exercises the authority of the first beast (13:12). The second beast compels people to worship the first beast and performs "great signs" on behalf of the beast (13:13–15). The second beast has the power to kill those who refuse to worship the image of the first beast (13:15) and to exclude them from participating in the economic practices of daily life ("no one can buy or sell" 13:17).

There is no escaping the intimidating nature of the dragon and the two beasts. Individually and together they exercise significant power and hold tremendous sway over earthly events. They have the ability to coerce the worship of false gods and to kill those who refuse to participate. They appear to rule over the whole created order and control all the nations. The dragon and the first beast are described in frightfully vivid ways. But in the world created by Revelation, the power of the dragon and the two beasts is ultimately limited and short-lived. The use of the passive voice to describe the power and authority that the beasts have been granted indicates that it is contingent on or granted by God.[46] As powerful and chaotic as these beasts may appear, they are not outside of God's sovereign control. And as the narrative of Revelation makes clear, their defeat and demise are certain, even if yet unrealized on earth.

The dragon and the beasts mirror the depiction of God and the Lamb in Revelation and the responses that their presence and activity generate. The depiction of these monstrous beings communicates their intimidating presence and fearful power. Their force and power are not imaginary; they inflict real and terrifying violence. Still, from the perspective of Revelation, they pale in comparison to the power and presence of God. The fear or terror evoked by the dragon and the beasts is relativized by the terror of God's presence and judgment. Finally, it is significant that Rev 12–13 depict combat between divine or semidivine beings. Narratives of these sorts were popular in the ancient world, and they relate to the topic of sublime rhetoric and the perspective of *On the Sublime*.[47] In *Subl.* 9.8, Longinus highlights one combat myth, the battle of the gods as recounted by Homer, as a particularly apt example of a "full-blooded idea" that is productive of sublime rhetoric.

The Nature and Function of Terror in Revelation

Porter's notion of the logic of the sublime provides a helpful framework for reading Revelation alongside of and with the perspective of *On the Sublime*. Even if Revelation does not fit with Longinus's working canon or the canon of other theorists on the sublime, the logic of the sublime is nevertheless present in significant ways. As the analysis above makes clear, Revelation's imagery and vivid description communicate the emotion of terror. They also facilitate the ecstatic effects of Longinus's understanding

---

46. Cf. Aune, *Revelation 6–16*, 743: "In vv 5–7, the singular aorist passive verb ἐδόθη, 'was given,' occurs five times in the identical phrase καὶ ἐδόθη αὐτῷ, 'and it was given'; in each instance the passive voice of the verb can be construed as a passive of divine activity, i.e., as a circumlocution for the direct mention of God as subject of the action of the verb. This makes it clear that John does not see the conflict between God and Satan (historically manifested in the conflict between Christians and the state) in terms of a cosmic dualism; rather he emphasizes the ultimate sovereignty and control of God over events that occur in the world."

47. For discussion of the allusion to combat myths in Rev 12–13, see Aune, *Revelation 6–16*, 712.

of sublime rhetoric. Revelation moves its audiences by both transporting them to the vivid scenes it describes and by stirring them emotionally.

As noted above, terror in Revelation is associated especially with God, God's presence, and God's coming judgment. The pronounced emphasis on what me might call religious terror provides the context for understanding the terror associated with Satan and his emissaries. There is no doubt that there is something terrible about Satan and the two beasts. They exercise tremendous power and hold significant control over the people of the earth. But their authority and influence are short-lived from the perspective of Revelation.

The nature of terror in Revelation relates to its rhetorical and theological purposes. In Revelation, terror and worship are interconnected. In key places, Revelation encourages its audiences to fear and worship God. We might say that Revelation seeks to instill the proper fear in its audiences so that they continue to worship the one who is worthy. Terror serves Revelation's hortatory purposes, exhorting its audiences to hold fast, to endure persecution, and to keep resisting the claims of the dragon and his earthly deputies.

This function of terror in Revelation aligns with the function of terror and sublime rhetoric more generally, as it is presented in *On the Sublime*. In the final chapter of the treatise, Longinus presents sublime rhetoric as an antidote to the pervasive apathy (ῥαθυμία) among his contemporaries. In that chapter, an important function of sublime rhetoric is to reorient hearers to what really matters and stir them on to what Longinus deems morally acceptable behavior. As a characteristic and product of sublime rhetoric, terror in Revelation serves similar ends. It arises from God's presence and judgment, which the text of Revelation depicts in vivid ways. Rhetorically and theologically, Revelation exhorts its audiences to worship God and to prove themselves conquerors by refusing to capitulate to the demands and pressures of other claimants to power.

Conclusion

This essay shows how *On the Sublime* is a useful tool for exploring the logic of the sublime in Revelation and the function of terror in it. The perspectives of Doran and Porter open up new avenues for reading Revelation. This analysis confirms Doran's suggestion that terror is frequently a feature of sublime rhetoric. Revelation's depictions of heavenly realities, God's promised judgment, and the opponents of God relate in various ways to the emotion of terror. The evocation of terror, moreover, relates to the logic of the sublime in Revelation. Revelation's terrifying, awe-inspiring scenes are pictures of incommensurability and moments characterized by the epiphanic appearance or disappearance of inconceivably large objects. They stretch the limits of language and of the imagination. Terror and the logic of the sublime serve Revelation's overall hortatory and theological purposes, which encourage its audiences to fear and worship God while dispelling misplaced fear of earthly rulers. In this way, terror and sublime rhetoric in Revelation foster endurance and hope for those who receive its powerful vision.

Sublime Terror in 1 Enoch

Vernon K. Robbins

Those who study Mediterranean antiquity know the treatise *On the Sublime* (Περὶ Ὕψους), attributed to Longinus (ca. 213–273 CE) but likely written during the first century CE.[1] Also they possibly know a discussion of the sublime by some other writer such as Dionysius of Halicarnassus (ca. 60–after 7 BCE). Those who study modern literature know Edmund Burke's *A Philosophical Enquiry into the Origin of Our Ideas of the Sublime and Beautiful* (1757). Those who are more philosophically minded know that book 2 in Immanuel Kant's *Critique of Judgment* (1790) presents an "Analytic of the Sublime."[2]

This essay begins with a brief review of Kant's thinking and then turns to Kant's language and ideas about the sublime as explained and interpreted by Rudolf A. Makkreel's *Imagination and Interpretation in Kant*, a book published exactly two hundred years after Kant's *Critique of Judgment* in 1790.[3] After explaining Kant's ideas of the mathematical and dynamical sublime, an interpretation of portions of 1 Enoch follows that uses both

---

1. Longinus, *On Great Writing (On the Sublime)*, trans. with an introduction by G. M. A. Grube (Indianapolis: Hackett, 1991.

2. Immanuel Kant, *Critique of Judgement*, Hafner Library of Classics (New York: Hafner, 1951), 82–181.

3. Rudolf A. Makkreel, *Imagination and Interpretation in Kant: The Hermeneutical Import of the "Critique of Judgment"* (Chicago: University of Chicago Press, 1990). I wish to express my gratitude to Professor Emeritus Rudolf Makkreel (regularly known as Rudi) for his help with this essay after a serendipitous moment when he sat down beside me at an Emory University Emeritus College luncheon prior to the Annual Meeting of the Society of Biblical Literature in San Diego in 2019. When I mentioned to him that I was writing a paper on the sublime, he asked me if I knew his discussion of Kant's approach to the sublime in his book on *Imagination and Interpretation in Kant*. I admitted that I did not. When I checked his book out of the library and started

of Kant's ideas. The final portion of the essay explores the possibility of a moral rhetorical effect of sublime terror that Andrew Shanks discusses as "the solidarity of the shaken," which is a concept Shanks relates to Hegel's *Phenomenology of the Spirit* in his book on *Hegel and Religious Faith*.[4]

Pure and Practical Reason

In order to understand Kant's approach to the sublime for this chapter, it is important for us briefly to review the relation of Kant's *Critique of Pure Reason* (1781) and *Critique of Practical Reason* (1788) to Kant's *Critique of Judgment* (1790), in which we see the analytic of the sublime. From Kant's perspective, when the mind uses pure and practical reason, the imagination synthesizes the progressive sequence of time that organizes representations determinantly, linearly, and subordinately.[5] In contrast, when the mind uses reflective judgment as described in the *Critique of Judgment*, it uses specification and spatial coordinating functions comprehensively. For Kant, then, time and space are constitutive of significantly contrasting functions in the mind. Pure and practical reason activates determinant judgment, which defines the particular intuitive content of experience in terms of universal concepts. Alternatively, reflective judgment is comparative and relates intuitions without any conceptual synthesis.[6]

The concepts of *understanding* make possible a temporal scientific reading of nature. But reason comes up with ideas that project a systematic

---

to read it, I began a new journey into my understanding of the sublime, which has been further enhanced through discussion with him.

4. After presenting the paper at the Annual Meeting of the Society of Biblical Literature in November 2019, I wanted to expand the end of it by exploring the possible moral dimensions of sublime terror. During the process of reading and searching for resources, another Emory colleague, Paul Zwier, professor of law in the Emory University School of Law, sent me a copy of Shanks's *Hegel and Religious Faith*. When I reached Shanks's discussion of "the solidarity of the shaken" on p. 31, I knew I wanted to blend this aspect of Shanks's discussion with the discussion of the terrible sublime in the first part of the essay. Thus the special approach in this chapter. See Andrew Shanks, *Hegel and Religious Faith: Divided Brain, Atoning Spirit* (New York: T&T Clark, 2011).

5. Rudolf A. Makkreel, "Imagination and Temporality in Kant's Theory of the Sublime," *Journal of Aesthetics and Art Criticism* 42 (1984): 303.

6. Makkreel, "Imagination and Temporality," 307.

whole that transcends experience. In contrast, *reflective judgment* allows us to experience nature imaginatively as a whole—not speculatively from on high but from the ground up. This means that pure and practical reason provide deductive grounding of doctrinal metaphysical systems of science and morals. In contrast, reflective judgment is inductive and orientational, enacting purposive interpretation of content in the universe. The functions of pure and practical reason proceed architectonically on the basis of fixed rational rules. Reflective judgment, in contrast, proceeds tectonically on the basis of revisable and indeterminate guidelines. Thus, interpretation within reflective judgment becomes hermeneutical, because the parts of a given whole are used to enrich and specify our initial understanding of it.[7]

Pure and practical reasoning erases emotions from their synthetic functions, while reflective judgment can assess emotions and feelings within formally purposive (teleological) and aesthetic reflection. *Understanding* within pure and practical reasoning uses temporality (sequential organization and subordination) to synthesize concepts and data in our world. *Interpretation* mediates reflective judgment that extends into aesthetic comprehension. Understanding is the faculty of finite knowledge attained through apprehension, using reason that strives to comprehend the infinite.[8] The sublime extends the imagination's power from apprehension to an aesthetic comprehension in which it is able instantaneously to grasp multiplicity (*Vielheit*) as a unity.[9] For Kant, the imagination has been assigned the dual function of *apprehension* and *comprehension*. *Apprehension* is a process that advances or progresses, so that to apprehend a magnitude is to grasp it part by part in a temporal succession. *Comprehension* of a magnitude involves the more difficult task of grasping or judging it as a whole.[10]

Kant's Analytic of the Sublime in Contrast to the Beautiful

Of special importance for this essay is Kant's definition of the sublime as "a state of mind."[11] This means that the sublime is as much about the

---

7. Makkreel, *Imagination and Interpretation*, 5.
8. Makkreel, "Imagination and Temporality," 307.
9. Makkreel, *Imagination and Interpretation*, 5.
10. Makkreel, "Imagination and Temporality," 305.
11. Makkreel, *Imagination and Interpretation*, 68.

mind as about physical objects such as a beautiful mountain or sunset. Kant reaches this definition by distinguishing between the feeling of the beautiful and the feeling of the sublime, a move he had already made by 1764 when he published his paper "Observations on the Beautiful and the Sublime." Kant summarized the difference between them in the statement: "The sublime touches, the beautiful charms."[12] The beautiful is a matter of taste, which was a topic of aesthetics that David Hume had discussed at some length before Kant.[13] With regard to the beautiful, Kant holds, "we feel so strongly in favor of the object that we imply that everyone else will and ought to be pleased by it."[14] In contrast, according to J. H. Bernard, "the principle underlying [people's] consent in judging of the sublime is 'the presupposition of the moral feeling in man.' The feeling of the sublimity of our own moral destination is the necessary prerequisite for forming such judgments."[15]

Since for Kant the sublime is a state of mind, *interpretation* is sublime rather than *some thing* being sublime. Below I will analyze sections of 1 Enoch on the basis of Kant's view of the *mathematical* sublime and the *dynamical* sublime. These two modes of the sublime build on and move beyond Kant's observation, stated above, that both ordinary and scientific processes of thought synthesize things using temporal modes of thinking, arranging representations in our minds sequentially, discretely, and subordinately. Sublime processes of thought, in contrast, institute "a 'regress' that annihilates the conditions of time and is related not to concepts of understanding, but to ideas of reason."[16] The imaginative regress of the sublime is important for comprehending *as a whole* what our minds normally apprehend as temporally discrete, namely as limited by a particular period of time.[17] This is what Kant means when he states, as we noted above, that the sublime is "a state of mind elicited by the representation of boundlessness or the infinite."[18]

---

12. Observations 2:208–9, in Bradley Murray, "Immanuel Kant, Critique of Judgment" (2014), https://tinyurl.com/SBL4831f.

13. Bradley Murray, "David Hume, On the Standard of Taste (pdf)" (2014), https://tinyurl.com/SBL4831g.

14. Murray, "Immanuel Kant, Critique of Judgment."

15. Bernard, "Translator's Introduction," in Kant, *Critique of Judgment*, xx.

16. Makkreel, *Imagination and Interpretation*, 67.

17. Makkreel, *Imagination and Interpretation*, 67–68.

18. Makkreel, *Imagination and Interpretation*, 68.

The Beautiful

Kant's *Critique of Judgment* begins by discussing the beautiful. It is important to know that his discussion of the beautiful merely expands on the functions of the mind associated with concepts of understanding needed for experience and not ideas of pure and practical reasoning that go beyond experience as the sublime does. The analytic of the beautiful shows judgments of *taste* to be reflective but nonconceptual appreciation of experience. In the analytic of the beautiful, a feeling of harmonious play between the imagination and the understanding is the result of *apprehension* of form that is subjectively purposive and produces aesthetic pleasure.[19]

For those of us who use the interpretive analytic of sociorhetorical interpretation (SRI), the process of apprehension of form Kant describes is what we would call the *rhetorical force* of the beautiful, namely, "the result of *apprehension* of form that is subjectively purposive and produces pure aesthetic pleasure."[20] For Kant, the felt harmony between imagination (as the faculty of a priori intuitions) and understanding (as the faculty of concepts) in the analytic of the beautiful is an indeterminate relation between two faculties in general, not a determinate relation where a specific intuition is subsumed under a specific concept to provide knowledge of an object. The idea of a free play between the faculties in the analytic of the beautiful indicates that the imagination is no longer directly controlled by understanding, although the rules of understanding remain in effect.[21]

The Sublime

As stated above, the sublime contrasts with the beautiful through representation of boundlessness or the infinite that excites and dislocates the mind. This excitement (*ekstasis*) and dislocation is an aspect of *rhetorical force* in sociorhetorical interpretation. The sublime is a "movement of the mind" whose subjective purposiveness is referred by the imagination either to the faculty of cognition or to the faculty of desire.[22] Kant's analytic of the sublime contains two aspects: (1) the *mathematical* sublime, related to the cognitive faculties and represented in terms of magnitude; (2) the *dynamical* sublime,

---

19. Makkreel, "Imagination and Temporality," 307.
20. Makkreel, "Imagination and Temporality," 307, emphasis added.
21. Makkreel, "Imagination and Temporality," 307.
22. Makkreel, "Imagination and Temporality," 303.

related to the faculty of desire and represented in terms of might or power.[23] The judgment of the sublime involves a polar relation between (1) aesthetic prehension, which is absolute in lying at the basis of all comparison or reflective judgment, and (2) the limit of aesthetic comprehension, which is the absolutely great beyond all comparison. Thus, the imagination contains a simultaneous reference to an absolute measure and the immeasurable.[24]

The Mathematical Sublime

Mathematical measurement related to the cognitive faculties and represented in terms of magnitude has the power of logical comprehension and is a function of determinant judgment as well as a faculty of sense and thus capable of establishing a measure for itself. Whereas numbers represent "relative magnitudes by means of comparison," as experienced successively in time, the intuitive estimation of functioning in the *mathematical* sublime "presents magnitude aesthetically and reflectively" apart from any comparison. This aesthetic comprehension occurs in an instant that Kant conceives as a vanishing limit of the time line.[25]

When the imagination's capacity to intuit a series of units as one simultaneous whole reaches a limit, aesthetic comprehension encounters the immeasurable and the emotion of the sublime. The maximum, "if it is judged as the absolute measure than which no greater is possible subjectively … brings with it the idea of the sublime and produces that emotion which no mathematical estimation of its magnitude by means of numbers can bring about (except so far as that aesthetical fundamental measure remains vividly in the imagination)." The sublime as the absolutely great is "great beyond all comparison" and can be projected only insofar as we remain conscious of the absolute fundamental measure that underlies numerical measure.[26]

The Dynamical Sublime

In the *dynamical* sublime absoluteness is estimated, not in terms of magnitude, but in terms of might or power. The sheer power of nature exhibited in a hurricane or waterfall tends to make humans regard themselves as

---

23. Makkreel, "Imagination and Temporality," 303–4.
24. Makkreel, "Imagination and Temporality," 304–5.
25. Makkreel, *Imagination and Interpretation*, 74.
26. Makkreel, "Imagination and Temporality," 304.

insignificant. Yet the power of nature can also cause humans to reflect on their own power and locate in themselves "a sublimity of disposition" that is superior to mere physical power and conformable to rational law. Individuals can only recognize the sublime and their rational, supersensible destination if they are morally cultivated. Thus Kant claims that "without development of moral ideas, that which we, prepared by culture, call sublime presents itself to uneducated people merely as terrible."[27]

Babies, for example, may very well experience waterfalls to be terrifying for their noise and force without any sense of amazing grandeur or beauty that may be created by rays of the sun on the sprays of water. In contrast, a sublime presentation leaves a highly cultivated human with a mental mood that influences "only indirectly ... the mind's consciousness of its strength and its resolution" with reference to rational purposiveness. In other words, the representation of the imagination produces an emotional sense of one's resources and the moral power of self-determination. In the *dynamical* sublime, the whole determination of the mind in the mathematical sublime regarding the integration of coexisting faculties (*Kräfte*) is informed by, and therefore dependent on, the integral power (*Macht*) of the moral person.[28]

An Example of the Mathematical Sublime in 1 Enoch 21.1–10

The Place of Punishment for the Disobedient Stars

> 1 I traveled to where it was chaotic. 2 And there I saw a terrible thing; I saw neither heaven above, nor firmly founded earth, but a chaotic and terrible place. 3 And there I saw seven of the stars of heaven, bound and thrown in it together, like great mountains, and burning in fire.
> 4 Then I said, "For what reason have they been bound, and for what reason have they been thrown here?"
> 5 Then Uriel said to me, one of the holy angels who was with me, and he was their leader, he said to me, "Enoch, why do you inquire, and why are you eager for the truth? 6 These are the stars of heaven that transgressed the command of the Lord; they have been bound here until ten thousand years are fulfilled—the time of their sins."[29]

---

27. Makkreel, "Imagination and Temporality," 313.
28. Makkreel, "Imagination and Temporality," 313.
29. Translation with modification from George W. E. Nickelsburg, *1 Enoch 1: A Commentary on the Book of 1 Enoch, Chapters 1–36; 81–108*, Hermeneia (Minneapolis: Fortress, 2001), 297.

To understand the scene in 1 En. 21.1–6 and then the following scene in 1 En. 21.7–10, we must recall some of the experiences of Enoch before these scenes occur. After God created all things in heaven and earth, "all who are in the heavens" know and see how all things in heaven and earth occur according to God's will, plan, and command (3.1–3). The reference to *all* in this statement immediately calls forth the sublime. There is no reference to certain groups who "know and seek," but *all* in the heavens know and see. There is, however, a problem. Certain beings both in heaven and earth engage in wicked, sinful acts. When this happens, these beings can be sure that God will execute judgment against them (2.6). The only question is about exactly how God will do this. In 1 En. 7, a most horrible transgression was performed by some of the angels. When some of them saw beautiful daughters of humans on earth, they chose them as wives, and this defiling activity brought forth Nephilim who began to kill and even eat humans (7.1–3; cf. 86.3–6). After God pronounces judgment on these angels, Enoch, who had been taken by God into heaven, becomes the intercessor between the transgressing angels and God. Enoch takes the petition of the sinful angels to God, asking God to forgive them for their transgressions, but God will not grant them forgiveness (1 En. 12–14). After it becomes clear that God will punish these angels, Enoch is taken on journeys throughout the created universe.

In 1 En. 21.1–5, recited above, Enoch relies on a provisional reflective judgment that takes the discourse into sublime reasoning about what he sees. Enoch's first reflection is on the space he sees. The space is chaotic, because there is no heaven above or earth beneath to give it a discrete location in space. It is like the chaos and void that existed before creation (Gen 1:2), containing no boundary of sky overhead and no earth beneath that rests on a firm foundation below it. The space is formless and therefore measureless. There is no high point like a boundary at the bottom of the sky, there is no conceptual low point, and there is no corner that could be a starting point for measuring in any direction east, west, north, or south. In other words, there is no definitive up, down, or sideways. The space Enoch sees is a mathematical sublime space that escapes any boundaries of magnitude or direction. He is disoriented and needs to be morally reoriented. He looks more intently at what he sees to find some orientation.

As Enoch looks into the sublime, chaotic space, he sees seven of the stars of heaven bound together and thrown into it, like great mountains and burning in fire. In other words, Enoch is able to see some stars, but these stars are not in orbits as they should be, but are in clumps like huge piles of garbage in a burning garbage dump. They have no special place, special form, or special order of arrangement. None are especially above or below the other, and none is more to the left or right of the other. They do not even make seven discrete mountains. They are simply thrown together and bound together in huge mounds of burning fire that cannot be described with any precision of measurement of size or distance.

The state of existence of the seven stars causes Enoch's mind to probe into his reflective judgment. "Why," he asks the angel Uriel, "have these stars been bound and thrown into this chaotic space in this indiscriminate manner?" Uriel answers with sublime reasoning that relates a sublime measurement of sins to a sublime length of time. The measure of the sins of the angels is ten thousand years, he says. So how long in time is the measurement of any sin? Within the discrete world of time in which we humans live, we learn that certain sins equal a certain length of time. Both parents and teachers have taught us the length of time of certain sins. When we were children at home, our parents may have decided that our hitting of a brother, sister, or playmate equaled one hour of sitting in our room without a favorite game to play, recording to hear, or favorite program to watch on television, or for those younger than we, no computer on which to play games. Or a teacher may have decided that our passing of a note to a classmate equaled one hour of sitting in the classroom outside the scheduled time of classes without fellow classmates or specially scheduled class activities. Our sin equaled one hour of time in a formless, chaotic space, and perhaps even an unknown aspect of what might actually happen in that space could be terrifying, like whether it was possible that someone might come and give us a scolding or do something even worse to us as a punishment. Then, when a person becomes an adult, stealing something like a van or truck may equal a very specific range of time in prison, in addition to a significant monetary fine. For example, in Georgia, "A person convicted of stealing a vehicle engaged in commercial transportation of cargo faces a minimum of three years in prison and a maximum of ten (the judge also has the discretion to place the defendant on probation or suspend the sentence), and a fine of $5,000 to $50,000."[30]

The measurement of the sins of the angels in 1 En. 21.6 is ten thousand years. Ten thousand years is a sublime temporal measurement here,

---

30. Rebecca Pirius, "Auto Theft laws in Georgia," *Criminal Defense Lawyer.* 22 December 2020. https://tinyurl.com/SBL4831h.

beyond any discrete length of measurement within daily human experience. Most adults attain discrete conceptualization of a day, although some live in liminal spaces of time that are not determined either by sunrise or sunset, or perhaps even specific times of sleep and work. Young women learn the length of a month through a physical cycle in their bodies, and then they may learn the length of a pregnancy until the birth of a child, then the length of time it takes for a child to learn to walk, and so forth. Thus humans develop conceptualization of certain extended times of life. They may conceptualize decades, like their teen years, their twenties, or other spans of time within a century of time. So how long is ten thousand years? As a multiple of ten, it might be a metaphor for a complete period of time. It is a sublime length of time beyond any discrete measurement within the minds of most humans. Uriel's answer is that the angels have committed sins that surpass any discrete measurement of time within the life of a human being, like ten, twenty, fifty, eighty, or even one hundred years. The quality of their sins is sublime, equaling a time of punishment in a chaotic, sublime space without discrete mathematical measurement.

The Prison of the Fallen Angels

After Enoch sees the place of the punishment of the disobedient stars in 1 En. 21.1–6, he travels further in the cosmos where he sees an even more sublime, more terrible, space than the first space. This leads us to 1 En. 21.7–10.

> 7 From there I traveled to another place, more terrible than this one. And I saw terrible things—a great fire burning and flaming there. And the place had a narrow cleft (extending) to the abyss, full of great pillars of fire, borne downward. Neither the measure nor the size was I able to see or to estimate.
> 8 Then I said, "How terrible is this place and fearful to look at!"
> 9 Then Uriel answered me, one of the holy angels who was with me, and said to me, "Enoch, why are you so frightened and shaken?"
> And I replied, "Because of this terrible place and because of the fearful sight."
> 10 And he said, "This place is a prison for the angels. Here they will be confined into cosmic spacetime [the age]."[31]

---

31. Translation with modification from Nickelsburg, *1 Enoch 1*, 297.

As Enoch approaches this second terrible place, he sees "a great fire burning and flaming." Then he sees a narrow cleft that extends boundlessly into an immeasurable abyss downward. Within this boundless abyss are "great pillars of fire." At this point Enoch's reflective judgment produces a sublime description. "Neither the measure nor the size was I able to see or to estimate" (21.7), he says. His reflective judgment fills his mind with mathematically sublime reasoning. Then he says, "How terrible is this place and fearful to look at!" (21.8). Anything so mathematically indeterminate, lacking any clear or specific aspects that can be discretely described, is sublimely terrible and terrifying. How fearful it is to look at it! When Uriel asks Enoch why he is "so frightened and shaken," Enoch says, "Because of this terrible place and because of the fearful sight" (21.9). Then Uriel tells Enoch the ultimate sublime temporal thought, "This place is a prison for the angels. Here they will be confined into cosmic spacetime" (the age, 21.10). In the speech of Uriel, this space receives fully sublime scope. The scope coordinates a particular boundless space with a period of time than can never be measured. At this point in the account, then, apocalyptic discourse has prompted hearers/readers to gaze into deep, cosmic spacetime beyond the boundaries of both heaven and earth. The sins of the angels are beyond measure, and the spacetime into which they have been placed is beyond apocalyptically conceived time and space in the created realm of heaven and earth. The hearer/reader has been led to conceptualize deep, cosmic spacetime in the context of immeasurable sins committed by eternally existing angels. The length of punishment of these ever-existing angels is related to the cosmic space of their imprisonment and cosmic time of the magnitude of their sins. The magnitude of their sins is beyond measurement either by time or by space in the created world of heaven and earth. Their sins are therefore *cosmic* in scope, both in terms of deep cosmic time and expansive cosmic space. Herein is a quintessential example of the mathematical sublime as Kant conceptualizes it. The angels will be confined to expansive, measureless cosmic space for a measureless amount of deep cosmic time. In the ordinary language of biblical and extrabiblical discourse, this is a fleeting glimpse into the cosmic spacetime of eternity.

An Example of the Dynamical Sublime in 1 Enoch 62.1–8

While our first two instances in 1 En. 21 are excellent examples of the *mathematical* sublime as Kant describes it, 1 En. 62 in the midst of the

Parables or Similitudes of 1 En. 37–71 nicely exhibits the *dynamical* sublime. In this chapter we see the power of the Chosen One, who is called "that Son of Man," who presides over the great judgment.

The Chosen One Presides over the Great Judgment: 1 Enoch 62.1–5, 11, 13–14

> 1 And thus the Lord commanded the kings and the mighty and the exalted and those who possess the land, and he said,
> "Open your eyes and lift up your horns, if you are able to recognize the Chosen One."
> 2 And the Lord of Spirits <seated him> upon the throne of his glory; and the spirit of righteousness was poured upon him.
> And the word of his mouth will slay all the sinners, and all the unrighteous will perish from his presence.
> 3 And there will stand up on that day all the kings and the mighty and the exalted and those who possess the land.
> And they will see and recognize that he sits on the throne of his glory; and righteousness is judged in his presence, and no lying word is spoken in his presence.
> 4 And pain will come upon them as [upon] a woman in labor, when the child enters the mouth of the womb, and she has difficulty in giving birth.
> 5 And one group of them will look at the other; and they will be terrified and will cast down their faces, and pain will seize them when they see that Son of Man sitting on the throne of his glory....
> 11 And he will deliver them to the angels for punishment, so that they may exact retribution from them for the iniquity that they did to his children and his chosen ones.
> 12 And they will be a spectacle for the righteous and for his chosen ones; and they will rejoice over them,
> because the wrath of the Lord of Spirits rests upon them, and his sword is drunk with them.
> 13 And the righteous and the chosen will be saved on that day; and the faces of the sinners and the unrighteous they will henceforth not see.
> 14 And the Lord of Spirits will abide over them, and with that Son of Man they will eat, and they will lie down and rise up in deep, cosmic spacetime [the age of the ages].[32]

---

32. Translation with modification from George W. E. Nickelsburg and James C. VanderKam, *1 Enoch 2: A Commentary on the Book of 1 Enoch, Chapters 37–82*, Hermeneia (Minneapolis: Fortress, 2012), 254.

From Kant's perspective, in the *dynamical* sublime "absoluteness is estimated, not in terms of magnitude, but in terms of might or power."[33] As Enoch is taken on travels throughout the universe, he sees all "the secrets of righteousness" (58.5), which includes all the secrets of the functioning of the created universe (59.1–60.23). Then he is shown how the first judgment occurred through the flood (60.1–25), and he sees the beginning activities of the final judgment (61.1–5). In 61.1, "all who are in the heights of heaven received a command, and power and one voice and one light like fire were given to them." This prepares for the scene that unfolds in 1 En. 62.

First Enoch 62.1–14 presents the sublime power and might of the Son of Man who is placed on the throne by God. One of the notable things about this scene is the repetitive occurrence of the word *all*. "The word of his mouth will slay *all* the sinners, and *all* the unrighteous will perish from his presence. And there will stand up on that day *all* the kings and the mighty and the exalted and those who possess the land" (62.2–3, emphasis added). The power of the one sitting on the throne is so great that "no lying word is spoken in his presence" (62.3). In this context, one group will be terrified (62.5). Another group however, "the righteous and the chosen," will be saved on that day. "The faces of the sinners and the unrighteous" will disappear from their sight (62.13), and "they will eat, and lie down and rise up in deep, expansive spacetime" with the Son of Man (62:14). Here we see the *dynamical* sublime.

Kant especially emphasizes the presence of *moral cultivation* for the dynamical sublime. This seems to stand in contrast to Edmund Burke's contention that "There is thus nothing morally educative (or rational) about the sublime as such. Fear 'robs the mind of all its powers of acting and reasoning.'"[34] But perhaps this is not in disagreement with Burke. Perhaps the dynamical sublime does not teach moral reasoning; rather if moral reasoning is present, then a person can recognize the dynamical sublime. Kant claims that "without development of moral ideas, that which we, prepared by culture, call sublime presents itself to uneducated people merely as terrible." In other words, "Individuals can only recognize

---

33. Makkreel, "Imagination and Temporality," 313.
34. Christine Battersby, "Terror, Terrorism and the Sublime: Rethinking the Sublime after 1789 and 2001," *Postcolonial Studies* 6 (2003): 70.

the sublime and their rational, supersensible destination if they are morally cultivated."[35]

Is it true that the sublime "floods the mind" so fully that it completely overwhelms and displaces (or bypasses?) moral reasoning? Not exactly. The primary question for Kant is *if* moral reasoning has been cultivated in a person. Kant thinks moral reasoning is *innate*, but moral reasoning induces moral *agency* only when it is cultivated, in other words, culturally or socially energized. So Kant says that both the mathematical and dynamical sublime are perceived simply as *terrible* if moral reasoning has not been cultivated in a person. If moral reasoning has been cultivated, the dynamical sublime may activate and energize moral agency and power within an individual. The sublime is an instantaneous moment that reorients people and leads them to recall their moral destination. There is no time for lessons here; merely a reminder or warning. For Kant, therefore, especially the dynamical sublime could be empowering. It is not especially educative, but it can energize moral agency. A constituent part of becoming educated is undoubtedly to become empowered. When the mind activates the sublime, even the imagination itself is transformed: it has to give up its pretension to intuit distinctly the infinite, but it gains an indeterminate felt power that opens up an "infinity within ourselves."[36]

A major question for me is the nature of empowerment by the sublime. We can quite easily perceive pure and practical reasoning as empowering because they are cumulative. Their progressive, temporal nature creates a "building up." But what about the sublime? Is there something the sublime builds up? This takes us to the series of *Bildung* words Kant uses to discuss *Bildungsvermögen*, which Makkreel translates as "the formative faculty in the imagination."[37] Makkreel lists the different species of *Bildungsvermögen* as:

1. *Bildung*: coordinating or giving form to intuition
2. *Abbildung*: direct image formation
3. *Nachbildung*: reproductive image formation
4. *Vorbildung*: anticipatory image formation
5. *Einbildung*: imaginative formation

---

35. Makkreel, "Imagination and Temporality," 313; Makkreel, *Imagination and Interpretation*, 74.
36. Makkreel, *Imagination and Interpretation*, 87.
37. Makkreel, *Imagination and Interpretation*, 12.

6. *Ausbildung*: completing formation
7. *Gegenbildung*: analogue or symbolic formation
8. *Urbildung*: archetypal formation.³⁸

According to Makkreel, items 1–7 are human capacities and item 8 is divine. The *lower* cognitive faculties (items 1–7) may be viewed as "aspects of a general formative faculty, or *Bildungsvermögen*."³⁹ They are *lower*, because they involve only imaging or imagining and not *Urbildung* or *original formation*. *Bildung* gives shape to something sensuous, like a carpenter gives form to wood. Items 2–4 are modes of mental *imaging* that are empirical or sense based. Item 5, *Einbildung*, is central to the *Critique of Pure Reason* and is considered the productive *imagination* that schematizes the categories to make them applicable to objects of experience. Here imagination is a higher mediating power.⁴⁰ In the *Critique of Judgment*, item 6, *Ausbildung* or *completing formation*, is more highly developed into the sublime comprehensive imagination, and item 7, *Gegenbildung* or *analogue formation*, becomes the symbolic imagination that allows us to refer to God by means of analogies.⁴¹ Beyond this, *Urbildung* is the drawing "finally from all objects of one type an archetype (*Urbild*)" and can thus be called "the power of archetypal formation."⁴² According to Kant, we cannot know (*wissen*) with certainty that there is a God, because all the proofs for God's existence fail. We do, however, have symbolic cognition (*Erkenntnis*) of God that entitles us to have faith that provides moral conviction. For Kant, there are no determinant judgments about God, but only reflective or provisional judgments that allowed him to think of God as our heavenly father.

John Shannon Hendrix praises Makkreel's clear summarization of Kant's *Bildungsvermögen* and discusses them in relation to unconscious

---

38. Makkreel, *Imagination and Interpretation*, 14. Roy R. Jeal cites Graham Wallas as presenting the following stages of creativity: preparation (focusing the mind); incubation (internalization in the unconscious mind); intimation (sensing a solution); illumination (conscious creative idea); verification (conscious verification and elaboration). See Jeal, "Creative Development: Blended Discourse in Colossians" (paper presented at the virtual Annual Meeting of the Society of Biblical Literature, Boston, MA, 7 December 2020), 3; Wallas, *The Art of Thought* (Kent: Solis, 2014), 37–55.

39. Makkreel, *Imagination and Interpretation*, 12.
40. Makkreel, *Imagination and Interpretation*, 20–21.
41. Makkreel, *Imagination and Interpretation*, 119–20.
42. Makkreel, *Imagination and Interpretation*, 14.

thought associated with the philosophical system of Plotinus.[43] Hendrix emphasizes that the lower imagination is connected to conscious thought and sense perception (*nous pathetikos*). This imagination is architechtonic as it is subject to the temporal categories in intuition in the inner experience and the spatial categories of intuition in sense perception.[44] *Abbildung* is limited to the present moment as it produces direct image formation depicting a sensuous object, *Nachbildung* adds a temporal dimension as it represents images formulated in the past by *Abbildung*, and *Vorbildung* adds the temporal dimension of the future as it reproduces images from the past and present in anticipation of future images. Working together, then, *Abbildung, Nachbildung,* and *Vorbildung* create "a storehouse of images, which becomes the vocabulary for sense experience and discursive reason.[45]

Hendrix then emphasizes that the higher imagination featuring *Einbildung, Ausbildung,* and *Gegenbildung* is not connected to sense perception or empirical experience, but is solely the product of intellectual cognition or the *nous poietikos*, unconscious thought.[46] *Einbildung* is an activity of the soul as it invents images not connected to sense perceptions, although its invented image (*Erdichtung*) must be derived from images of sense perception.[47] Thus it is an unconscious process, which Makkreel says "loves to wander in the dark."[48] *Ausbildung* completes the invented images in unconscious thought or *nous poietikos*. The completion then leads to *Gegenbildung*, "formation of symbolic or analogical invented image, an

---

43. John Shannon Hendrix, *Unconscious Thought in Philosophy and Psychoanalysis* (London: Palgrave Macmillan, 2015), 158–60.

44. Hendrix, *Unconscious Thought*, 158.

45. Hendrix, *Unconscious Thought*, 158; cf. Makkreel, *Imagination and Interpretation*, 14. Hendrix's further thoughts on these are: "Each is tied to the mechanisms of sense perception and material images, but also depends on active intellect and intellectual cognition in its formative powers. The manifold, for example, is present even in *Abbildung* as individual perceptions, conscious and unconscious, immediately participate in a totality, in a process of 'running through' (*durchläuft*) the manifold. The mind is conscious in sense perception of forming and receiving images which are composites of many points of view, in the process of apperception" (159).

46. Hendrix, *Unconscious Thought*, 158.

47. Hendrix, *Unconscious Thought*, 158–59; cf. Makkreel, *Imagination and Interpretation*, 15.

48. Hendrix, *Unconscious Thought*, 159; Makkreel, *Imagination and Interpretation*, 15.

archetype or intelligible, formed by the schemata from the categories in a priori intuition."[49] For Hendrix, the pure form of archetypal formation in the *Gegenbildung* is the *Urbildung*, which has no connection whatsoever to the material world, but is solely a pure quality of the soul. The *Urbildung* precedes the mechanisms of imagination in cognition and is produced from a source that is inaccessible to conscious thought.[50]

An important question for us is what aspects of "the formative faculty in the imagination" (*Bildungsvermögen*) either the mathematical or dynamical sublime use. Perhaps a contribution of my interpretation of 1 Enoch is an explanation of apocalyptic sublime terror as including substantive mathematical sublime in modes of *Einbildung*, *Ausbildung*, *Gegenbildung*, and *Urbildung* (items 5–8 of the *Bildungensvermögen*). The concreteness of the imagery in apocalyptic literature creates a cumulation of mathematical sublime imagination. In other words, apocalyptic sublime terror in 1 Enoch reintroduces temporality into a context of aesthetic comprehension and imaginative regress through imaginative experiencing of the vast space of the cosmos. The temporality of consciousness, therefore, need not simply be the temporality of the end of the world or end of the age. Rather, it is a temporality of exploration and comprehension of the vastness of the cosmos imaginatively with extended specification and spatial coordination. The temporality of this extended exploration reintroduces the cumulative cognitive effect of arranging things sequentially, discretely, and subordinately.[51]

---

49. Hendrix, *Unconscious Thought*, 159.
50. Hendrix, *Unconscious Thought*, 159.
51. Hendrix, *Unconscious Thought*, 176–77, adds: "While the judgment of beauty in nature, though derived from intuition, is based on the perception of the object in nature, the sensation of the sublime is based on the failing of reason in apprehension, the failing of the representation in the imagination by apprehension. The sublime invokes the terror of the unknowability of the self to itself. The feeling of the sublime is 'a feeling of displeasure, arising from the inadequacy of imagination in the aesthetic estimation of magnitude to attain to its estimation by reason' (Kant, *Critique of Judgment*, §27, 257, 12–15), spatial and temporal magnitude in the a priori categories.... The sublime, in severing the tie between perception and reason, or the relation of reason to itself, 'makes reason confront its own unconscious,' in the words of Joel Faflak in *Romantic Psychoanalysis* [Faflak, *Romantic Psychoanalysis*: *The Burden of the Mystery* (Albany: State University of New York Press, 2008), 47]. Reason loses itself in an abyss: 'The point of excess for the imagination (towards which it is driven in the apprehension of the intuition) is like an abyss in which it fears to lose itself...' (*Critique*

According to Makkreel, moral and religious themes are most commonly associated with the dynamical rather than mathematical sublime.[52] However, if moral and religious aspects of life are substantive aspects of the mathematical sublime, then perhaps a rhetorical force of the cumulative number of deaths and the spatial size of destruction during World Wars I and II could contribute to a particular kind of new or emergent moral and religious point of view. Perhaps this can be understood as an instance of *Ausbildung*, or "completion," that Shanks describes as a religious movement during the last half of the twentieth century among Czech philosophers that he calls "the solidarity of the shaken."

The Solidarity of the Shaken

In his book on *Hegel and Religious Faith*, Shanks discusses transmetaphysical theology, which he considers to be concerned with "*evoking* the moral demands of perfect truth-as-openness," which becomes a poetic enterprise.[53] In my understanding, truth-as-openness as Shanks describes it invites the sublime into cognition both as the mathematical sublime and the dynamical sublime. The theology that emerged in the midst of the Czech philosophy "aims at a maximum energizing of metaphor, in celebration of truth-as-openness."[54]

In contexts where thought has gone stale in self-enclosed intellectual cultures, it is necessary to have a challenge from "outsiders whose experience of life may lead them to view the world quite differently."[55] For Shanks, the way in which some Czech philosophers blended their trauma memories from the two world wars of the twentieth century with the pre-Socratic poetic-philosophic thought of Heraclitus created a special environment for seeing the world quite differently. In this context the Czech philosopher Jan Patočka coined a phrase, the "solidarity of the shaken" to describe "the solidarity that binds together, simply, *all* those who have been 'shaken' by the demands of perfect truth-as-openness; 'shaken,' that is, out of shelter of fixed preconceptions, standard

---

of Judgment, §27, 258, 6–9) (Kant, 1952). The sublime is a conflict between reason and imagination, in the inadequacy of the understanding."

52. Makkreel, *Imagination and Interpretation*, 68.
53. Shanks, *Hegel and Religious Faith*, 26.
54. Shanks, *Hegel and Religious Faith*, 26.
55. Shanks, *Hegel and Religious Faith*, 26.

judgements, and clichés. In the Christian context, trans-metaphysical theology is, first and foremost, a project of rendering the confessional solidarity of Christians with Christians, to the greatest possible extent, *transparent* to the solidarity of the shaken."[56]

In relation to the special trauma memories of twentieth-century Czech philosophers during the 1970s, Patočka poses the question, "Why [did] European civilization fail to generate a more effective resistance" against all the horrors of the "front-line experience" of "the First World War nightmare of trench-warfare, the barbarities associated with the Second World War, [and] the oppressive menace of the Cold War?" He gives the simple name "Force" to the answer and focuses especially on "the propaganda operations of Force."[57]

From the perspective of sociorhetorical interpretation, repetition is a mathematical rhetorical force that introduces a temporality that arranges things sequentially, discretely, and subordinately. During the years 2016–2020, the world saw the repetitive rhetorical force of counterfactual claims by President Donald J. Trump that are related to the rhetorical force of the government propaganda of the Third Reich in Germany. Shanks explains that the culture of governmental politics during and after the world wars allowed and encouraged individuals to project their experiences individually "to their summit" and then to "retreat back to everydayness."[58] In this context, governmental organizations embodying the solidarity of the shaken did not come forward with positive programs for government but focused their resources on researchers who applied research, namely inventors and engineers, "to the everydayness of the fact-crunchers and routine minds." It proved to be virtually impossible to get governmental leaders to focus on projects that pursued human rights, justice, and what Shanks calls "true peace" rather than "the false peace of devout thought-gone-stale."[59]

The challenge is "to try and get to grips with the challenge of the solidarity of the shaken to the solidarity of Christians with other Christians." Since "shakenness is so very much an inner condition, without immediately obvious external markers to identify it," Shanks explains, "we are faced with a strategic need to mix the highest will-to-truth with other motives,

---

56. Shanks, *Hegel and Religious Faith*, 27, emphasis original.
57. Shanks, *Hegel and Religious Faith*, 27–28.
58. Shanks, *Hegel and Religious Faith*, 28.
59. Shanks, *Hegel and Religious Faith*, 30.

so as to stiffen it, give it staying-power: the solidarity of the shaken always needs mixing with other, easier-to-recognize solidarity principles."[60]

The question then, using my sociorhetorical terminology, is how to blend memory of sublime terror with persistent will-to-truth grounded in the demands of truth-as-openness. Shanks thinks Hegel's drive toward "perfect truth-as-openness" provides primary resources for "a Christian theological stiffening of the solidarity of the shaken." The problem is that "Shakenness, by the imperatives of perfect truth-as-openness, is a condition of soul that is completely beyond any rational calculation of self-interest." Agapeic community, which in the first instance is a form of pastoral organization, must continually energize itself as a form of campaigning organization through "a constant insistence on the imperatives of shakenness in all their distinctiveness."[61] This requires a type of "knowing" that is "an ideal kind of strategic nous" that identifies the truth of faith with the solidarity of the shaken. And here the special challenge is that "every potentially successful strategy for the solidarity of the shaken, *in order to be successful*, is more or less bound to introduce fresh ambiguities."[62]

The primary source for "fresh ambiguities," it appears to me, is empathy guided by a life directed "by the imperatives of perfect truth-as-openness." From my point of view, this is what Jesus in the Gospel of Matthew means by "Be perfect as your heavenly Father is perfect" (5:48) and in the Gospel of Luke by "Be merciful as your heavenly Father is merciful" (6:36). So, is there any possibility for humans to live on a daily basis with the terrible sublime? Is there any possibility that people who live a life grounded in the imperatives of perfect truth-as-openness can sustain the presence of the terrible sublime in a strategic mind of knowing that identifies the truth of faith with the solidarity enacted through intersubjective empathy with other living beings on earth? The next couple of decades ahead of us will tell us a significant story about the possibility or impossibility of a solidarity like this among Christians.

Conclusion

Beginning with a discussion of the sublime in Kant's *Critique of Judgment*, this chapter explored the mathematical sublime as exhibited in 1 En.

---

60. Shanks, *Hegel and Religious Faith*, 31–32.
61. Shanks, *Hegel and Religious Faith*, 32.
62. Shanks, *Hegel and Religious Faith*, 33, emphasis original.

21.1–10 and the dynamical sublime as exhibited in 1 En. 62.1–14. Then the essay turned to Shanks's discussion of the solidarity of the shaken, which he discusses in his book on *Hegel and Religious Faith*. The overall goal has been to explore what the rhetorical force of sublime terror may be in literature that existed in the environment of the emergence of Christian discourse and in discourse in our world today.

Our conclusion is that the rhetorical effect of sublime terror may simply be a private journey of individuals into an imaginative realm beyond reason and beyond moral effect. Following Kant, however, if a person already has a cultivated moral sense of being, it is possible that the rhetorical force of sublime terror rhetoric can be an energizing of one's moral resources and power of self-determination. Following Shanks, it is possible, in a context where terror has become traumatic for a large group of people, that a response of solidarity of the shaken may emerge. If this happens, a movement may arise that embodies action for the purpose of advancing justice, fairness, and love for humans of all kinds in the world. For Shanks, the greatest possibility for this is if people live in a mode of truth-as-openness, which is most fully developed and articulated in Hegel's *Phenomenology of Spirit*. From this perspective, the Spirit struggles on a daily basis "against habits of oversimplification, structures of stubborn distorting prejudice, [and] refusals of genuine conversational reciprocity, in all kinds of different context."[63] If a person regularly lives in this truth-as-openness mode of conceptualization and action, an experience of sublime terror in either its mathematical or dynamical mode, or a blend of both, may have a rhetorical force that propels people to call forth and participate in moral communal, intersubjective political action to correct injustices and inequalities that assure suffering and hardship. The warning Shanks gives is that "Shakenness, by the imperatives of perfect truth-as-openness, is a condition of soul that is completely beyond our rational calculation of self-interest."[64] So here is the rub. How sustainable is an approach to life that is "completely beyond our rational calculation of self-interest"? A few people might sustain it until death, but surely it will always be only a chosen few.

---

63. Shanks, *Hegel and Religious Faith*, 21.
64. Shanks, *Hegel and Religious Faith*, 33.

The Sublime Terror of Ignatius of Antioch

Harry O. Maier

This essay focuses on the letter of Ignatius of Antioch to the Roman church as an instance of sublime rhetoric. Specifically, it considers Ignatius's description of his death by being torn apart by wild beasts and his mutilated body as rhetoric designed to transport listeners from their everyday experiences to the arena, to invoke in them an experience of sublime terror. The letter has traditionally been dated to the later reign of Trajan. I am increasingly persuaded that the letter, like the middle recension of the Ignatian corpus as a whole, is largely pseudonymous and of a later date, although arguments about dating and authorship do not for the most part affect the argument proposed here.[1] Where they do affect outcomes is that,

---

1. In what follows, when I refer to Ignatius, I am describing an implied author and audience and am using the name *Ignatius* and *the audience* as shorthands for a literary creation. Arguments for pseudonymity and a later second century dating ranging from the second quarter to the final quarter of the second century are presented by Thomas Leuchner, *Ignatius adversus Valentinianos? Chronologische und theologiegeschichtliche Studien zu den Briefen des Ignatius von Antiochien*, VCSup 47 (Leiden: Brill, 1999); Reinhard Hübner, *Der Paradox Eine: Antignostischer Monarchianismus im zweiten Jahrhundert; Mit einem Beitrag von Markus Vinzent*, VCSup 50 (Leiden: Brill, 1999); Timothy D. Barnes, "The Date of Ignatius," *ExpTim* 120 (2008): 119–30; Michael Theobald, *Israel-Vergessenheit in den Pastoralbriefen: Ein neuer Vorschlag zu ihrer historisch-theologischen Verortung im 2. Jahrhundert n. Chr. Unter besonderer Berücksichtigung der Ignatius Briefe*, SBS 229 (Stuttgart: Katholische Bibelwerke, 2016), 252–314; Markus Vinzent, *Writing the History of Early Christianity: From Reception to Retrospection* (Cambridge: Cambridge University Press, 2019), 266–464; Jan N. Bremmer, "The Place, Date, and Author of the Ignatian Letters: An Onomastic Approach," in *Das Baujahr hinter der Fassade: Probleme bei der Datierung neutestamentlicher Pseudepigraphen und neuere Lösungsansätze*, ed. Wolfgang Grünstäudl and Karl Matthias Schmidt, WUNT 470 (Tübingen: Mohr Siebeck, 2021), 405–34. For a defense of the Trajanic date, Allen Brent, *Ignatius of Antioch: A Martyr Bishop and the Origin of*

if later, the letter finds a place amidst a developing form of martyrological discourse designed for particular rhetorical purposes. Following Candida Moss, I argue that its rhetoric reflects a need to form a certain kind of social identity and set of commitments to a set of shared religious ideals centered on sole allegiance to Christ, developing in the second and third quarters of the second century.[2] In the case of Ignatius, this is extended to include commitment to bishops that the memory of Ignatius is conscripted to promote.[3]

In the letter to the Romans, Ignatius seeks to persuade his implied audience not to intervene on his behalf and to let him die as a martyr in a Roman spectacle. In a strikingly Ignatian phrase, he appeals to audience members to remain silent that he become "a word of God" (ἐγὼ λόγος θεοῦ). If they intervene on his behalf, he shall be "only a cry" (πάλιν ἔσομαι φωνή, Ignatius, *Rom.* 2.1 [Lake]). In Ignatius's other letters, the *word* is a power of silence, or rhetorically, well-placed, properly timed speech that affects powerful outcomes (e.g., Ignatius, *Eph.* 6.1; 14.2; 15.1, 2; 19.1; *Magn.* 8.2; *Phld.* 1.1).[4] But here Ignatius refers neither to the silence of the bishop nor of God, but to that of the Romans and the future martyr's potency as *word* (or speech), an association that gains a good understanding when we consider silence as a consequence of encounter with the sublime. Ignatius wants the Romans to experience through his letter the shocked silence that comes from being transported through his rhetorical crafting to his violent death, a highly emotional depiction that aims to put the listeners in the arena and to carry them away in terror and the experience of a terrifying death. This is the sublime terror of Ignatius's letter to the Romans: It represents a rhetorical strategy to generate an awed silence through vivid description of a horrifying death in order to motivate the Romans to avoid an intervention that would otherwise short circuit the transport of Ignatius to his desired goal. If

---

the Episcopacy (London: T&T Clark, 2009), 95–143; Mark J. Edwards, "Ignatius and the Second Century: An Answer to R. Hübner," *ZAC* 2 (1998): 214–26.

2. Moss, *Ancient Christian Martyrdom: Diverse Practices, Ideologies, and Traditions*, ABRL (New Haven: Yale University Press, 2012).

3. Similarly, Theobald, *Israel-Vergessenheit*, 309–14.

4. In an earlier article, I argue against the idea that Ignatius is creating a cosmic-ecclesiastical homology between God and the bishop and defend the thesis that Ignatius is drawing on a rhetorical ideal of properly delivered and timed speech as a means of persuasion. Harry O. Maier, "The Politics of the Silent Bishop: Silence and Persuasion in Ignatius of Antioch," *JTS* NS 55 (2004): 503–19.

we read the letter as a pseudonymous, mid-second-century instance of martyrological rhetoric, we can see that the writing crafts a rhetorical situation in order to absorb its audiences into a death and that it uses the sociorhetorical, literary creation of a martyr's death to effect allegiance to an institutional order outlined by the Ignatian corpus as whole, with *To the Romans* occupying a central role in making that goal persuasive. Sublime rhetoric carries the letter's audience members away to another world by putting a terrifying experience of death in their minds. I hope to show that part of the power of Ignatius's use of the terrifying sublime is to play off of audiences' probable experiences of the ancient arena as a place of entertainment where one went to watch people torn apart by beasts. The letter takes listeners to the arena where they are no longer observers but participants in a first-person narration of martyrdom. Vivid language takes the letter's audience(s) out of their seats and into a death, where they gain an epiphanic experience of the divine.

Ignatius out of His Mind

"Sublimity ... tears everything apart like a thunderbolt" (*Subl.* 1.4.9–10).[5] Ignatius is like a thunderbolt, sublime. He tears everything apart, puts common sense on notice, brings his audience members to the limit of human experience, and then carries them beyond it. Certainly, as several generations of exegetes have argued, he ruptures anything resembling reason. A modern exegetical tradition shaped in the Enlightenment categories of madness and civilization have diagnosed Ignatius as paranoid, pathological, a maniac, a man suffering from an inferiority complex, a lunatic with a perverse desire for death, a man breaking apart under the stress of his impending death.[6] In other words, he was crazy.

> From Syria all the way to Rome I am fighting with wild beasts, on land and sea, by night and day, chained amidst ten leopards (that is, a company of soldiers) who only get worse when they are well treated. Yet because of

---

5. ὕψος ... τά τε πράγματα δίκην σκηπτοῦ πάντα διεφόρησε. Citations for Longinus are from Donald A. Russell, *"Longinus" On the Sublime: Introduction and Commentary* (Oxford: Clarendon, 1964), 1–56.

6. For a review of the variety of diagnoses, see Harry O. Maier, *The Social Setting of the Ministry as Reflected in the Writings of Hermas, Clement, and Ignatius*, SCJud 12 (Waterloo: Wilfrid Laurier University Press, 2002), 156–58.

their mistreatment I am becoming more of a disciple; nevertheless I am not thereby justified. May I have the pleasure of the wild beasts that have been prepared for me; and I pray that they prove to be prompt with me. I will even coax them to devour me quickly, not as they have done with some, whom they were too timid to touch. And if when I am willing and ready they are not, I will force them. Bear with me—I know what is best for me. Now at last I am beginning to be a disciple. May nothing visible or invisible envy me, so that I may reach Jesus Christ. Fire and cross and battles with wild beasts, mutilation, mangling, wrenching of bones, the hacking of limbs, the crushing of my whole body, cruel tortures of the devil—let these come upon me, only let me reach Jesus Christ! (Ignatius, *Rom*. 5.1–3 [Holmes])[7]

It is impossible to know the psychological state of the historical Ignatius (or of the letter's author), but Ignatius is certainly presented engaging in sublime speech. He is terrifying and his terror shakes the world like thunder; indeed in Ignatius, *Phld*. 7.1 he claims for his own speech that it is "with a loud voice, God's voice" (μεγάλη φωνῇ, θεοῦ φωνῇ) that he has addressed his audience, and that by divine revelation he has received knowledge of the divisions roiling the Philadelphians, even that it was the Spirit preaching when the Philadelphian assembly heard him say, "The Spirit itself was preaching, saying these words: 'Do nothing without the bishop. Guard your bodies as the temple of God. Love unity. Flee from divisions. Become imitators of Jesus Christ, just as he is of his Father'" (Ignatius, *Phld*. 7.2).[8] If there is truth to modern exegetes' claims about Ignatius's mental status, it is that from the perspective of the sublime he is a man in ἔκστασις—that is, he is someone literally outside of himself. In the case of his desire for martyrdom, he presents a desire for and love of martyrdom, an eros the letter to the Romans aims to awaken in the implied audience by also lifting them outside of themselves onto the sand of the arena to hear with Ignatius the sound of crunching bones and to fight a wild beast alongside him. Not only are they not to intervene on his behalf to fend off his martyrdom; they are to experience it with him.

---

7. Michael W. Holmes, *The Apostolic Fathers: Greek Texts and English Translations*, 3rd ed. (Grand Rapids: Baker Academic, 2007), 114. Translations of Ignatius are from Holmes except where noted.

8. τὸ δὲ πνεῦμα ἐκήρυσσεν, λέγον τάδε· Χωρὶς τοῦ ἐπισκόπου μηδὲν ποιεῖτε· τὴν σάρκα ὑμῶν ὡς ναὸν θεοῦ τηρεῖτε· τὴν ἕνωσιν ἀγαπᾶτε· τοὺς μερισμοὺς φεύγετε· μιμηταὶ γίνεσθε Ἰησοῦ Χριστοῦ, ὡς καὶ αὐτὸς τοῦ πατρὸς αὐτοῦ.

Definitions of the sublime—ὕψος in Greek and *sublimis* in Latin—are elusive.[9] For Longinus and for Quintilian (although he does not use the term), they are exemplary of the grand style of rhetoric (although not all rhetoric in the grand style is sublime).[10] Sublime speech carries one away. It transports one out of the realm of the everyday to another time and place. The sublime can be a scene or a word or even an arrangement of words that affects powerful emotions and awakens audience participation. It uses speech, thought, and arrangement to take one out of the realm of speech, of what can be thought in any conventional sense, away from the routine arrangement of things, into a new arena marked by heroic excess, supernatural achievement, a picture of the world that redefines what is reasonable and achievable under a common sense understanding of the order of things. Its origins, as James Porter has argued, long before Longinus got around to writing about the topic, is to be found in thought about the heavens and the divinities who inhabit them.[11] It was oriented from its start to capture a sense of the divine excess and the limits of human reason and understanding. It refers to the astonishing, the sudden, and the epiphanic. Longinus's treatise, which has come to be known as Περὶ ὕψους due to the presence of its eponymous title in the manuscript tradition, describes something that speech does through a variety of elements. Porter has constructed what he describes as a rough typology of ὕψος, to present elements "the sublime typically gather[s] around." The list includes a number of items that even a cursory reading of Ignatius's description of his martyrdom and his desire for it matches: descriptions of immense heights and profound depths; sudden or extreme, often violent, motions or changes; gaps such as fissures, rips and tearing, abuses, vast distances; transgressions of limits; unthinkably large masses and quantities and surfaces, bold or sudden expansions and contractions; cosmic magnification of noncosmic events; unsurpassed qualities; sharp collisions and

---

9. For a discussion of definitions, James I. Porter, *The Sublime in Antiquity* (Cambridge: Cambridge University Press, 2015), 1056; for the paradox of a definition, see Ned O'Gorman, "Longinus's Sublime Rhetoric, or How Rhetoric Came into Its Own," *RSQ* 34.2 (2004): 71–89.

10. Quintilian, *Inst.* 12.10.61–65 likens the grand style to a torrent that "force[s] [the audience] to go wherever it takes them," i.e., outside of themselves through a powerful expression.

11. I follow here the general working typology of the sublime as garnered from Porter, *Sublime in Antiquity*, 51–53.

contrasts; sharp antagonisms and tensions; uncontainable forces; vivid and terrifying collapse of form and order; indefinability; ephemerality as signs of eternity; blinding moments of excessive light or noise or silence; overwhelming focus on details; moments of intense and vital danger and risk and crisis; profound awareness of vitality; natural, mythical divine or literary phenomena that embody elements of the sublime; forces that work against nature's laws.

For Longinus, vivid speech gathered around the sublime creates images in the minds of listeners to carry them away and to create within them strong emotions. Longinus describes a chief goal of the sublime as being "to introduce a great deal of excitement and emotion into one's speeches, but when combined with factual arguments it not only convinces the audiences, it positively masters them" (*Subl.* 15.9).[12] Such strong emotions work to make people feel things very deeply, whether very angry, jealous, terrified, and so on. Using the example of Demosthenes description of the threat to Athens, Longinus describes ὑπέρβατα, the rhetor's use of vivid description, through the arrangement of elements by juxtaposition and rapid-fire description. The device, Longinus explains, allowed Demosthenes to create "a great effect of vehemence, and indeed of improvisation, but also drags his audience along with him and to share the perils of these long hyperbata" (*Subl.* 22.3) to communicate and awaken terror in his listeners and share the list of things described.[13] Through the arranging of words and experiences out of natural sequence, Demosthenes was able "to bring forward one extraneous idea after another in a strange and unlike order, making the audience terrified of a total collapse of the sentence, and compelling them to sheer excitement, to share the speaker's risk" (*Subl.* 22.4).[14] When applied to Ignatius's letter to the Romans, the sublime adds the critical dimension of shared experience or terror and risk to the way Ignatius's rhetoric has been understood. Othmar Perler identified Ignatius's Greek as an instance of Asianism that includes such

---

12. τοῖς λόγοις ἐναγώνια καὶ ἐμπαθῆ προσεισφέρειν, κατακιρναμένη μέντοι ταῖς πραγματικαῖς ἐπιχειρήσεσιν οὐ πείθει τὸν ἀκροατὴν μόνον, ἀλλὰ καὶ δουλοῦται.

13. κατακορέστατος καὶ πολὺ τὸ ἀγωνιστικὸν ἐκ τοῦ ὑπερβιβάζειν καὶ ἔτι νὴ Δία τὸ ἐξ ὑπογύου λέγειν συνεμφαίνων, καὶ πρὸς τούτοις εἰς τὸν κίνδυνον τῶν μακρῶν ὑπερβατῶν τοὺς ἀκούοντας συνεπισπώμενος.

14. εἰς ἀλλόφυλον καὶ ἀπεοικυῖαν τάξιν ἄλλ' ἐπ' ἄλλοις διὰ μέσου καὶ ἔξωθέν ποθεν ἐπεισκυκλῶν, εἰς φόβον ἐμβαλὼν τὸν ἀκροατὴν ὡς ἐπὶ παντελεῖ τοῦ λόγου διαπτώσει, καὶ συναποκινδυνεύειν ὑπ' ἀγωνίας τῷ λέγοντι συναναγκάσας.

elements as juxtapositions, sentences comprised of short cola, hyperbole, paronomasia, comparisons, oxymorons, anaphora, and homeoteleuta.[15] However, what such an attribution does not express is the way that attention to the sublime helps to recognize Ignatius's use of vivid speech to bring an audience into a terrifying experience of death and the way that it works to create a sense of awe and silence.

Dragging the Audience to the Arena

In *Rom.* 4.1–2, Ignatius deploys vehemence, excess, and ekphrastic description to drag his audience with him to experience his death.

> Let me be food for the wild beasts, through whom I can reach God. I am God's wheat, and I am being ground by the teeth of the wild beasts, so that I may prove to be pure bread. Better yet, coax the wild beasts, so that they may become my tomb and leave nothing of my body behind, lest I become a burden to anyone once I have fallen asleep. Then I will truly be a disciple of Jesus Christ, when the world will no longer see my body. Pray to the Lord on my behalf, so that through these instruments I may prove to be a sacrifice to God.

The Greek shows pronounced juxtapositions especially where present tense narration joins assonance and emphatic word order and exotic grammatical construction: ἄφετέ με θηρίων εἶναι βοράν, δι' ὧν ἔνεστιν θεοῦ ἐπιτυχεῖν σῖτός εἰμι θεοῦ, καὶ δι' ὀδόντων θηρίων ἀλήθομαι, ἵνα καθαρὸς ἄρτος εὑρεθῶ. The same stylistic elements continue in 5.1–3 (see above), with Ignatius counterintuitively making the image of being mangled to death the object of jealousy in 5.3 (also in 7.2). This theme of envy belongs to the letter's wider application of a civic *homonoia* topos in which jealousy brings about political discord and faction, a rhetorical commonplace that Allen Brent has convincingly shown to be anti-imperial in orientation with the assemblies joining with Ignatius in championing the real death of

---

15. Perler, "Das vierte Makkabäerbuch, Ignatius von Antiochien und die ältesten Märtyrerberichte," *Revista di archaeologia cristiana* 25 (1949): 47–72; also, Harald Riesenfeld, "Reflections on the Style and the Theology of St. Ignatius of Antioch," *StPatr* 4/*TU* 79 (1961): 312–22; William R. Schoedel, *Ignatius of Antioch: A Commentary on the Letters of Ignatius of Antioch*, Hermeneia (Philadelphia: Fortress, 1985), 7–8.

Jesus as the construction of an alternative order.[16] The paradox of envy and death creates a further disorientation where Ignatius piles up in rapid fire a set of terms to describe his execution, with odd elements added such as "cross" and "fire," and then a set of terms that are not necessarily in temporal order or consistent with each other, such as "cutting," "tearing asunder," "mangling of limbs, crushing of my whole body," and then links this to "cruel tortures of the devil," with all of this leading up to the main point, "only in order that I may attain to Jesus Christ." Ignatius's piling of terms in present tense narration results in his transporting the implied readers out of themselves into the arena and placed in a terrifying situation. As such he achieves a main goal of both Longinus's sublime and ekphrasis, namely, to make listeners into viewers and to awaken the experience of what is seen within them.[17]

Earlier in 5.1, Ignatius again creates a striking and terrifying juxtaposition where he likens his journey with Roman soldiers to a fight with wild beasts: "From Syria to Rome I am fighting with wild beasts through land and sea, by night and day, bound to ten leopards (which is a company of soldiers), who when treated kindly become worse." By setting off "which is a company of soldiers" in parentheses, the English translation of ἐνδεδεμένος δέκα λεοπάρδοις, ὅ ἐστιν στρατιωτικὸν τάγμα reduces the dramatic juxtaposition as does the comma, which would not have been present in the original text. All of this Ignatius prefaces in 1.2 with the introduction of a paradox that "the beginning has been well ordered, if I may obtain grace unhindered to my end," thus making being chained to savage beasts a good start and a tumultuous ending to the kind of order Ignatius has in mind. This kind of surprising juxtaposition occurs elsewhere in the letter where he contrasts: "nothing visible is good, for your God, Jesus Christ, being now in the Father, is the more plainly visible. Christianity is not the work of persuasiveness but of greatness when it is hated by the world" (3.3). Ignatius probably invokes the term *Christian*-

---

16. Allen Brent, *Ignatius of Antioch and the Second Sophistic*, STAC 36 (Tübingen: Mohr Siebeck, 2006), 231–311; also on *homonoia*, Ignatius, and Roman imperial nuances, see John-Paul Lotz, *Ignatius and Concord: The Background and Use of the Language of Concord in the Letters of Ignatius of Antioch*, PatSt 8 (Frankfurt am Main: Lang, 2007), 157–87.

17. For ekphrasis and rhetorical theorization of turning listeners into viewers, see Ruth Webb, *Ekphrasis, Imagination, and Persuasion in Ancient Rhetorical Theory and Practice* (Farnham: Ashgate, 2009).

ismos in its original popular use as a word of mockery of Jesus followers. Again, he presents an unexpected set of juxtapositions. Hatred, greatness, and persuasiveness, a reversal of social expectations where hatred leads to dissent and the end of persuasion, as well as the redefinition of visibility that makes a peculiar syllogism of nothing visible being good—that is, Ignatius's hoped for invisibility through his disappearance from the world by his being devoured by beasts, but Jesus being invisible and hence visible in God is good, not to mention the dramatic equation of God and Jesus. Kirsopp Lake points to the clumsiness of the whole construction: "The sentence has been clumsily expressed ... he has sacrificed clearness to a paradoxical playing with words."[18] But it is not a sacrifice of clarity, it is a semantic disruption that typifies the sublime in order to bring about a paradoxical redefinition of common sense.

Sublime Silence

An important outcome of sublime speech, Longinus observes, is a kind of shock that issues forth in silence. He speaks of the need of the aspiring student of rhetoric to "train our minds into sympathy with what is noble" (τὰς ψυχὰς ἀνατρέφειν πρὸς τὰ μεγέθη). "Sublimity is the echo of a noble mind," he writes, "and so even without being spoken the bare idea often of itself wins admiration for its inherent grandeur. How grand, for instance, is the silence of Ajax in the Summoning of the Ghosts, more sublime than any speech" (*Subl.* 9.2).[19] Such silence, he later states, is made through terrible and repulsive images, which magnifies power and creates what he calls, in a description of Homer's treatment of the powers of heaven as "the high-neighing horses of heaven" to create "a cosmic interval to measure their stride" (τόσσον ἐπιθρώσκουσι θεῶν ὑψηχέες ἵπποι, 9.5). In an account of Homer's vivid description of the violent battle of the gods, he remarks:

> Terrible as these passages are, they are utterly irreligious and breach the canons of propriety unless one takes them allegorically. I feel indeed that in recording as he does the wounding of the gods, their quarrels, ven-

---

18. Kirsopp Lake, *The Apostolic Fathers*, 2 vols., LCL (Cambridge: Harvard University Press, 1977), 1:229.

19. ὕψος μεγαλοφροσύνης ἀπήχημα. ὅθεν καὶ φωνῆς δίχα θαυμάζεταί ποτε ψιλὴ καθ' ἑαυτὴν ἡ ἔννοια δι' αὐτὸ τὸ μεγαλόφρον, ὡς ἡ τοῦ Αἴαντος ἐν Νεκυίᾳ σιωπὴ ἔγα καὶ παντὸς ὑψηλότερον λόγου.

geance, tears, imprisonment, and all their manifold passions. However, he has done his best to make the men in the Iliad gods and the gods men. (9.7)[20]

In his letter, Ignatius seeks to be a word and not a cry (*Rom.* 2.1). He urges the Romans to silence and thus creates a typical parallelism and reversal of speech and silence: "I would not have you people-pleasers but God-pleasers, even as you do indeed please him. For neither shall I ever have such an opportunity of attaining God nor can you, if you be but silent, have a better deed ascribed to you. For if you are silent concerning me, I am a word of God, but if you love my flesh, I shall again be only a cry" (ἐὰν γὰρ σιωπήσητε ἀπ' ἐμοῦ, ἐγὼ λόγος θεοῦ· ἐὰν δὲ ἐρασθῆτε τῆς σαρκός μου, πάλιν ἔσομαι φωνή [Lake]). Elsewhere, Ignatius links divine silence with being a word. In his description of the birth of Jesus in *Eph.* 19.1, he states, "And the virginity of Mary, and her giving birth were hidden from the Prince of this world, as was also the death of the Lord. Three mysteries of a cry that were wrought in the silence of God" (τρία μυστήρια κραυγῆς, ἅτινα ἐν ἡσυχίᾳ θεοῦ ἐπράχθη). He goes on to describe these three cries as the means by which an entire new order was brought about:

> A star shone in heaven beyond all the stars and its light was unspeakable, and its newness caused astonishment, and all the other stars, with the sun and moon, gathered in a chorus round this star, and it far exceeded them all in its light; and there was perplexity whence came this new thing, so unlike them. By this all magic was dissolved and every bond of wickedness vanished away, ignorance was removed, and the old kingdom was destroyed, for God was manifest as a human for the newness of eternal life and that which has been prepared by God received its beginning. Hence all things were disturbed because the abolition of death was being planned. (Ignatius, *Eph.* 19.1–3 [Lake])

This remarkable passage expresses well the two kinds of notions of the sublime associated both with the disruption of the cosmos as well as its cosmic dimensions of grandeur, distance, and depth identified in Porter's typology. It also expresses Ignatius's theology of well-timed silence

---

20. ὕψος μεγαλοφροσύνης ἀπήχημα. ὅθεν καὶ φωνῆς δίχα θαυμάζεταί ποτε ψιλὴ καθ' ἑαυτὴν ἡ ἔννοια δι' αὐτὸ τὸ μεγαλόφρον, ὡς ἡ τοῦ Αἴαντος ἐν Νεκυίᾳ σιωπὴ ἔγα καὶ παντὸς ὑψηλότερον λόγου.

and inchoate divine silence accomplishing cosmic altering and dramatic effects through utterance.

In *Rom.* 2.1, Ignatius seeks to be a reality-altering word made possible not by the silence of God, but rather the silence of the Romans. When placed within the broader corpus of Ignatius's letters, silence by the Romans is not merely an appeal not to intervene on his behalf. Rather, it does double duty by also participating in a divine silence, whence Ignatius as word can acclaim and thereby result in the kind of dramatic alterations that the word expressed from silence achieves cosmically. But the silence of the Romans may also issue forth from the experience of the sublime through Ignatius's vivid description of his death. That death is intended to provoke shock and awe at Ignatius's nobility and, by the dramatic manifestation of his dedication to God, to achieve a dramatic social outcome. The outcome is, of course, that Ignatius will (using his terms) achieve God or, to put it more strikingly still, a cosmic ending:

> Grant me that I may be poured out to God, while an altar is still ready, that forming yourselves into a chorus of love, you may sing to the Father in Christ Jesus, that God has vouchsafed that the bishop of Syria shall be found at the setting of the sun, having fetched him from the sun's rising. It is good to set to the world toward God, that I may rise to him. (Ignatius, *Rom.* 2.2)[21]

Ignatius has become astronomical. His gory death accomplishes a great deal. Arguably it seeks to move the Romans to a stunned silence wherein they are mute before the terrifying spectacle of Ignatius's sacrificial death, but where they also participate in God's paradoxical silence that by saying little an entire cosmos is upended and a brand-new rule is brought about through the execution of a defeated victim that is a gateway to a greater victory.

Finally, we may relate this to the use of vivid speech to transport audiences to the scene of description, in this case the arena. Consistent with Longinus's observation cited above, that vivid speech is most effective in transporting an audience outside of itself when combined with factual arguments, Ignatius relies upon his audiences' experiences of arena spec-

---

21. πλέον δέ μοι μὴ παράσχησθε τοῦ σπονδισθῆναι θεῷ, ὡς ἔτι θυσιαστήριον ἕτοιμόν ἐστιν, ἵνα ἐν ἀγάπῃ χορὸς γενόμενοι ᾄσητε τῷ πατρὶ ἐν Ἰησοῦ Χριστῷ, ὅτι τὸν ἐπίσκοπον Συρίας κατηξίωσεν ὁ θεὸς εὑρεθῆναι εἰς δύσιν ἀπὸ ἀνατολῆς μεταπεμψάμενος. καλὸν τὸ δῦναι ἀπὸ κόσμου πρὸς θεόν, ἵνα εἰς αὐτὸν ἀνατείλω.

tacles, attendance at which was especially popular across the empire. In his letter to the Romans, however, the audience is not only in the cavea being excited by the events transpiring in the arena below them. They are also on the ground with Ignatius and watching the events through his eyes. This makes the audience both observer and observed, at once in their seats and the executed. The result of this is to use death as a form of the sublime, to awaken terror by placing listeners in the process of being torn apart, to hear bones being crunched, and to see their flesh devoured.

Conclusion

Ignatius "the word" is the outcome of the sublime silence that issues forth from both the observation and the experience of death. Attention to the sublime in *To the Romans* moves us away from a study of pathology toward engagement with a sophisticated use of rhetoric to achieve a particular end. This invites us to consider other instances of sublime rhetoric in emergent martyrology in both Jewish and Christian tradition, whether in the Maccabean writings (4 Maccabees has long been identified as *Romans* closest cousin) or in other second century texts.[22] Longinus's theory of the sublime and its relation to silence combined with vivid description conveyed through jarring syntax allows us to recognize aspects of Ignatius's rhetoric that are otherwise passed over.

---

22. Perler, "Das vierte Makkabäerbuch," 47–72. Among the candidates for sublime rhetoric in Christian martyrology are the report of Blandina's death in the martyrdom of Lugdunum, Eusebius, *Hist. eccl.* 5.1.40–42; Martyrdom of Perpetua and Felicitas, esp. 10, 19; Mart. Pol. 13–15; Martyrdom of Carpus, Papylus, and Agathonice 36–41; and Martyrdom of Pionius 20–22, to name only a few.

Subliming the Sublime: The Bible and the Sublime in Eighteenth-Century Britain

Alan P. R. Gregory

During the eighteenth century, claiming that the Bible contains "the highest instances of the sublime" became a cliché of British criticism.[1] Religious and cultural authority made the Bible fit for more or less any laudatory hyperbole going, but, in the case of the sublime, some novel argument warranted this claim for biblical precedence. Recognizing the sublimities of scripture involved an account of how the Bible, or at least a good deal of its poetic content, worked, how it affected readers in ways that were religiously formative, even salvific. On the relatively thin foundations provided by Longinus, critics built a philosophical and theological psy-

---

1. Hugh Blair, *Lectures on Rhetoric and Belles Lettres*, 2nd ed., 3 vols. (London: Strahan & Cadell; Edinburgh: Creech, 1785), 1:77. The general bibliography for the early modern sublime has grown considerably during the last few decades, though many works downplay the theological component. I have found the following especially helpful: Samuel Holt Monk, *The Sublime: A Study of Critical Theories in Eighteenth-Century England* (Ann Arbor: University of Michigan Press, 1960); Patricia Ann Meyer Spacks, *The Insistence of Horror: Aspects of the Supernatural in Eighteenth Century Poetry* (Cambridge: Harvard University Press, 1962); David B. Morris, *Religious Sublime: Christian Poetry and Critical Tradition in Eighteenth-Century England* (Lexington: University Press of Kentucky, 1982); Marjorie Hope Nicolson, *Mountain Gloom and Mountain Glory: The Development of the Aesthetics of the Infinite* (Seattle: University of Washington Press, 1997); James Kirwan, *Sublimity: The Non-rational and the Irrational in the History of Aesthetics* (New York: Routledge, 2005); Timothy M. Costelloe, ed., *The Sublime: From Antiquity to the Present* (Cambridge: Cambridge University Press, 2012); Philip Shaw, *The Sublime*, 2nd ed., New Critical Idiom (London: Routledge, 2017); Robert Doran, *The Theory of the Sublime from Longinus to Kant* (Cambridge: Cambridge University Press, 2017).

chology into their aesthetics of sublimity. Mining scripture for the sublime also advanced, especially through the lectures of Robert Lowth and Hugh Blair, attention to poetic form in the Old Testament and to the necessity of reading Hebrew poetry and thus appreciating its sublimity, in the terms of its ancient context. The Bible provided preeminent examples of the sublime, not only because its treatment of God, "of all objects ... by far the most sublime," but because scripture represented God, God's works, and the lives of God's servants, in a sublime manner.[2] Sublimity was realized through both the content and the form of the Bible's poetry, in line with the distinction between the sublime object and its representation in writing. Taking the long view, eighteenth century enthusiasm for the biblical sublime recurs to a problem that goes back well before Augustine: the perceived tension between the Bible, particularly the Old Testament, and the canons of a contemporary literary taste. The reader expecting "the graces of correct writing,... just proportion of parts, and skilfully conducted narration" will look in vain to the scriptures.[3] The form, urgency, and pulse of biblical poetry, however, is fitted above all for sublimity and to realize sublimity is the highest calling of the poet who, in giving sublime force to his words, serves the highest.

Applauding the Bible for its sublimity had some significant implications deriving from the nature of a properly sublime object and from the ways in which the sublime was understood to work its beneficent, enlarging, vivifying and, in some presentations, quite definitely *manly* operations. Some of these were theologically and hermeneutically fundamental, especially as they amounted to a shift in the place and function of scripture within Christian faith and practice. This essay explores those implications and the reasoning behind them. Primarily drawing on the poetry of Edward Young, I begin with the way in which the sublime was accorded a religious authority. Proceeding to the literary and biblical criticism of John Dennis, Lowth, and Blair, I then illustrate how enthusiasm for the sublime had a formative influence upon reading Scripture and how it also involved new approaches to locating the Bible's authority. This essay concludes with a brief comment on the long influence of the sublime on the popular religious imagination in the English-speaking world.

---

2. Adam Smith, "The Principles Which Lead and Direct Philosophical Enquiries; Illustrated by the History of Astronomy," in *Essays on Philosophical Subjects* (Dublin: Wogan, Byrne, et al., 1795), 113–30.

3. Blair, *Lectures on Rhetoric and Belles Lettres*, 3:194.

This Prospect Vast ... Scripture Authentic (Edward Young)

In 1745, Young published the ninth and final book of his blank verse poem, *The Complaint: or Night-Thoughts on Life, Death, and Immortality*.[4] This is the poet's final attempt to inspire the young Lorenzo to forsake a life confined to sense, wine, and inadvisable young ladies and embrace orthodox Christianity and its virtues. Young attempts a sublime tour de force, hurling the poem from a frenetic last judgment in which "rocks eternal pour their melted mass" and hell "belches forth her blazing seas" to an extended meditation on the night sky as witness to God's majesty, glory, and benevolence (ll. 165, 185). As so often elsewhere, a capacity for sublime feeling and enthusiasm appears as the potency for divine elevations. "Were moon and stars for villains only made?," the poet asks Lorenzo. "No; they were made to fashion the Sublime / Of human hearts, and wiser make the wise" (ll. 996–997). Within this frame, Young offers a novel reckoning of the Christian's apologetic resources. He begins with the properly Pauline admission, "True, all things speak a GOD" to introduce a decidedly un-Pauline distinction:

> but in the small,
> Men trace out him; in great, He seizes man,
> Seizes, and elevates, and rapts, and fills
> With new inquiries. (ll. 774–777)

Since Young has made much of Earth's insignificance before the "immensely great," the "swarms/of worlds that laugh at Earth," the "small" is surely this planet and all that therein lives (ll. 1102, 1103, 1715). This limited world, later compared to a "barrier" through which "contemplation" pierces under sublime impulsion, permits a tracing of God via the rational reflections of "physico-theology." The works of John Ray and William Derham, in particular, stimulated an enduring regard for arguments from design.[5]

---

4. Edward Young, *Young's Night Thoughts; or, Thoughts on Life, Death, and Immortality* (New York: Worthington, 1889).

5. John Ray, *The Wisdom of God Manifested in the Works of Creation*, 2nd ed. (London: Smith, 1692); Ray, *Three Physico-Theological Discourses*, 2nd ed. (London: Smith, 1693); William Derham, *Physico-Theology: Or a Demonstration of the Being and Attributes of God from His Works of Creation, Being the Substance of Sixteen Sermons Preached in St Mary-Le-Bow-Church, London, as the Honourable Mr Boyle's Lectures, in the Years 1711 and 1712*, Boyle Lectures (London: Innes, 1723).

Derham's Boyle Lectures, given in 1711, had gone into eleven editions by the 1750s. In his various writings on natural theology, Derham distinguishes *physicotheology*, which surveys the "terraqueous globe," from similar work on astronomy or *astrotheology*. Young commandeers the latter as, above all, the field of the sublime, which leaves the physicotheologian mapping his teleologies, tracing God in the small, appealing to the shape of teeth or those "Species of Insects" who load "ample provisions, into their dry and barren Cells."[6] The astronomical, however, as the superlatively sublime, sweeps the ploddingly discursive aside and then reverses the cognitive relationship. God overwhelms, "seizes" the person, mind, and heart, "rapts, and fills with new inquiries."

Young's sublime version of astrotheology claims a privileged place for astronomical observation as an occasion for sublime experience. This is quite in line with the common emphasis on vastness as characteristic of objects experienced as sublime. "Vast Objects occasion vast Sensations" John Baillie assures his readers and, while he prefers "mighty power or force" as the taproot of sublimity, Blair insists that "all Vastness produces the impression of Sublimity."[7] Young privileges the astronomical order, however, not only as supremely sublime but as the mediator of a religious sublimity, a converting experience of deity. "Devotion! Daughter of Astronomy!," he gasps, "An undevout Astronomer is mad."[8] Though God was acknowledged as "of all objects ... by far the most sublime," it was not the case that whatever was experienced as sublime was experienced religiously. Critics routinely listed, as potential occasions for evoking sublime enthusiasm, objects that were not guaranteed to inspire a devotional enthusiasm. Dennis, for instance, includes "Enchantments, Witchcraft, Serpents, Lions, Tygers" and "War."[9] Nonetheless, accounts of sublimity and expectations of sublime experience possessed an underlying theological drift toward the sublime as religiously significant, as mediating experience of God. Having noted the connection between vastness and sublimity, it is a mere logical hop for Blair to point out how "infinite space,

---

6. Ray, *Wisdom of God Manifested*, 127.

7. John Baillie, *An Essay on the Sublime* (London: Dodsley, 1747), 7; Blair, *Lectures on Rhetoric and Belles Lettres*, 1:59.

8. Young, *Young's Night Thoughts*, ll. 772–773.

9. John Dennis, *The Grounds of Criticism in Poetry: Contain'd in Some New Discoveries Never Made before, Requisite for the Writing and Judging of Poems Surely* (London: Strahan, 1704), 87–88.

endless numbers, and eternal duration fill the mind with great ideas." Since this is so, the theological conclusion seems obvious, albeit made at the cost of a sizeable reduction in divine transcendence:

> no ideas, it is plain are so sublime as those taken from the Supreme Being; the most unknown but the greatest of all objects, the infinity of whose nature, and the eternity of whose duration, joined with the omnipotence of his power, though they surpass our conceptions yet exalt them to the highest.[10]

Baillie makes a similarly incautious claim, observing that as our minds are, in a sense, present to what they conceive, then the larger the object, the greater appears our mental power and capacity, and the closer it approaches the divine. As "an Universal Presence is one of the sublime attributes of the Deity; then how much greater an existence must the Soul imagine herself, when contemplating the Heavens, she takes in the mighty Orbs of the Planets, and is present to a Universe, than when confined within the narrow space of a Room, and how much nearer advancing to the Perfections of the Universal Presence?"[11] The theological drift of this logic, motivated by the conviction that God is the acme of sublime objects, also underlies the claim that "of all writings ... the Sacred Scriptures afford us the highest instances of the Sublime."

What, then, of the "Sacred Scriptures"? Sublime uplift required either the direct experience of a suitably sublime object or such an object sublimely represented. The object had priority in that only absurdity would result from trying to render sublime what was inherently not so, garden flowers, dentists, and small children, for instance. That said, experience of a sublime object did not guarantee experience of sublimity, an experience that depended upon a particular kind of seeing or reading. The sublime, as Young roars repeatedly, overwhelms and astonishes, God seizing his creature in this experience. However, this is still not quite like getting hit by a falling tree. Devotion may come naturally to an astronomer but still only through a proper attention to a sublime cosmos, a meditative or, as Dennis terms it, "contemplative" attention.[12] No sublime exhilaration follows from Lorenzo glancing at the moon while shinning up a ladder to

---

10. Blair, *Lectures on Rhetoric and Belles Lettres*, 1:69.
11. Baillie, *Essay on the Sublime*, 6.
12. Dennis, *Grounds of Criticism in Poetry*, 20.

his mistress's window.[13] This notion that the sublime is potent for moral and religious improvement was commonplace, as was the suggestion that the capacity for the experience was morally conditioned. Sublime alpine scenery elevates Anne Radcliffe's heroine, Emily St. Aubert, beyond "every trifling thought, every trifling sentiment," while the dodgy Madame Montoni remains unmoved save by the calculation of her ill-gotten gains.[14] Expounding the sublimities of Scripture occurs within the terms of this moral psychology and theological anthropology. Young, again, provides a fulsome example of this framework:

> That Mind immortal loves immortal aims:
> That boundless Mind affects a boundless space:
> That vast surveys, and the Sublime of things,
> The soul assimilate, and make her great:
> That, therefore, Heaven her glories, as a fund
> Of inspiration, thus spreads out to man.
> Such are their doctrines; such the Night inspired.
> And what more true? What truth of greater weight?
> The Soul of man was made to walk the skies;
> Delightful outlet of her prison here!
> There, disencumber'd from her chains, the ties
> Of toys terrestrial, she can rove at large;
> There freely can respire, dilate, extend,
> In full proportion let loose all her powers,
> And, undeluded, grasp at something great.
> Nor as a stranger does she wander there;
> But, wonderful herself, through wonder strays;
> Contemplating their grandeur, finds her own. (ll. 1019–1027)

Sublimity is the vehicle of human exaltation to God and, therefore, to realization of our own divinity, our "birth celestial." Young sweeps aside Alexander Pope's admonition to remember our "middle state," undeterred by any danger that in soaring into "th' empyreal sphere" we confound ourselves and "quitting sense call imitating God."[15] Whereas Pope urged humble acceptance of an enduring uncertainty, Young found an immedi-

---

13. Young, *Young's Night Thoughts*, ll. 958–964.
14. Ann Radcliffe, *The Mysteries of Udolpho*, in *Complete Novels of Mrs. Ann Radcliffe* (London: Folio Society, 1987), 173–74, 176–77.
15. Alexander Pope, *The Rape of the Lock and Other Major Writings*, ed. Leo Damrosch, Penguin Classics (London: Penguin, 2011), 106–7.

ate, self-securing surety in sublime rapture. In sublimity, we discover the "boundless mind" or, as Baillie argued, the soul thereby "conceives something infinitely grand of Herself."[16] Tracing out God by argument gives way to sublime conviction and the alternative to allowing oneself to be thus caught up is madness: "Who sees, but is confounded or convinced, / Renounces Reason, or a GOD adores" (ll. 861–862). Nature's sublimity secures the attentive mind as a divine guarantee by which we may trust all other, less evident, design: "The Grand of Nature is the' Almighty's oath, / In Reason's court, to silence Unbelief" (ll. 845–846).

Young places the Bible within this account of human calling. By virtue of its sublimity, the night sky mediates a felt certainty in the knowledge of God. As sublime, it possesses a magisterial authority as God's "first volume," an "elder Scripture, writ by GOD'S own hand" (l. 646). As "authentic" Scripture, "uncorrupt by man," the starry heavens, experienced as sublime, provide the hermeneutic light within which the Bible should be read.

> Preface and comment to the sacred page!
> Which oft refers its reader to the skies,
> As pre-supposing his first lesson there,
> And Scripture's self a fragment, *that* unread. (ll. 1070–1073)

In traditional terms, sublime enthusiasm comes close here to an identification with the enlightening role of the Holy Spirit as the inward interpreter of the scriptures. Young rarely draws breath between hyperboles, but, as we shall see, he is not alone in making this kind of claim, albeit elsewhere it is more modestly expressed. From the perspective of classical accounts of scripture, Young has reversed the relationship between scripture and creation. Whereas John Calvin compares scripture to eyeglasses through which we read the creation, and Thomas Aquinas admits only a shadowy and uncertain theological knowledge outside the biblical revelation, Young makes creation, known in the passionate certainty of the sublime, the illuminator of scripture.[17] The structure of religious knowing here finds an analogue in the contemporary preaching of John Wesley, who also published and edited an abridgment of *Night-Thoughts*. In an important sermon, "The Witness of the Spirit:

---

16. Baillie, *Essay on the Sublime*, 13.

17. John Calvin, *Genesis 1–11*, ed. John L. Thompson, Reformation Commentary on Scripture 1 (Downers Grove, IL: IVP Academic, 2012), 13.

Discourse I," published in 1746, Wesley distinguished between a discursive knowledge of salvation, based on reasoning from scripture, and an "immediate consciousness," an inner certainty by which "you will know if your soul is alive to God."[18] In the former, we might say, reason "traces out" the conditions of salvation and applies them tentatively to one's own condition while the latter gifts a personal assurance of God's mercy. Reasoning proffers the "witness of *our own* spirit" but true heart's ease demands that intuitive certainty that is nothing less than the witness of God's Spirit within us.[19] On the basis of that witness, Christians ask further concerning the working of the Spirit in the community of faith. In like fashion, sublime experience "seizes" then "fills/With new inquiries." Though the religious claim is more muted in some, theories of the sublime approach and connect with the evangelical "religion of the heart" in acknowledging the authority of "enthusiastic" experience, a unity of feeling and intuition.[20]

Since Young bellows his sublimities and goes in for rhetorically cudgeling his readers into a righteous hope, he might appear too extreme and exceptional a witness. Certainly, Young stands in some contrast with Edmund Burke whose *Philosophical Enquiry into the Origin of Our Ideas of the Sublime and Beautiful* dominated accounts of the sublime in eighteenth century Britain. Burke does admit that representations of God offer the greatest potential for sublimity.[21] Since terror is the root of sublime experience and God appears to our minds, first and foremost, as infinite and, therefore, immeasurably terrible power, sublime feeling is produced wherever human beings have a religiously adequate idea of God.[22] Burke does not, however, present the sublime as spiritually transformative, as salvifically significant. By comparison

---

18. John Wesley, *The Complete Sermons* (Amazon CreateSpace, 2013), 45, §I.5.

19. The title of Wesley's sermon, "The Witness of Our Own Spirit," in *Sermons*, 55–59, emphasis added.

20. For an excellent history of early modern enthusiastic movements, see Ted A. Campbell, *The Religion of the Heart: Study of European Religious Life in the Seventeenth and Eighteenth Centuries* (Columbia: University of South Carolina Press, 1991).

21. Edmund Burke, *A Philosophical Enquiry into the Sublime and Beautiful: And Other Pre-revolutionary Writings*, ed. David Womersley (New York: Penguin, 1998), 109–11.

22. Burke acknowledges that we may think about God in a purely intellectual fashion and, therefore, without emotional investment. However, we rarely reflect upon God in such a "refined and abstracted" way. Rather, when we contemplate God, our

with Young, Burke's account of the teleology of the sublime remains earthbound. "Terror" belongs to those passions that serve "self-preservation" and an energizing sublime delight is the product of a terrifying threat ameliorated by safe distance.[23] This is, however, where Burke discerns the operation of providence, in the connection between delight and heightened alertness, a stretching of the nerves that readies us for action. "Providence has so ordered it" that the experience of the tolerable "pain and terror" effected by the sublime serves to preserve the vigorous functioning of our minds from that lassitude to which they tend owing to the body's need for rest. Since lassitude undermines survival, our physiological system needs "to be shaken and worked to a proper degree."[24] God has provided for this in giving us such a shaking in a form we enjoy.

Despite Burke's influence on philosophical accounts of the sublime, however, other contemporaries came closer to Young's theologically enthusiastic claims for sublimity. "At the presence of the sublime," James Ussher announces, "although it be always awful, the soul of man ... assumes an unknown grandeur.... It is rapt out of the sight and consideration of this diminutive world into a kind of gigantic creation."[25] Sublimity, Dennis had argued more than half a century earlier, engages the "greatest and strongest" passions and since the "ideas" of God and of God's power are the greatest and most sublime ideas, then sublime religious poetry, in bringing passion and reason into accord upon the highest truth, effects a restoration to paradisal order.[26] Unlike Young, though, the object of Dennis's argument was the sublime as encountered not in the natural world as "preface and comment" to Scripture but in religious poetry, preeminently the poetry of the Old Testament. To those "highest instances of the sublime" we now turn.

---

imagination, which draws upon the senses, is engaged and, therefore, also the passions (*Philosophical Enquiry*, 110–11).

23. Burke, *Philosophical Enquiry*, 85–86.
24. Burke, *Philosophical Enquiry*, 165.
25. James Ussher, *Clio, or a Discourse on Taste; Addressed to a Young Lady*, 3rd ed. (London: Davies, 1772), 103.
26. John Dennis, *The Advancement and Reformation of Modern Poetry: A Critical Discourse; In Two Parts* (London: Parker, 1701), 172.

Religion Is That Thing from Which the Sublime Is Chiefly to Be Derived (John Dennis)

Young invokes the sublime as a dislocating experience, one that "seizes," and raptures. Nature's astonishing vastness enacts "Heaven's indulgent violence," its sublimity rushing upon the mind (l. 1046). We are assaulted by wonder and overwhelmed (l. 685). Yet this ecstatic disturbance serves to recover order. The night sky was made to astound and elevate the heart, not to cover Lorenzo's nocturnal escapades but to restore the proper ordering of mind and heart, the attunement to divinity that reveals the soul's own "boundless" scope (ll. 1011–1012).

That the sublime serves the restoration of a due order, thus belonging within the teleology of God's design, is common to Joseph Addison, Dennis, Baillie, and Ussher, among others.[27] We have found a theologically modest version of it in Burke's argument that sublime experience provides "due exercise," a stretching and excited tension that, by God's design, brings the mental powers into lively and recreational play.[28] Within this teleological framework, upon which much eighteenth century theology thrived, human beings appear as existing within an "order of interlocking natures." They thrive or fail to thrive according to whether the inward ordering of their faculties and operations mesh properly with one another and so also harmonize with the larger design of concordant natures that is God's creation.[29] Locating the sublime in relation to a divine ordering, within which it serves as a means of restoring and maintaining the vocation of humanity within that order, measures the distance between eighteenth century and later, particularly postmodern accounts of sublimity.[30] Understood as a disruptive

---

27. For Addison, see Joseph Addison and Richard Steele, *Selections from "The Tatler" and "The Spectator,"* Penguin Classics (London: Penguin, 1988), 364–406; see also, John Aiken and Anna Letitia Aiken, "On the Pleasure Derived from Objects of Terror; With Sir Bertrand, a Fragment," in *Miscellaneous Pieces in Prose* (Belfast: Magee, 1774), 117–37.

28. Burke, *Philosophical Enquiry*, 164–65.

29. Charles Taylor, *Sources of the Self: The Making of the Modern Identity* (Cambridge: Cambridge University Press, 1992), 276, 280–84.

30. Jean-François Lyotard, "The Sublime and the Avant-Garde" and "Newman: The Instant," in *The Lyotard Reader*, ed. Andrew Benjamin (Oxford: Blackwell, 1989), 196–211; 240–49; Lyotard, *Lessons on the Analytic of the Sublime*, trans. Elizabeth Rottenberg (Stanford, CA: Stanford University Press, 1994); Clayton Crockett, *A Theology of the Sublime* (London: Routledge, 2001).

return to due order, or as Dennis argued, using the source of misery as the means of joy, the sublime's dynamic has roots in a biblical, particularly Pauline, dialectic. When that dialectic, however, is transposed within the terms of the eighteenth-century sublime and its philosophical psychology, the theological consequences are considerable and their implications in tension with the Protestant orthodoxy professed by most of its advocates.[31]

In two treatises, *The Advancement and Reformation of Modern Poetry* (1701) and *The Grounds of Criticism in Poetry* (1704), Dennis provides a good deal of the theological and psychological logic that underlies Young's sublime effusions, as well as much critical advocacy of the sublime later in the century.[32] Dennis's stated objective is to encourage the renewal of English poetry. That, however, depends on the recovery of proper order. We appreciate poetry correctly only when we recognize the primacy of religious poetry and how the operation of the sublime within religious poetry engages our strongest passions. In doing this, the sublime restores the inward order of reason and passion so that they harmonize in ordering the human soul toward God. In Dennis's view, poetry is where the operations of language are most powerfully geared to the operations of reason and passion. In turn, poetry and religion mesh in having human happiness as their common goal, while that happiness consists in the harmonious "satisfaction of all the Faculties, the Reason, the Passions, the Sences [sic]."[33] Above all, our most vigorous passions, "chiefly… admiration, terror, horror, joy, sadness, desire," require satisfaction since these driving passions bring us our heights of joy, as well as ruin us most entirely when not ordered to reason.[34] When poetry and religion collaborate to achieve our happiness, therefore, they reset that primary dislocation of the soul that is the consequence of sin. Such is God's designing of nature:

> Poetry seems to be a noble attempt of Nature, by which it endeavours to exalt itself to its happy primitive state; and he who is entertain'd with

---

31. Dennis, e.g., mounts a stern critique of deism as failing to provide the religious motivation of orthodox Christianity precisely because, unlike Christian revelation, it fails to recognize the necessary demands of both passion and reason. Among notable writers on the sublime, only Ussher was a Roman Catholic.

32. Monk argues that Dennis's direct influence was relatively slight. His interpretation of the sublime, though, and especially his emphasis on terror and the "enthusiastic" was characteristic of much British writing on the sublime (Monk, *Sublime*, 54).

33. Dennis, *Advancement and Reformation of Modern Poetry*, 169.

34. Dennis, *Grounds of Criticism in Poetry*, 16.

an accomplish'd Poem, is for a time at least restor'd to Paradice [sic]. That happy man converses boldly with Immortal Beings. Transported he beholds the Gods ascending and descending, and every Passion in its turn is charm'd, while that his Reason is supreamly [sic] satisfied.[35]

If this is true, up to a point, for the poetry of pagan Greece and Rome, how much more so for a religious poetry inspired by Christianity which, as the true religion, "makes the best provision for the happiness of those who profess it."[36]

Since the eighteenth century, discourse about our passions has given way to that of *emotions*.[37] Our use of the latter does overlap with Dennis's *passions*, but, since we often use *emotion* as synonymous with *feeling*, we may think of *passions* as more transient and less dispositional that would Dennis. Dennis follows John Locke in treating passions as motivational: passions orient and direct a person toward action, most primitively, aversive or acquisitive action. Passions, Locke argues, are "modifications of pleasure or pain," different ways in which we experience our relationship to what is good or evil for us.[38] Anger, therefore, is "an uneasiness or discomposure of the mind, upon the receipt of any injury [mental or physical], with a present purpose of revenge."[39] The various forms of uneasiness, such as fear, terror, envy, hatred, and so on, or of delight, as love, hope, or joy, occur at all degrees of intensity from the overwhelming to an excitation indistinguishable from the simple act of will that satisfies it.[40] A passion may also be short-lived or cultivated into a lasting disposition. This is important to the claims made for the sublime. Terror belongs to the experience of sublimity but, since the danger is not present and immediate, the storm raging in metaphors, terror rises just to a level of intensity that subordinates pain to pleasure and stimulates a delight in the mind's belonging to spheres powerful and gigantic.

---

35. Dennis, *Advancement and Reformation of Modern Poetry*, 172.

36. Dennis, *Advancement and Reformation of Modern Poetry*, 168.

37. Louis C. Charland, "Reinstating the Passions: Arguments from the History of Psychopathology," in *The Oxford Handbook of Philosophy of Emotion*, ed. Peter Goldie (Oxford: Oxford University Press, 2012), 237–60.

38. Locke, *An Essay Concerning Human Understanding*, Penguin Classics (London: Penguin, 2021), 217.

39. Locke, *Essay Concerning Human Understanding*, 218.

40. Locke, *Essay Concerning Human Understanding*, 217.

Reading the catastrophe of Adam and Eve through his faculty psychology, Dennis locates the primary cause of human misery in the disorder of reason and the passions. Without the guidance of reason, human passions go rogue, they are excited by what is unworthy of rational creatures, they pursue their satisfactions despite reason and so overwhelm conscience. The classical philosophical prescription for this disorder requires suppressing rebellious desires under the rule of reason. This fails, Dennis argues, because even were reason strong enough to achieve this, it flies in the face of our making as creatures both rational and passionate and denies us the experience of pleasure, which is the basis of happiness. In contrast, the genius of Christianity is to recover the divinely designed working of our inward operations by exciting the passions in the service of reason: she "exalts our Reason by exalting the Passions."[41] Nothing excites, gathers, and directs the passions more than poetry. The capacity of poetry to move the heart is incomparable so when poetic representation proceeds from knowledge of the true God the passions enter a harmonious fusion with reason, which now possesses their weight, force, and motivating power. True ideas of God, poetically represented, engage our most urgent and commanding passions: admiration, joy, terror, and desire.[42] In Dennis's logic, this appears as a case of the greatest passions adhering to the greatest representations of the greatest ideas of the greatest object, which is God. The argument locks together, in a system of meshing operations, a set of emotional conditions, a particular literary content and form, and God as represented with special reference to particular divine attributes. Since these elements warrant each other, in order to avoid a grand circularity, Dennis's argument depends heavily upon his psychology of human disorder and recovery.

In relation to this psychology and the effects upon it of religious poetry, we should notice the importance and frequency of terms such as *force*, *strength*, and *power*. Dennis commends Virgil for his "Enthusiasm; which is nothing but the elevation, and vehemence and fury proceeding from the Great and Terrible and Horrible Ideas." Even in this pagan setting, though, "what prodigious force all this must have in the connexion, where Religion adds to the Terror, increases [sic] the Astonishment, and augments the Horror."[43] Only the "greater poetry" can express a "great

---

41. Dennis, *Advancement and Reformation of Modern Poetry*, 159.
42. Dennis, *Grounds of Criticism in Poetry*, 21–22.
43. Dennis, *Advancement and Reformation of Modern Poetry*, 44–45.

passion," from which it follows, Dennis concludes that the idea of God, which animates the greatest passion, demands religious poetry that "is the worthiest Language of Religion."[44] The shift from "great" to "worthy," here reflects the ambiguity of "greatest" in which Dennis confounds "worthiest," "highest," and most "ennobling" with strongest, most forceful, and most powerful. In service of "true religion," the sublime forces the soul's reordering. Thus, violent passion cures the violence of passion. Religious representation, when it takes poetic form, will "ravish and transport the Reader, and produce a certain admiration mingled with astonishment and surprise."[45] Among the "greatest passions," terror in particular, takes its force from the associated elements of admiration, astonishment, and surprise. Dennis, therefore, gives terror pride of place as the paradigm religious passion. "Perhaps the violentest of all the passions," terror is so irresistible and unforgettable that it drives out all rivals and so wrenches the soul before God.[46] In the form of poetry, religious sublimity "is an invincible force which commits a pleasing rape upon the very soul of the reader."[47] Pleasing because the sublime contains a double movement, a shuttling between terror and relief: "greater joy" proceeds from "our reflecting that we are out of danger at the very time that we see it before us."[48] In Dennis's apologia for the sublime, this "invincible force" effects the violence needed to restore the operations of mind and heart within the larger operations of a creation, conceived as a system of natures within an ordering that ultimately serves human happiness as knowledge of God though a harmony of reason and passion. The insistence on sublime force, on a violent healing, however, also traps Dennis as he attempts the Christian side of his apologia, particularly against deism.[49] The great advantage of Christianity over its more rationalist rivals is precisely that it nurtures both reason and the passions, above all the passion of charity, which is the end of God's design. Charity alone, "the most pleasing of all the Passions," heals by "gently restraining" all the more tumultuous ones.[50] As a Christian sentiment, this is unsurprising,

---

44. Dennis, *Grounds of Criticism in Poetry*, 23.
45. Dennis, *Grounds of Criticism in Poetry*, 86.
46. Dennis, *Grounds of Criticism in Poetry*, 86.
47. Dennis, *Grounds of Criticism in Poetry*, 79.
48. Dennis, *Grounds of Criticism in Poetry*, 86.
49. Dennis, *Advancement and Reformation of Modern Poetry*, 156–64.
50. Dennis, *Advancement and Reformation of Modern Poetry*, 160.

but it also exercises no leverage whatsoever on the trajectory of Dennis's argument in either treatise. All of Dennis's examples from poetry or Scripture involve divine power, exercised in creative disposition or, most typically, in wrath and judgment. None imagine divine love. Dennis's psychology works with force and counterforce and the change in his imagery when he writes on "gently restraining" charity, who "exalts all the pleasing affections," suggests that such a love resists sublime treatment. Of course, there is a love possessed of a sweeping force that brooks no rival, but Dennis can hardly exalt the erotic, though that would warm the heart of Young's Lorenzo.

Insofar as it achieves sublimity in its representations of the divine, Christian religious poetry does more than reach the acme of the poet's vocation, it is salvific, a medium of paradisal renewal. By way of his theologically motivated psychology, Dennis provided a novel account of the *practical* authority of Scripture, of how it works in the mind and heart. The novelty, though, comes with his linking excitement of the passions to the renewed strength of reason. Dennis knows that religious rhetoric can stir passion even to civil disorder and he remarks on the heightened, scripturally inflected discourse of "our modern fanatics in England." In summoning the power of the heart, then, sublimity is enthusiastic but such enthusiasm is free of "the Imaginary Dictates of the private Spirit."[51] It is rather, public, intelligible in its workings, concordant with nature's design, and for the sake of a "reasonable religion": enthusiasm without the tears of unrest, its violence inward and restorative. As religiously privileged poetic discourse, the sublime also privileges those parts of scripture that exhibit it. The "noblest and most important" writings of the Old Testament, therefore, are those of the prophets, which include the psalms as Davidic. As a direct expression of their religious authority, the prophets spoke in the primal and primary language of religion: they "were poets by the institution of their order, and poetry was one of their prophetic functions."[52] By way of a close reading, Dennis argues for the superiority of Ps 18 over a thematically similar passage in Virgil's *Georgics*, both in the original Latin and in its English translation by John Dryden.[53] Both passages treat of divine anger and its expression in nature and Dennis argues for the psalmist's poetic excellence in terms of the harmony of its rational discourse

---

51. Dennis, *Grounds of Criticism in Poetry*, 85.
52. Dennis, *Grounds of Criticism in Poetry*, 119.
53. Dennis, *Advancement and Reformation of Modern Poetry*, 181–87.

with the vigorous passions, principally terror and wonder, that it excites. Dennis simply assumes the background rationality of Christian monotheism over against pagan polytheism. Reason is specifically satisfied here in literary terms, allowing for the psalm's excellence as poetry relatively independently of theological truth.[54] Reason in the psalm, Dennis argues, improves on Virgil by way of satisfying more fully our intellectual and imaginative expectations of God's wrath, "for the more amazing effects that we see of Divine displeasure, the more it answers our Idea of infinite wrath."[55] At the same time, the visual imagery here raises the emotional temperature to a religious awe: "how terribly is the Eye delighted here, which is a sence [sic] that the Poet ought chiefly to entertain; because it contributes more than any other to the exciting of strong Passion?" Dennis concludes with a question that is both Protestant in appealing to a purity of biblical origin and distinctively modern in historicizing that origin as an ancient and natural integrity: "there is more Terror here, both ordinary and Enthusiastick, and consequently more spirit in a faint Copy, nay, a Prosaick Copy, translated in the Imperfection of our Tongue, and by men who in all likelihood had no manner of notion of Poetry.... What force and what infinite Spirit must there not have been in the original Hebrew?"[56] Almost fifty years later, Lowth answered just this question in treating the forms of Hebrew poetry and, in particular, the power of their sublimity.

Lowth's *Lectures* owed their popularity and influence to his detailed discovery and examination of the devices of Hebrew poetry. He grounded in exegetical demonstration the claims of predecessors, such as Dennis, as to the excellence of Hebrew poetry, evidenced especially in its sublimity. The Hebrew sublime, Lowth claimed, whether one considers subject matter, the evocative circumstances described, or the magnificence of its imagery, has "obtained an unrivalled pre-eminence."[57] Much like Dennis, Lowth found in poetry the confluence of reason and pas-

---

54. An example that supports Morris's observation that, in connection with the sublime, the excellence of the Bible took a literary form in addition to the excellence of its truth (Morris, *Religious Sublime*, 35–37).

55. Dennis, *Advancement and Reformation of Modern Poetry*, 184.

56. Dennis, *Advancement and Reformation of Modern Poetry*, 186.

57. Robert Lowth, *Lectures on the Sacred Poetry of the Hebrews; Translated from the Latin of the Right Rev. Robert Lowth ... By G. Gregory ... to Which Are Added the Principals of Professor Michaelis, by the Translator and Others* (London: Johnson, 1753), 348.

sion. While rational discourse is "cool," the passions riot in an excess of energetic expressions, unconsidered, forceful, and prey to confusion.[58] Poetry, however, aims both to excite passion and to "direct," "temper," and "discipline the affections," and in so doing to give pleasure.[59] None of this is unfamiliar, any more than Lowth's account of the subject-matter of sublime poetry, which, though his biblical examples are notably extensive, consists of the display of divine power in creation and judgment and descriptions of grief, joy, and righteous anger before God. Since he is keen to stick to his literary brief, Lowth does not develop a doctrine of salvific, sublime effects, and, though he acknowledges its contribution to the repertoire of sublimity, he does not emphasize terror or horror. The sublime "proceeds from the imitation of the passions of admiration, of joy, indignation, grief, and terror."[60] Lowth, however, does break new ground, over and above his analysis of Hebrew poetry itself, in developing what Dennis only hints at: the connection between the primitive and the integrity of sublime expression.

Lowth distinguishes between the Hebrew *mizmor* as referring to the form of a poem and *mashal* as having to do with its "diction and sentiments," the latter "properly expressive of the poetical style."[61] *Mashal* is an important term for Lowth, and he criticizes the restrictive character of its familiar translation as *parable*. When applied to style, *mashal* implies "something eminent or energetic, excellent or important."[62] Reading Num 23:7–11, Lowth observes that though Balaam's speech is called a *mashal*, it contains none of the features associated with *mashal* in the sense of poetry involving "figurative language."[63] When figurative language is bracketed out of our understanding of *mashal*, we discover at the core of this term reference to "those exalted sentiments, that spirit of sublimity, that energy and enthusiasm, with which the answer of [Balaam] is animated."[64] Sublimity, Lowth concludes, thus belongs to Hebrew poetry in "its very name and title."[65] This analysis finds the sublime at the primitive origins of

---

58. Lowth, *Lectures*, 308.
59. Lowth, *Lectures*, 369–70.
60. Lowth, *Lectures*, 365.
61. Lowth, *Lectures*, 78.
62. Lowth, *Lectures*, 304.
63. Lowth, *Lectures*, 306.
64. Lowth, *Lectures*, 306.
65. Lowth, *Lectures*, 307.

poetry itself. Poetry begins in "the vehement affections of the mind," and its early history is found in the "singular frenzy of poets" crying out in "a style and expression directly prompted by nature herself."[66] Art and time brought such frenzy into an ordering that was delightful and instructive. This is the setting in which Lowth places Hebrew poetry, not only in terms of history but qualitatively, with respect to its excellence.

Hebrew poetry reflects the providential blessing of its social and cultural setting. Lowth describes the Hebrews in terms of a primitive nobility opposed to the corrupting seductions of "superior civilization ... if luxury, levity, and pride, be the criterions of [superiority]."[67] Simplicity of life and manners made for a life uncorrupted by the seductions of excess or refinement and, given their only limited interest in commercial life, the energies of this people flowed into the arts necessary to life, in which, by not being diffused, they retained their natural force.[68] Under these conditions, the Hebrew poets take their images largely from the creation around them and from the simple materials of their pastoral lives. Psalmists and prophets, therefore, add to the natural dignity of ordinary things, the vigor and force of the sublime.[69] Lowth opposes this primitive simplicity to the confusions, distractions, and deceits of a refined, civilized existence. From this simplicity follow two vitalizing features of the Hebrew sublime, spontaneity and economy. Passion is not smothered in sophistication, nor is it cultivated or feigned according to social manners. Praise breathes the spirit of nature and of passion as "joy, admiration, and love ... burst forth spontaneously in their native colours," while grief, too, takes on sublime expression on "the model of those complaints which flow naturally and spontaneously from the afflicted heart."[70] Both Lowth and Blair, who follows Lowth in his own lectures on the sublime, illustrate how sublimity depends upon the economy and tense force of words. The sublime flags and falls with diffuseness, a piece of advice Young largely ignored. Hebrew poetry again sets the standard, giving us "great and magnificent conceptions and sentiments ... in language bold and elevated, in sentences concise, abrupt and energetic."[71] The implication here, strengthened when Lowth compares Hebrew poetry

---

66. Lowth, *Lectures*, 79.
67. Lowth, *Lectures*, 145.
68. Lowth, *Lectures*, 145–46.
69. Lowth, *Lectures*, 248.
70. Lowth, *Lectures*, 127.
71. Lowth, *Lectures*, 377.

with that of the Greeks and Romans, is that among the Hebrews we find the conditions for a pure sublime, a sublimity untainted by corrupt interests or the dissipated energies of civilized life. "In the progress of society," Blair warns, "the genius and manners of men undergo a change more favourable to accuracy, than to strength or sublimity."[72] Reading Hebrew poetry for its sublimity, therefore, becomes the occasion for a historicized version of the disorder of reason and passion described by Dennis. The authority of the biblical text, especially in the sublime heights of its poetry, derives also from the conditions of Hebrew life as "close to nature," simple and uncorrupted, and allowing for a freer, more wholesome expression of the passions. In this, civilized life meets its corrective example.

> Before the Christian Religion Had, as It Were,
> Humanized the Idea of the Divinity ... There Was Very Little
> Said of the Love of God (Edmund Burke)

"Of all writings, Sacred Scriptures afford us the highest instances of the sublime. The descriptions of the Deity, in them, are wonderfully noble; both from the grandeur of the object, and the manner of representing it." [73] Blair's summary of the biblical sublime seems innocent enough and leaves him free to argue that the Bible also affords the "highest instances" of other literary forms. Well before 1783, when Blair's lectures were published, however, the sublime had gathered a theological weight and significance that set it apart from other literary modes, giving it a unique place within the Bible itself. Along with others, Dennis appealed to Longinus's treatise *On the Sublime* as fount, origin, and prime authority for this advocacy of the sublime. [74] Somewhat to Dennis's irritation, though, Longinus had failed to draw the broader conclusions obvious to his eighteenth-century advocate. Longinus's interest was in a potential of literary and rhetorical discourse, the sublime as "a certain distinction and excellence in expression." [75] Compared with

---

72. Blair, *Lectures on Rhetoric and Belles Lettres*, 1:77.
73. Blair, *Lectures on Rhetoric and Belles Lettres*, 1:77.
74. The fragment *Peri Hypsous*, long attributed to the third century CE writer, Cassius Longinus, was probably written during the first century. It bounded from history's minor leagues in the late seventeenth century in France and, a little later, in Britain. For a survey of this history, see Monk, *Sublime*, chs. 1 and 2.
75. Longinus, *On the Sublime*, in *Critical Theory since Plato*, rev. Hazard Adams (New York: Harcourt Brace Jovanovich, 1971), 77.

Dennis, his purpose was modest and certainly did not involve arguing that the sublime functioned in God's design as a means of restoring an original human integrity. Dennis, therefore, raps Longinus over his ancient knuckles for suggesting that sublimity need not necessarily involve passion, a point that contradicts everything the eighteenth century built upon the sublime. We might say that eighteenth century critics sublimed the sublime, raising it out of Longinus's confines to become a potential of objects and ideas, as well as of their poetic representations.[76] Above all, sublimity is a potential of the human mind in its relatedness to God, a vital and vitalizing element in God's design, especially for coordinating the human heart and mind with God's works in nature and, thereby, with God's own power and majesty. When truly realized, the sublime possesses a salvific power, even restoring humanity to its paradisal origins or bringing it in frame with the nobility of that ancient life from which the prophets drew their poetry. Furthermore, the sublime is coordinated with human greatness, the infinity of the mind's reach. Attuned to sublimity, the soul assumes its proper reach.

In this coordination, via sublimity, of anthropology with the doctrine and experience of God we see most keenly the problematic theological consequences of "subliming the sublime." The religious privilege given to the sublime identifies terror and similar reactions to power, including astonishment, as basic in our knowledge of God. Correspondingly, God is known, first and foremost as "a force which nothing can withstand."[77] Burke goes on to argue in a way that recalls Young's distinction between concluding from reflection and getting oneself "rapt" by sublimity: next to our recognition of God's power "some comparing is necessary to satisfy us of his wisdom, his justice, and his goodness." On the other hand, in imagining his power, "we shrink into the minuteness of our nature and are, in a manner, annihilated before him."[78] That, however, turns out only to be the downbeat of the sublime rhythm as we are no sooner thus put in our place than we discover the relative infinity and immensity of the human mind. Immediately, the sublime is an experiential acknowledgment of

---

76. For the sublime in eighteenth-century and early nineteenth-century painting, see Edward J. Nygren, *James Ward's Gordale Scar, An Essay in the Sublime* (London: Tate Gallery, 1982); Matthew Craske, *Art in Europe, 1700–1830: A History of the Visual Arts in an Era of Unprecedented Urban Economic Growth*, Oxford History of Art (Oxford: Oxford University Press, 1997), 107–23.

77. Burke, *Philosophical Enquiry*, 111.

78. Burke, *Philosophical Enquiry*, 111.

divine majesty and power but equally it serves to exalt the humanity that so experiences it. Though Young protests at any idea that our notions of vastness might serve to measure the divine immensity, the general drift is toward implying that, however, different in scale, terms such as knowledge and power are predicated univocally of God and creatures. Baillie reminds us, for instance, that however complete the power of a master over his slaves, it never reaches the sublimity found in the sway of a prince "extending to multitudes, and from nations bowing at his commands." Then he concludes, "but it is in the Almighty that this sublime is completed, who with a nod can shatter to pieces the Foundations of a universe, as with a Word he called it into Being."[79] As we saw earlier, Baillie and Young happily include the human mind in such a rising scale.[80] Ironically, the divine immensity, which referred to God's omnipresence and that Christopher Smart found exemplified in the "linnet's throat" no less than "along the spangled sky," looks, in connection with the sublime, strangely like the "'bad infinity" of an endlessly encompassing physical space.[81] The cultivation of the sublime belongs to what William Placher nicely termed early modernity's "domestication of transcendence," the other side of which is the coordinated exaltation of human imagination and desire.[82]

In terms of scripture, pursuit of the sublime foregrounded images of divine power and judgment in an undialectical way, without due regard for the complexity of the Old Testament's representation of God's relationship with Israel. It also opened up a tension between the Old and New Testaments evidenced most vividly in attempts to relate sublimity to Christology. Among frenzied appeals to the night sky, Young does manage to find a brief place for christological reference, though in poetry that is as awkward as the content is unsupported by the broader theme:

Thou canst not 'scape uninjured from our praise.
Uninjured from our praise can He escape,

---

79. Baillie, *Essay on the Sublime*, 20.
80. As with Young's "That Mind immortal loves immortal aims / That boundless Mind affects a boundless space / That vast surveys, and the Sublime of things, / The soul assimilate, and make her great" (1019–1022) or "The more our spirits are enlarged on earth, / The deeper draught shall they receive of heaven" (577–578).
81. Christopher Smart, "On the Immensity of the Supreme Being" (Eighteenth Century Poetry Archive, 2015), https://tinyurl.com/SBL4831c.
82. William Placher, *The Domestication of Transcendence: How Modern Thinking about God Went Wrong* (Louisville: Westminster John Knox, 1996).

> Who, disembosom'd from the Father, bows
> The heaven of heavens, to kiss the distant earth?
> Breathes out in agonies a sinless soul;
> Against the cross, Death's iron sceptre breaks;
> From famish'd Ruin plucks her human prey. (ll. 2349–2355)

At no point does Young succeed in intimating, let alone establishing, an intrinsic, christological relationship between the religious force of converting sublimity and the person or work of Christ. His drama notices the atonement but the sublime holds an entire sway over the spiritual struggle addressed in book 9. Christology does no theological work here; sublimity alone redeems the soul. The spiritual struggle concludes in visions of the last judgment in which the riot of sublime destruction almost swallows the figure of the returning Son of Man, acknowledged here solely by the entire contrast between his earthly life and his present power.

> Amazing period! when each mountain-height
> Out-burns Vesuvius; rocks eternal pour
> Their melted mass, as rivers once they pour'd;
> Stars rush; and final Ruin fiercely drives
> Her ploughshare o'er Creation!—while aloft
> More than astonishment, if more can be!
> Far other firmament than e'er was seen,
> Than e'er was thought by man! far other stars!
> Stars animate, that govern these of fire;
> Far other Sun!—A Sun, O how unlike The Babe at Bethlehem! (ll. 164–174)

There is no hint of the paradox found, for instance, in the Apocalypse's representation of "the Lamb" in wrath (e.g., Rev 6:16).

Dennis tackles the christological issue head on, dissociating Jesus from the sublime on theological grounds. That the teaching of Jesus lacks the sublime oomph of Isaiah or Jeremiah is an embarrassment for Dennis so he argues that Jesus "instructed the world as God, and as God he could not feel either admiration or terrour, or the rest of the Enthusiastick Passions."[83] Having resorted to this oddly docetic defense, Dennis rescues Jesus's authority for his high doctrine of religious poetry by noting how, though not sublime, the "method of [Jesus's] instruction was entirely

---

83. Dennis, *Grounds of Criticism in Poetry*, 120.

poetical, that is by fable or parables, contriv'd and plac'd and adapted to work very strongly upon human passions." Burke appeals to the Bible for evidence that in any knowledge of God the attribute of power is primary. "In the scripture, wherever God is presented as appearing or speaking, everything terrible in nature is called up to heighten the awe and solemnity of the divine presence."[84] In consequence, divine attributes such as mercy or love get treated as secondary qualifiers of divine power. The doctrine of God is thus molded to Burke's account of the relationship between the sublime and the beautiful. Sublime experience is primary, both theologically as a response to representations of divine power, and anthropologically, as stimulating "the passions belonging to self-preservation."[85] Beauty, by contrast, associated with both the need to reproduce the species and also with the "lesser ... domestic virtues," engages such passions as love and amiability that excite the body and mind to relaxation. Beauty is thus secondary, a temporary counterbalance to the necessary weight of the self-preserving passions. In Burke's gendered argument, the sublime is productive, therefore, of the manly virtues, the beautiful of the feminine. In an indirect but telling reference to Christ, Burke observes that "before the Christian religion had, as it were, humanized the idea of the divinity, and brought it somewhat near to us, there was very little said of the love of God." The person and work of Christ, together with the New Testament insistence upon the divine love, fall thereby into association with the beautiful, the feminine, and are implicitly subordinated to the sublime of God's power and the manly virtues of self-preservation. What produces this configuration of associations is the framework of connections between the aesthetics of the sublime, an anthropology of human transcendence, and the theology the two latter generate.

In 1853, the huge triptych, *The Last Judgement* by the Northumbrian painter, John Martin, began a tour of galleries and assembly halls in England, Scotland, Ireland, New York, and, eventually, Australia. Long before the trip to Sydney, the number who had viewed the paintings was estimated at eleven million.[86] The company of those who knew *The Last Judgement* from the huge supply of prints was greater still. Martin had made his name as a painter of sublime and, particularly biblical, catastrophe: the deluge overwhelming the fleeing crowd, terrorized by lightning

---

84. Burke, *Philosophical Enquiry*, 112.
85. Burke, *Philosophical Enquiry*, 88.
86. Martin Myrone, ed., *John Martin: Apocalypse* (London: Tate, 2011), 174–83.

that snakes viciously towards them; fire and hail churning an Egyptian harbor as pharaoh laments another plague; guests scattering over a blood-red palace at Belshazzar's feast; the last man on a vertiginous rock, lamenting a wasted earth under a bloody sun.[87] The central panel of *The Last Judgement* depicts the "Great Day of His Wrath." On the right of the painting, lightning topples a huge mountain that crushes a city as it falls into a central circle of fire, welling up from the opened earth. In the foreground, to right and left, tiny men and women, many clearly of wealth and rank, fall into the abyss. The tops of two other mountains rush toward the fiery center from the left. Between Martin's painting and Young's rhetoric, there is a close sympathy.[88] Both give apocalyptic the sublime treatment and both effect a similar displacement of Christology, as the dwarfing and cataclysmic immensities of nature hold center stage as the privileged representatives of divine power.[89] Though Martin earns small place and little praise in most histories of art, his work permeated the imaginations of millions, visually defining the sublime and the sublimity of God. His art "penetrated the culture of the nineteenth-century English-speaking world more deeply and more profoundly than that of any other modern artist."[90]

Martin belongs to the trajectory of the popular sublime. The British critics discussed above, along with Young, certainly belong to histories of the philosophical sublime where they, especially Burke, are found on the way to Immanuel Kant's defining account in *The Critique of Judgement*.[91] They also contribute, however, to the more continuously enduring tradition of popular sublimity, to which they mediated the sublime dynamic of uplift and terror, the heady association of sublimity and human potential, and the vastness and prodigious force of nature as the likeness of divine power. The popular sublime has provided a literary and visual language for biblical imaginings, political enthusiasm, technological advances and

---

87. Myrone, *John Martin*, 101–2, 119, 131, 156.

88. Given Young's popularity and Martin's interest in poetry, it is very likely that Martin had read *Night Thoughts*, though I have not yet found biographical confirmation of this.

89. Alan P. R. Gregory, *Science Fiction Theology: Beauty and the Transformation of the Sublime* (Waco, TX: Baylor University Press, 2015), 158–59.

90. Myrone, *John Martin*, 11.

91. Immanuel Kant, *Critique of Judgement*, Hafner Library of Classics (New York: Hafner, 1951).

aspirations, for fantasy and science fiction, and for tourism, advertisements, sports events, and contemporary spiritualities.[92] In its way, as I have suggested, it has also, in the popular imagination, obscured the complexities of scripture, contributed to a crude picture of the God of Israel, anthropomorphized the divine, and unhappily wedded the language of divine power to sublimity's prodigious force.

---

92. For examples, see David E. Nye, *American Technological Sublime* (Cambridge: Massachusetts Institute of Technology, 1996); Gregory, *Science Fiction Theology*.

Sublime Terror in Context: A Response

Roy R. Jeal

Terrifying images evoked by the rhetography of written texts dislocate us.[1] They are meant to do so. They press the emotions of terror into our minds, even into our bodies. Fright pushes people off-center. It causes a range of adrenaline-produced reactions like increased heart and respiration rates, sudden perspiration, muscle contractions, and fight or flight responses. Terrifying images can cause panic; they can debilitate. Observation of powerful and dominating forces, invasions, destruction, ferocious beasts, cataclysmic events, torture, suffering, and death prompt fear and anxiety. Sometimes they evoke feelings of guilt or repugnance. Sometimes they stimulate a kind of high. Some people are attracted to horror, perhaps perversely intrigued by it. Terror can draw the mind and body toward a sense of—even desire for—participation in what texts cast on the imagination. It can produce ἔκστασις ("astonishment," "bewilderment"). Argumentation can function by creating terror. There is an ideology of terror. There even seems to be a sacredness of terror: if God causes terror then it must be a holy thing. Terror in all these ways is sublime and in texts it functions as a sublime texture. It floods minds and bodies with unexpected and unsettling reactions meant to drive people to belief and action.

Sociorhetorical interpretation describes these effects as *rhetorical force*. The rhetorical force of New Testament, early and later Christian, and pseudepigraphal discourse is about what the texts *do* to their audiences.[2] Rhetorical force makes people feel or do things. Audiences are moved by

---

1. In SRI, *rhetography*, an elision of the words rhetoric and graphic, addresses the ways in which textures of texts prompt images or pictures in the minds of listeners and readers. The images imply truths and realities.

2. See Roy R. Jeal, *Exploring Philemon: Freedom, Brotherhood, and Partnership in the New Society*, RRA 2 (Atlanta: SBL Press, 2015), 13–14, 203–10.

the dynamics of the rhetography and texturing (interweaving of discourses) that are meant to elicit belief, behavior, and formation. The rhetorical force of the discourses shapes people's lives. It functions to create new cognitive, social, discursive, and physical spaces that are occupied by listeners and readers. Sublime terror shapes the mind; it creates a disposition of mind among those who dwell in the new spaces. This means, of course, that the texts, even those that evoke terror, are meant to have, in SRI terms, a *wisdom function*.³ Wisdom is about how people, believers, are to live in their social, cultural, and religious contexts. They face pressures all around to conform to expectations of all kinds. How should they live? What should they do? Wisdom is about doing the right thing, about doing good and living faithfully, fruitfully, and ethically. In our texts wisdom relies on the conviction that God is the creator and sustainer of all things and is to be honored and that humans are responsible to God. Sublime terror is meant to shape them toward this conviction. Sometimes it does not work that way. The employment of terror can have negative consequences.⁴ Often it hits people in their σπλάγχνα, in, rhetorically speaking, their guts.⁵ The effects are dramatic.

Many will recall the famous 1979 Francis Ford Coppola film *Apocalypse Now*, which is a take on Joseph Conrad's *Heart of Darkness* (1899) with allusions to T. S. Eliot ("The Hollow Men," 1925). In the film, a monologue by the character Colonel Kurtz (played by Marlon Brando) subtly, obscurely, frighteningly suggests the sublime, rhetorical nature, and rhetorical force of terror: Colonel Kurtz says (abridged),

> I've seen the horrors, horrors that you've seen.... It's *impossible* for words to describe what is necessary, to those who do not know what horror means. Horror, *horror has a face* and you must make a friend of horror. Horror and moral terror are your friends. If they are not, then they are enemies to be feared. They are truly enemies.⁶

Friends or enemies: terror can function both ways. The essays in part 2 of this volume point to this paradox.

---

3. On wisdom see Jeal, *Exploring Philemon*, 7–8.
4. As the essays in this volume by Harry Maier and Alan Gregory indicate.
5. The Greek word σπλάγχνα (σπλάγχνον) is often translated as "heart," but in fact means *bowels, intestines*, hence "guts."
6. Cf. the original lines "He cried in a whisper at some image, at some vision—he cried out twice, a cry that was no more than a breath: 'The Horror! The Horror!,'" in Joseph Conrad, *Heart of Darkness*, https://tinyurl.com/SBL4831a.

While in his essay, "Terror and the Logic of the Sublime in Revelation," Christopher T. Holmes recognizes that there is much more to consider as a guide to terror in the sublime than the ancient treatise *On the Sublime* (Περὶ Ὕψους), attributed to Longinus, he reasonably draws from the "important perspective" of this work for his analysis of terror in Revelation. He renders the word ὕψος as sublime rhetoric and notes that it addresses "the quality and intended effect of language" on people. That it addresses intention strikes me as a very important feature of what Holmes tells us. A major notion, therefore, is about how sublime language aims to influence the mind and, consequently, how it provokes behavior. Sublime language "leads to ekstasis," transport or transcendence.[7] The sublime "dislocates" and "reorients." Holmes points to two of Longinus's sources for the sublime, "impressive ideas" and "vehement emotion," as being particularly important for consideration of terror. Terror is dramatically impressive and certainly evokes strong emotions. Holmes quotes Robert Doran, who claims that terror is the strongest emotion and "is most associated with a displacement with the mundane condition, such as that which accompanies a divine vision."[8] Terror is a source and an effect. Referencing James Porter, Holmes notes that sublime sensibilities are provoked by "extremes, contrasts, intensities, and incommensurabilities of transgressed limits, excesses, collisions, and structures on the edge of collapse or ruin."[9] Impressive ideas, vehement emotion, and vivid description work together in Revelation to convey terror. Holmes argues that the apocalyptic heights and depths, grand spaces, dramatically large masses and surfaces, massive climatic forces, strange creatures, catastrophic destruction and disorder, war, killing, flowing blood, the collapse of political and economic structures and systems all convey sublime, heightened, and terrifying thoughts and emotions to audience mindsets. The vivid imagery creates terror in minds and bodies. Audiences of spectators can be transported to frightening levels while they are offered the comfort and assurance that God is in control and all will be well, all manner of things will be well in the end and the evil, cowardly things will be destroyed.

---

7. So Robert Doran, referenced by Holmes.

8. Robert Doran, *The Theory of the Sublime from Longinus to Kant* (Cambridge: Cambridge University Press, 2015), 43.

9. James Porter, *The Sublime in Antiquity* (Cambridge: Cambridge University Press, 2016), 53.

In Rev 1, the fearsome "incommensurable"[10] imagery of Jesus causes John to fall "as though dead" (1:17). Apparently John suffers from shock, hypotension (a blackout), at the sight of the imagery. "Don't be afraid," says Jesus, at the terrifying vision. So the sublime terror is not meant to evoke fear but a sublime peace, a freedom from death and Hades. The intention of the terror is to point to good (perhaps we could say "abundant") life. Terror begets comfort. The real and true Lord, not some human or imperial usurper, is in control. The story here is reminiscent of the narrative of Exodus where the underlying question is "Who will be God? Yahweh or pharaoh?" The pharaoh of Egypt caused terrible things to be done to the Hebrews living in his land. But Yahweh caused terrifying things to occur in Egypt until pharaoh gave it up and let God's people go.

In Rev 4, visual reminders of the fearsome presence of God at Mount Sinai evoke a sense of sublime awe from God's throne room. The throne is guarded and unapproachable, and the one sitting on it is utterly "holy" (the trisagion "holy, holy, holy"), alone worthy of all honor. None of us dare to get close to the throne and we live with fear of proximity to it. We can only look with John through the doorway.

Revelation 6–16, as Holmes indicates, present dramatic judgments that arouse terror again and again. There is no hiding, no escape, only crushing destruction for evil and for refusing to honor the true God. Embedded within this, Rev 12–13 cause human minds to visualize the great red dragon—the term itself strikes fear—who aims to harm and destroy, to stop the goodness of the woman and the child, to devour the goodness that comes from the woman. The two beasts, similarly, have only destruction and power in mind and people are going to be hurt. The beasts aim to bring fear to humans, to the faithful worshipers. Sublime intimidation is the goal of these powers. Their message is the message of fright and horrible oppression.

We could add the horrifying description of destruction visualized in Rev 18 where the fallen Babylon and those kings and nations who have committed fornication with her are laid waste in one hour. The profiteers "stand far off in fear of her torment" (18:15 NRSV).[11]

The eventual sublime response from heaven to the horror elicits a great "Hallelujah!" (19:1, 3) because the great whore has been defeated and

---

10. "No common standard of measurement; impossible to measure or compare."
11. Holmes mentions this. Scripture translations are from the NRSV.

the saints avenged. These events move the twenty-four elders and the four living creatures to sublime recognition and disposition that moves them to worship (19:4). The great and sublime marriage and marriage banquet follow (19:7–9).

Vernon K. Robbins's "Sublime Terror in 1 Enoch" takes us deep into Immanuel Kant's philosophical theory of the sublime as a way to understand sublime horror in 1 Enoch. Robbins tracks Kant's ideas particularly as they are interpreted by his colleague Rudolf A. Makkreel. Very important is Kant's understanding that things—material realia—are not themselves sublime. Rather, (quoting Makkreel) the sublime is "a state of mind elicited by the representation of boundlessness or the infinite."[12] For Kant the sublime is of the mind, the movement of the mind, not of physicality. It is of interpretation, not of things themselves. James Porter, by some contrast, argues that "sublimity, though it frequently tends to draw the eye and the mind away from matter and the sensuous domain, cannot exist without reference to these same things. Sublimity originates in an encounter with matter."[13] So Porter, while recognizing Kant, speaks of "conjoined" *material* and *immaterial* sublimes.[14] Language itself, whether spoken or written, is a material thing and is what we read and interpret in the texts we study. But of course we use—must use—our minds to interpret and understand. Understanding is cognitive and emotional.[15]

Still, as Robbins clearly demonstrates, Kant's categories of the sublime—the *mathematical* sublime and the *dynamical* sublime—open an exciting world of understanding and interpretive possibilities. The mathematical sublime is "related to the cognitive faculties and represented in terms of *magnitude*" and the dynamical sublime is "related to the faculty of desire and represented in terms of might or *power*" (emphasis added). Kant understands the mind to employ "pure and practical reason" that produces discrete, linear progressions of time. On the other hand, the

---

12. Rudolf A. Makkreel, *Imagination and Interpretation in Kant: The Hermeneutical Import of the "Critique of Judgment"* (Chicago: University of Chicago Press, 1990), 68.

13. James Porter, *The Sublime in Antiquity* (Cambridge: Cambridge University Press, 2016), 391.

14. Porter, *Sublime in Antiquity*, 382–536, esp. 391–97. "Not even silence, one of the basic conditions of language, can be perceived except against the background of the noise of language" (401).

15. For a more medical discussion of the connections of cognition, body, and emotion see Gabor Maté, *When the Body Says No: The Cost of Hidden Stress* (Toronto: Vintage Canada, 2004).

mind also employs "reflective judgment" that produces "spatial coordinating functions." "Pure and practical reasoning *erases* emotions from their synthetic functions, while reflective judgment *can assess* emotions and feelings within formally purposive (teleological) and aesthetic reflection." Interpretation is what "mediates reflective judgment that extends into aesthetic comprehension" (emphasis added). This aesthetic interpretation is sublime, leading to aesthetic comprehension. This is wonderfully helpful. The sublime, on this understanding, occurs in the mind. It *is* interpretive, *a movement of the mind*. This is rhetoric at work, the rhetorical force of texts and human discourses.

Robbins points out that the sublime is "a state of mind elicited by the representation of boundlessness or the infinite." The mathematical sublime is about magnitude but not about counting or measuring. It is "aesthetic comprehension" that can establish "a measure for itself." It measures intuitively prior to comparison. That is, the imagination "reaches a limit" and "aesthetic comprehension encounters the immeasurable and the ... sublime." The emotion of magnitude is beyond counting or estimation. This is like Abram being asked if he can count the stars or being told that his descendants will be as numerous as grains of sand at the seashore (Gen 15:5; 22:17). The dynamical sublime is, in contrast to the mathematical, about grasping a sense of power, not of size. The mind is moved by power and might. The power is extremely impressive, often emotionally overwhelming.

Robbins provides studies of both the mathematical and dynamical sublime. First Enoch 21:1–10 evokes dramatic mathematical sublime terror of magnitude and space for those who "transgressed the command of God." They are bound for a metaphorically complete time of ten thousand years. A more terrifying sublimity is the immeasurable burning space of eternal confinement. Dynamical sublime terror is evoked in the mind by the power and might indicated in 1 En. 62.1–14. Powerful terror and pain come on kings and mighty and exalted persons when the powerful Son of Man is observed on his throne. They will be handed over to angels for retributive punishment. Robbins's analyses of both texts in 1 Enoch reveal senses of sublime terror of God's judgment from deep-cosmic spacetime. According to Kant, the sublime "builds up" humans cognitively and emotionally through a series of *Bildungsvermögen*, "the formative faculty in the imagination" (Makkreel's translation).[16] John Shannon Hendrix draws on

---

16. Makkreel, *Imagination and Interpretation*, 12, cited in Robbins's essay.

Makkreel's analysis of Kant, demonstrating the connections of the sublime to unconscious thought. The sublime, unconscious thought, according to Makkreel, "loves to wander in the dark."[17] Humans experience the sublime unconsciously, yet are moved, transported by it to believe and behave. This is rhetorical force. Robbins hopes, somewhat skeptically, that humans will be shaken by the rhetorical force of the sublime, energizing moral resources for good, for the working of the Spirit. Self-interest, of course, gets in the way.

Harry O. Maier in "The Sublime Terror of Ignatius of Antioch" takes us directly into the sublime madness of Ignatius of Antioch through his letter to the Romans. Ignatius is unreasonable, weird, gone right over the edge. Crazy, as Maier points out. He has a sublime madness. He wants the recipients of his letter to validate his death wish. He wants "the pleasure, ["the thrill" in Richardson's translation] of the wild beasts" (5.2). Does he seek some kind of cleansing? He wants to become "a pure loaf" (4.1, καθαρὸς ἄρτος, a clean loaf? clean bread?). Has his madness moved him to think Christ does not make him clean enough? Does he think the death and resurrection of Christ are inadequate? Ignatius seems to be in a hurry "to get to Jesus Christ" (5.3).

Maier is right to say that the letter evokes "shocked silence" that invites mental and visualized participation by the Roman believers. The terror invites a silent, passive involvement.[18] It is highly sensory. Audiences enter the symbolic world of horror with Ignatius in their own minds. Spectators (θεωροί) become participants in the visualized scenes. They also become probably unwilling critics, judges (κριταί) who are called to make righteous decisions about what they are hearing and visualizing. This is bound to evoke an intense sense of terror among them (perhaps even among us?): Will we be next? Are we to face the same terrors of the arena? Does Ignatius want the Romans to *feel* the horror of suffering? As Maier states, "Ignatius's piling of terms in present tense narration results in his transporting the implied readers out of themselves into the arena and placed in a terrifying situation." He goes on to say that the audience is "both observer and observed" and that "The result of this is to use death as a form of the sublime." The suffering, the fire, the cross, and the mutilation have purifying, sanctifying force. Strangely, it has a sublime result, something that may be

---

17. Makkreel, *Imagination and Interpretation*, 15, cited in Robbins's essay.

18. See Donald D. Evans, *The Logic of Self-Involvement* (London: SCM Press, 1963); Kenneth Burke, *A Rhetoric of Motives* (Berkeley: University of California Press, 1969).

beyond comprehension, yet very real. Suffering can bring about understanding. Ignatius sounds a little self-righteous about it all. He says "My desire has been crucified and there burns in me no passion for material things. There is living water in me, which speaks and says inside me 'Come to the Father'" (7.2).

While reading Maier's essay, I was reminded of something I read about understanding suffering in nineteenth-century French author Victor Hugo's famous novel *Les Misérables* (1862). Perhaps it captures something of the force of terrible suffering. Hugo wrote: "Martyrdom is a sublimation, but a sublimation that corrodes. It is a torment that sanctifies. One may endure it at first, the pincers, the red hot iron, but must not the tortured flesh give way in the end?"[19] Hugo calls martyrdom a sublimation, which here means that it is something shaped into a culturally and socially acceptable activity. Martyrdom sanctifies without clear logic. The tortured flesh gives up and dies, and only sanctification, holiness, exists. Perhaps Ignatius has come to such a sublimation regarding his own forthcoming horror, and calls for such a sublime view among his audience of believers in Rome. Yet to desire it seems to be a bizarre holiness, something only an unstable person would want. Don't get in the way of my terror, my suffering! Ignatius thinks of his own martyrdom as an acceptable, even welcomed event. He imagines it as a sacred act, as something that sanctifies him. The horror has become his friend. Suffering makes the justified strong; Paul the apostle says so, will boast of it (Rom 5:3–5).[20] But it still kills you in the end. The flesh gives way to death. Sanctifying perhaps, but it kills. It is difficult for many modern persons to see it this way.[21] Ignatius presents not only as being crazy, but also vain. His sublime terror draws his Roman audience mentally into the arena to suffer with him. He wants them to feel his suffering. Ignatius is the center of attention, not Christ. Perhaps Ignatius imagined it as taking up his own cross (*Rom.* 5.3; cf. Mark 8:34), but his pride wants him to be seen doing it.

---

19. Victor Hugo, *Les Misérables*, Penguin Classics (London: Penguin, 1982), 1143.

20. "We also boast in our sufferings, knowing that suffering produces endurance, and endurance produces character, and character produces hope, and hope does not disappoint us, because God's love has been poured into our hearts through the Holy Spirit that has been given to us."

21. Could this be because people forget or refuse to be moved by the horrors of wars, of the holocaust, genocides, and other gruesome history?

Ignatius aims to be rhetorically effective. The sublime terror is meant to change people's minds. In other words, it calls people to a kind of μετάνοια, repentance. It may be a misguided repentance. It is to make his audience of Roman Christ-believers feel the pain with him, to imagine themselves in the arena and to persuade them not to intervene on his behalf. Terror disorients, and the disorientation frightens and calls for changed perspectives on perceived reality.[22] Ignatius, despite his madness and apparent self-interest, is calling for trust in Christ and for the expectation of being with him.

In "Subliming the Sublime: The Bible and the Sublime in Eighteenth-Century Britain," Alan P. R. Gregory persuades us to consider the importance and relevance of understandings of the sublime in the contexts of Christianity and the use of the Bible in Britain during the 1700s. Gregory draws us into this era of reception history, demonstrating that there was a hermeneutic of the sublime in play for many interpreters during the time period that is much different than what biblical scholars would imagine appropriate for today, but of which echoes are still heard.[23] The Bible had become by that time, he says, "fit for more or less any laudatory hyperbole going." What interpreters did, shaped by the culture, religion, and ethos of the time, was construct "on the relatively thin foundations provided by Longinus ... a philosophical and theological psychology into their aesthetics of sublimity." These views led to "a shift in the place and function of scripture within Christian faith and practice." The Bible was imagined to have a sublime psychological, formative force that was in itself "salvific."

In his survey, Gregory draws on the reasoning of eighteenth-century thinkers Edward Young, Edmund Burke, John Dennis, Robert Lowth, and Hugh Blair, demonstrating that the sublime *itself*, as sublime experience, was believed to have religious authority, "how enthusiasm for the sublime had a formative influence upon reading Scripture" and that the sublime had profound effect "on the popular religious imagination in the English-speaking world." Developed understandings of the place of the sublime brought about a "shift in the place and function of scripture."

Gregory explains this with the example of the sublime *astrotheology* of Young. Astronomical observations were thought to bring about sublime

---

22. See Maier's essay.
23. Cf. the essay by Tom Olbricht in this volume.

mediating experiences, "a converting experience of deity." The vastness of astronomical observations caused people to be seized by the notion that God exists. This kind of sublimity, when perceived by those morally prepared for it, led to "moral and religious improvement."[24] This is reminiscent, of course, of Pss 19:1; 50:6; 97:6. According to Young, the astronomical sublime, the starry night sky for example, has authority "as God's 'first volume,' an 'elder Scripture, writ by GOD'S own hand.'"[25] The sublime astronomical thereby indicates how the Bible should be read and interpreted. The sublime becomes "the illuminator of scripture." This reverses the relationship between scripture and creation. Unlike John Calvin and Thomas Aquinas and more like John Wesley, the sublime experience was perceived to have authority in the way it seizes and transports the mind.

Gregory contrasts Young's views with those of Burke, Dennis, Lowth, and Blair, who, in varying degrees, considered sublime terror to have a transporting effect on people. For Burke, "since terror is the root of sublime experience and God appears to our minds, first and foremost, as infinite and, therefore, immeasurably terrible power, sublime feeling is produced wherever human beings have a religiously adequate idea of God." Terror prevents "lassitude" (but see 2 Tim 1:7). For Dennis, terror has "pride of place," is "irresistible," and "drives out all rivals." As Gregory points out, "The religious privilege given to the sublime identifies terror and similar reactions to power, including astonishment, as basic in our knowledge of God. Correspondingly, God is known, first and foremost as 'a force which nothing can withstand.'" Faith and faithfulness are generated and driven by putting fear and judgment in people's hearts and bodies. Terror is employed, we might say, to scare the hell out of people rather than proclaim good news as indicated in the New Testament. This approach, of course, persists in some places: first you frighten people to get them in; then you keep them terrorized to keep them in.[26]

---

24. Apparently, contra Kant who claimed the sublime is "of the mind" (as in Robbins's essay).

25. Edward Young, *Young's Night Thoughts; or, Thoughts on Life, Death, and Immortality* (New York: Worthington, 1889), l. 646.

26. A literary example of this abusive tradition is observed in James Joyce's famous novel, *A Portrait of the Artist as a Young Man*: "The faint glimmer of fear became a terror of spirit as the hoarse voice of the preacher blew death into his soul. He suffered in its agony.... The unjust he casts from Him, crying in His offended majesty: *Depart from me, ye cursed, into everlasting fire which was prepared for the devil and his angels.*"

In the end, Gregory points to how the "prodigious force" of the sublime of the eighteenth century led to the graphic horror presented in John Martin's 1853 painting of *The Last Judgement*. Cataclysm is the central motif. There is no good news here, only the fear of judgment, the horror of the descent to flames and suffering and to separation from all that is imagined to be good. There is no Christology, no gospel, no comfort from the scriptures, nothing of the love of God. There is only the sublimity of terror. Gregory shows us that the sublime became sublimed, that the rhetorical force of words of texts became "obscured" and was replaced by power.

Friend or enemy? Sublime terror can function both ways. The essays in part 2 of this volume point to this paradox. Words and visualizations artistically and subtly arouse terror. The sublime terror might move one to the goodness of wisdom or to the evil of destructiveness. It can be righteously persuasive or unrighteously coercive. It might move people toward faith or, perhaps perversely, away from it. The sublime shapes minds and bodies, reconfiguring them as it and they go along. Sublime terror is not only created, it creates and re-creates. This is its rhetorical force. This sublimity is at the heart of what rhetoric is about—creating dispositions of mind, emotions, physiological responses that, rather than producing rationalized understanding, transport them to new realities. Sublime terror is a texture that SRI calls an *arrangement* or *interweaving* of threads that, along with other threads and textures forms a tapestry. A text as tapestry is "a thick network of meanings and meaning effects that an interpreter can explore by moving through the text from different perspectives."[27] The explorations of sublime terror in a broad sweep from 1 Enoch (300–100 BCE) to Revelation to Ignatius of Antioch (early second century CE) to the eighteenth century demonstrate that this texture is equally as important, perhaps sometimes more important, than determining things in rational, linear, tightly defined ways. Not everything is categorical cause and effect. It is reasonable to trust in many things that we understand only in partial ways or do not understand at all. Terror reveals unexpected insights. It evokes movement not practiced otherwise. Sublime terror texture surprises, and its existence means that it's not over yet.

James Joyce, *A Portrait of the Artist as a Young Man* (New York: Viking, 1962), 111, 135, emphasis original.

27. Jeal, *Exploring Philemon*, xxviii.

Bibliography

Addison, Joseph, and Richard Steele. *Selections from "The Tatler" and "The Spectator."* Penguin Classics. London: Penguin, 1988.

Aiken, John, and Anna Letitia Aiken. "On the Pleasure Derived from Objects of Terror; With Sir Bertrand, a Fragment." Pages 117–37 in *Miscellaneous Pieces in Prose*. Belfast: Magee, 1774.

Agnew, Lois. "The Civic Function of Taste: A Re-assessment of Hugh Blair's Rhetorical Theory." *RSQ* 28 (1998): 25–36.

Aristotle. *The Art of Rhetoric*. Translated by J. H. Freese. LCL. Harvard: Harvard University Press, 1926.

Aune, David E. *Revelation*. 3 vols. WBC 52A, 52B, 52C. Dallas: Word, 1998.

Auerbach, Erich. *Mimesis: The Representation of Reality in Western Literature*. Translated by Willard R. Trask. Princeton: Princeton University Press, 1974.

Baillie, John. *An Essay on the Sublime*. London: Dodsley, 1747.

Barbeau, Jeffrey W., ed. *Coleridge's Assertion of Religion: Essays on the "Opus Maximum."* StPT 33. Leuven: Peeters, 2006.

Barfield, Owen. *What Coleridge Thought*. London: Oxford University Press, 1972.

Barnes, Timothy D. "The Date of Ignatius." *ExpTim* 120 (2008): 119–30.

Barth, Markus. *Ephesians*. 2 vols. AB 34, 34A. Garden City, NY: Doubleday, 1974.

Battersby, Christine. "Terror, Terrorism and the Sublime: Rethinking the Sublime after 1789 and 2001." *Postcolonial Studies* 6 (2003): 67–89.

Baumgarten, Alexander Gottlieb. *Aesthetica*. Frankfurt an der Oder: Kleyb, 1750.

Bauckham, Richard. "The Worship of Jesus in Apocalyptic Christianity." *NTS* 27 (1981): 322–41.

Beecher, Henry Ward. *Lectures to Young Men: On Various Important Subjects: New Edition with Additional Lectures.* Boston: Ticknor & Fields, 1868.

Bernard, J. H. "Translator's Introduction." Pages xiii–xxxv in *Critique of Judgement.* By Immanuel Kant. Hafner Library of Classics. New York: Hafner, 1951.

Bitzer, Lloyd F. "The Rhetorical Situation." *Philosophy and Rhetoric* 1 (1968): 1–14.

Blair, Hugh. *Lectures on Rhetoric and Belle Lettres.* 2 vols. London: Strahan & Cadell; Edinburgh: Creech, 1783.

———. *Lectures on Rhetoric and Belles Lettres.* 2nd ed. 3 vols. London: Strahan & Cadell; Edinburgh: Creech, 1785.

Bloom, Harold, ed., *William Wordsworth's, "The Prelude."* Modern Critical Interpretations. New York: Chelsea House, 1986.

Blount, Brian K. *Revelation: A Commentary.* NTL. Louisville: Westminster John Knox, 2009.

Boileau-Despréaux, Nicolas. *Oeuvres diverses du Sieur D*** avec le traité Du Sublime ou Du Merveilleux dans le discours, traduit du Grec de Longin.* Paris: Billaine, 1674.

Boring, M. Eugene *Revelation.* IBC. Louisville: Westminster John Knox, 1989.

Brady, Emily. "The Environmental Sublime." Pages 171–82 in *The Sublime: From Antiquity to the Present.* Edited by Timothy M. Costelloe. Cambridge: Cambridge University Press, 2012.

———. *The Sublime in Modern Philosophy: Aesthetics, Ethics, and Nature.* Cambridge: Cambridge University Press, 2013.

Bremmer, Jan N. "The Place, Date, and Author of the Ignatian Letters: An Onomastic Approach." Pages 405–34 in *Das Baujahr hinter der Fassade: Probleme bei der Datierung neutestamentlicher Pseudepigraphen und neuere Lösungsansätze.* Edited by Wolfgang Grünstäudl and Karl Matthias Schmidt. WUNT470. Tübingen: Mohr Siebeck, 2021.

Brent, Allen. *Ignatius of Antioch: A Martyr Bishop and the Origin of the Episcopacy.* London: T&T Clark, 2009.

———. *Ignatius of Antioch and the Second Sophistic.* STAC 36. Tübingen: Mohr Siebeck, 2006.

Brigance, William Norwood. *Speech Composition.* New York: Crofts, 1937.

Brown, Raymond E. *The Birth of the Messiah: A Commentary on the Infancy Narratives in Matthew and Luke.* ABRL. New York: Doubleday, 1993.

Burke, Edmund. *A Philosophical Enquiry into the Origin of Our Ideas of the Sublime and Beautiful.* Edited by James T. Boulton. Oxford: Blackwell, 1987.

———. *A Philosophical Enquiry into the Origin of Our Ideas of the Sublime and Beautiful: And Other Pre-revolutionary Writings.* Edited by David Womersley. New York: Penguin, 1998.

Burke, Kenneth. *A Rhetoric of Motives.* Berkeley: University of California Press, 1969.

Calvin, John. *Genesis 1–11.* Edited by John L. Thompson. Reformation Commentary on Scripture 1. Downers Grove, IL: IVP Academic, 2012.

Campbell, George. *The Philosophy of Rhetoric.* New ed. 2 vols. Edinburgh: Creech, 1808.

———. *Philosophy of Rhetoric.* Edited with an introduction by Lloyd F. Bitzer. Carbondale: Southern Illinois University Press, 1988.

Campbell, Ted A. *The Religion of the Heart: Study of European Religious Life in the Seventeenth and Eighteenth Centuries.* Columbia: University of South Carolina Press, 1991.

Canuel, Mark. *Justice, Dissent, and the Sublime.* Baltimore: Johns Hopkins University Press, 2012.

Caplan, Harry. *[Cicero] Rhetorica ad Herennium.* LCL. Cambridge: Harvard University Press, 1954.

Charland, Louis C. "Reinstating the Passions: Arguments from the History of Psychopathology." Pages 237–60 in *The Oxford Handbook of Philosophy of Emotion.* Edited by Peter Goldie. Oxford: Oxford University Press, 2012.

Clarke, Michael. "Sublime." Pages 238–39 in *The Concise Oxford Dictionary of Art Terms.* 2nd ed. Oxford: Oxford University Press, 2010.

Clewis, Robert R., ed. *The Sublime Reader.* London: Bloomsbury Academic, 2019.

Cohick, Lynn H. *Ephesians: A New Covenant Commentary.* Cambridge: Lutterworth, 2013.

Conrad, Joseph. *Heart of Darkness.* Blackwood's Magazine, 1902. https://tinyurl.com/SBL4831a.

Coleridge, Samuel Taylor. *The Collected Works of Samuel Taylor Coleridge.* 16 vols. Bollingen Series. Princeton: Princeton University Press, 1969–2002.

———. *The Notebooks of Samuel Taylor Coleridge.* Edited by Kathleen Coburn. 3 vols. London: Routledge & Kegan Paul, 1962–1973.

———. *The Notebooks of Samuel Taylor Coleridge, Vol. 5: 1827–1834*. Edited by Kathleen Coburn and Anthony John Harding. Bollingen Series 50. Princeton: Princeton University Press, 2002.

Costelloe, Timothy M. "The Sublime: A Short Introduction to a Long History." Pages 1–10 in *The Sublime: From Antiquity to the Present*. Edited by Timothy M. Costelloe. Cambridge: Cambridge University Press, 2012.

———, ed. *The Sublime: From Antiquity to the Present*. Cambridge: Cambridge University Press, 2012.

Craske, Matthew. *Art in Europe, 1700–1830: A History of the Visual Arts in an Era of Unprecedented Urban Economic Growth*. Oxford History of Art. Oxford: Oxford University Press, 1997.

Crockett, Clayton. *A Theology of the Sublime*. London: Routledge, 2001.

Daniels, Stephen, and Lucy Veale. "Revealing Repton: Bringing Landscape to Life at Sheringham." *Landscape Research* 40 (2005): 5–22.

Das, A. Andrew. *Paul and the Jews*. Library of Pauline Studies. Peabody, MA: Hendrickson, 2003.

———. *Solving the Romans Debate*. Minneapolis: Fortress, 2007.

De Bolla, Peter. *The Education of the Eye: Painting, Landscape, and Architecture in Eighteenth-Century Britain*. Stanford: Stanford University Press, 2003.

Dennis, John. *The Advancement and Reformation of Modern Poetry: A Critical Discourse; In Two Parts*. London: Parker, 1701.

———. *The Grounds of Criticism in Poetry: Contain'd in Some New Discoveries Never Made before, Requisite for the Writing and Judging of Poems Surely*. London: Strahan, 1704.

Derham, William. *Physico-Theology: Or a Demonstration of the Being and Attributes of God from His Works of Creation, Being the Substance of Sixteen Sermons Preached in St Mary-Le-Bow-Church, London, as the Honourable Mr Boyle's Lectures, in the Years 1711 and 1712*. Boyle Lectures. London: Innys, 1723.

Dodd, C. H. *The Epistle to the Romans*. London: Hodder & Stoughton, 1932.

Dodds, E. R. *The Greeks and the Irrational*. Berkeley: University of California Press, 1951.

Doerr, Anthony. *All the Light We Cannot See*. New York: Scribner, 2014.

Doran, Robert. *The Theory of the Sublime from Longinus to Kant*. Cambridge: Cambridge University Press, 2015.

Dunn, James D. G. *Romans 1–8*. WBC 38A. Dallas: Word, 1988.
Dyer, Bryan R. *Suffering in the Face of Death: The Epistle to the Hebrews in Its Context of Situation*. LNTS 568. London: Bloomsbury T&T Clark, 2017.
Edwards, Mark J. "Ignatius and the Second Century: An Answer to R. Hübner." *ZAC* 2 (1998): 214–26.
Evans, Donald D. *The Logic of Self-Involvement*. London: SCM, 1963.
Evans, Murray J. "Coleridge's Sublime and Langland's Subject in the Pardon Scene of *Piers Plowman*." Pages 155–74 in *From Arabye to Engelond: Medieval Studies in Honour of Mahmoud Manzalaoui on His Seventy-Fifth Birthday*. Edited by A. E. Christa Canitz and Gernot R. Wieland. Actexpress. Ottawa: University of Ottawa, 1999.
———. *Coleridge's Sublime Later Prose and Recent Theory: Kristeva, Adorno, Rancière*. New York: Palgrave Macmillan, 2023.
———. "C.S. Lewis and Coleridge, Revisited: *The Abolition of Man*." Pages 42–56 in *The Inklings and Culture: A Harvest of Scholarship from the Inklings Institute of Canada*. Edited by Monika B. Hilder, Sara L. Pearson, and Laura N. Van Dyke. Newcastle upon Tyne: Cambridge Scholars Publishing, 2020.
———. *Rereading Middle English Romance: Manuscript Layout, Decoration, and the Rhetoric of Composite Structure*. Kingston: McGill-Queen's University Press, 1995.
———. *Sublime Coleridge: The "Opus Maximum."* New York: Palgrave Macmillan, 2012.
———. "Sublime Discourse and Romantic Religion in Coleridge's *Aids to Reflection*." *Wordsworth Circle* 47 (2016): 27–31.
Faflak, Joel. *Romantic Psychoanalysis: The Burden of the Mystery*. Albany: State University of New York Press, 2008.
Ferguson, Francis. "A Commentary on Susan Guerlac's 'Longinus and the Subject of the Sublime.'" *New Literary History* 16 (1985): 291–97.
Flaubert, Gustave. *Bouvard et Pécuchet*. Paris: Lemerre, 1881.
Forsey, Jane. "Is a Theory of the Sublime Possible?" Pages 1–16 in *The Possibility of the Sublime: Aesthetic Exchanges*. Edited by Lars Aagaard-Mogenson. Cambridge: Cambridge Scholars Press, 2017.
Fredriksen, Paula. "Judaism, the Circumcision of Gentiles, and Apocalyptic Hope: Another Look at Galatians 1 and 2." *JTS* 422 (1991): 532–64.
———. "Why Should a 'Law-Free' Mission Mean a 'Law-Free' Apostle?" *JBL* 134 (2015): 637–50.

Frank, David. "Arguing with God, Talmudic Discourse, and the Jewish Countermodel: Implications for the Study of Argumentation." *Argumentation and Advocacy* 41 (2004): 71–86.

———. "Engaging a Rhetorical God: Developing the Capacities of Mercy and Justice." Pages 51–76 in *Responding to the Sacred: An Inquiry into the Limits of Rhetoric*. Edited by Michael Bernard-Donals and Kyle Jensen. University Park: Pennsylvania State University Press, 2021.

Gager, John G. *Moses in Greco-Roman Paganism*. Nashville: Abingdon, 1972.

Gaudio, Michael. "At the Mouth of the Cave: Listening to Thomas Cole's *Kaaterskill Falls*." *Art History* 33 (2010): 448–65.

Gaventa, Beverly Roberts. *Mary: Glimpses of the Mother of Jesus*. Columbia: University of South Carolina Press, 1995.

Gigerenzer, Gerd. *Gut Feelings: The Intelligence of the Unconscious*. London: Penguin, 2007.

Godolphin, F. R. B. "The Basic Critical Doctrine of 'Longinus,' *On the Sublime*." *TAPA* 68 (1937): 172–83.

Golden, James L., and Edward P. J. Corbett. *The Rhetoric of Blair, Campbell, and Whately*. Carbondale: Southern Illinois University Press, 1990.

Gombis, Timothy O. *The Drama of Ephesians: Participating in the Triumph of God*. Downers Grove, IL: IVP Academic, 2010.

Goodspeed, Edgar J. *The Meaning of Ephesians*. Chicago: University of Chicago Press, 1933.

Gotlieb, Marc. "Sublime." In *Encyclopedia of Aesthetics*. Edited by Michael Kelly. 2nd ed. Online ed. Oxford: Oxford University Press, 2014.

Green, Joel B. *The Gospel of Luke*. NICNT. Grand Rapids: Eerdmans, 1997.

Gregory, Alan P. R. *Coleridge and the Conservative Imagination*. Macon, GA: Mercer University Press, 2003.

———. "Coleridge's Higher Sublime?" *Coleridge Bulletin* NS 38 (2011): 100–105.

———. "Philosophy and Religion." Pages 107–8 in *Romanticism: An Oxford Guide*. Edited by Nicholas Roe. Oxford: Oxford University Press, 2005.

———. *Science Fiction Theology: Beauty and the Transformation of the Sublime*. Waco, TX: Baylor University Press, 2015.

Griffiths, Jonathan I. *Hebrews and Divine Speech*. LNTS 507. London: Bloomsbury T&T Clark, 2014.

Grube, G. M. A. "Notes on the ΠΕΡΙ ΥΨΟΥΣ." *AJP* 18 (1957): 355–74.

Güting, Eberhard, and David L. Mealand. *Asyndeton in Paul: A Text-Critical and Statistical Enquiry into Pauline Style*. Lewiston, NY: Mellen, 1998.
Hagaman, John. "On Campbell's 'Philosophy of Rhetoric' and Its Relevance to Contemporary Invention." *RSQ* 3 (1981): 145–54.
Hall, Robert G. "Paul, Classical Rhetoric, and Oracular Fullness of Meaning in Romans 1:16–17." Pages 163–85 in *Paul and Ancient Rhetoric: Theory and Practice in the Hellenistic Context*. Edited by Stanley E. Porter and Bryan R. Dyer. Cambridge: Cambridge University Press, 2016.
Halmi, Nicholas. "Coleridge on Allegory and Symbol." Pages 345–58 in *The Oxford Handbook of Samuel Taylor Coleridge*. Edited by Frederick Burwick. Oxford: Oxford University Press, 2009.
Halmi, Nicholas, Paul Magnuson, and Raimonda Modiano, eds. *Coleridge's Poetry and Prose: Authoritative Texts, Criticism*. Norton Critical Edition. New York: Norton, 2004.
Heath, Malcolm. "Longinus and the Ancient Sublime." Pages 11–23 in *The Sublime: From Antiquity to the Present*. Edited by Timothy M. Costelloe. Cambridge: Cambridge University Press, 2012.
———. "Longinus, *On Sublimity*." *PCPS* NS 45 (1999): 43–74.
Hendrix, John Shannon. *Unconscious Thought in Philosophy and Psychoanalysis*. London: Palgrave Macmillan, 2015.
Hertz, Neil, ed. *The End of the Line: Essays on Psychoanalysis and the Sublime*. New York: Columbia University Press, 1985.
Hester, J. David. "The Wuellnerian Sublime." Pages 3–22 in *Rhetorics and Hermeneutics: Wilhelm Wuellner and His Influence*. Edited by James D. Hester and J. David Hester. ESEC 9. London: T&T Clark, 2004.
Hester, James D., and J. David Hester, eds. *Rhetorics and Hermeneutics: Wilhelm Wuellner and His Influence*. ESEC 9. London: T&T Clark, 2004.
———. "The Contribution of Wilhelm Wuellner to New Testament Rhetorical Criticism." Pages 93–126 in *Genealogies of New Testament Rhetorical Criticism*. Edited by Troy W. Martin. Minneapolis: Fortress, 2014.
Hill, James J. "The Aesthetic Principles of the *Peri Hupsous*." *JHI* 27 (1966): 265–74.
Hill, John. *An Account of the Life and Writings of Hugh Blair*. Edinburgh: Ballantyne, 1807.

Holmes, Christopher T. *The Function of Sublime Rhetoric in Hebrews: A Study in Hebrews 12:18–29*. WUNT 2/465. Tübingen: Mohr Siebeck, 2018.

———. "(Religious) Language and the Decentering Process: McNamara and *De sublimitate* on the Ecstatic Effect of Language." *JCH* 2 (2015): 53–65.

Holmes, Michael W. *The Apostolic Fathers: Greek Texts and English Translations*. 3rd ed. Grand Rapids: Baker Academic, 2007.

Holmes, Richard. *Coleridge*. Oxford: Oxford University Press, 1982.

———. *Coleridge: Darker Reflections*. London: Harper Collins, 1998.

———. *Coleridge: Early Visions, 1772–1804*. London: Penguin, 1990.

Howell, Wilbur Samuel. *Eighteenth Century British Logic and Rhetoric*. Princeton: Princeton University Press, 1971.

———. *Logic and Rhetoric in England, 1500–1700*. Princeton: Princeton University Press, 1956.

Hübner, Reinhard. *Der Paradox Eine: Antignostischer Monarchianismus im zweiten Jahrhundert; Mit einem Beitrag von Markus Vinzent*. VCSup 50. Leiden: Brill, 1999.

Hugo, Victor. *Les Misérables*. Penguin Classics. London: Penguin, 1982.

Ingersoll, Robert. *The Works of Robert Green Ingersoll*. 12 vols. New York: Dresden Publishing, 1900.

Innes, Doreen C. "Longinus and Caecilius: Models of the Sublime." *Mnemosyne* 4th series 55 (2002): 259–84.

Jeal, Roy R. "Creative Development: Blended Discourse in Colossians." Paper presented at the virtual Annual Meeting of the Society of Biblical Literature. Boston, MA, 7 December 2020.

———. *Exploring Philemon: Freedom, Brotherhood, and Partnership in the New Society*. RRA 2. Atlanta: SBL Press, 2015.

———. *Integrating Theology and Ethics in Ephesians: The Ethos of Communication*. Studies in the Bible and Early Christianity 43. Lewiston, NY: Mellen, 2000.

———. "Visual Interpretation: Blending Rhetorical Arts in Colossians 2:6–3:4." Pages 55–87 in *The Art of Visual Exegesis: Rhetoric, Texts, Images*. Edited by Vernon K. Robbins, Walter S. Melion, and Roy R. Jeal. ESEC 19. Atlanta: SBL Press, 2017.

Jewett, Robert. *Romans: A Commentary*. Hermeneia. Minneapolis: Fortress, 2007.

Jipp, Joshua W. "The Son's Entrance into the Heavenly World: The Soteriological Necessity of the Scriptural Catena in Hebrews 1.5–14." *NTS* 56 (2010): 557–75.

Jonge, Casper C. de. "Dionysius and Longinus on the Sublime: Rhetoric and Religious Language." *AJP* 133 (2012): 271–300.

Joyce, James. *A Portrait of the Artist as a Young Man*. New York: Viking, 1962.

Kahneman, Daniel. *Thinking Fast and Slow*. New York: Farrar, Strauss & Giroux, 2011.

Kant, Immanuel. "B. Of the Dynamically Sublime in Nature, Second Book: *Analytic of the Sublime*; From *Critique of Judgment*." Pages 266–71 in *The Critical Tradition: Classic Texts and Contemporary Trends*. Edited by David H. Richter. New York: St. Martin's Press, 1989.

———. *Critique of Judgement*. Hafner Library of Classics. New York: Hafner, 1951.

———. *Observations on the Feeling of the Beautiful and Sublime*. Translated by John T. Goldthwait. Berkeley: University of California Press, 1960.

Keck, Leander E. "*Pathos* in Romans? Mostly Preliminary Remarks." Pages 71–96 in *Paul and Pathos*. Edited by Thomas H. Olbricht and Jerry L. Sumney. SymS 16. Atlanta: Society of Biblical Literature, 2001.

Keefe, Rosaleen Greene-Smith. "'A Peculiar Power of Perception': Scottish Enlightenment Rhetoric and the New Aesthetic of Language." PhD diss., University of Rhode Island, 2016.

Kelhoffer, James A. "Persecution, Perseverance, and Perfection in Hebrews." Pages 127–42 in *Persecution, Persuasion, and Power: Readiness to Withstand Hardship as a Corroboration of Legitimacy in the New Testament*. WUNT 1/270. Tübingen: Mohr Siebeck, 2010.

Kennedy, George A. *New Testament Interpretation through Rhetorical Criticism*. Chapel Hill: University of North Carolina Press, 1984.

Kirwan, James. *Sublimity: The Non-rational and the Rational in the History of Aesthetics*. New York: Routledge, 2005.

Koester, Craig R. "Conversion, Persecution, and Malaise: Life in the Community for Which Hebrews Was Written." *HvTSt* 61 (2005): 231–51.

———. *Hebrews: A New Translation with Introduction and Commentary*. AB 36. New York: Doubleday, 2001.

Korn, Marianne. *Ezra Pound: Purpose, Form, Meaning*. London: Pembridge, 1983.

Kristeva, Julia. *This Incredible Need to Believe*. Translated by Beverley Bie Brahic. New York: Columbia University Press, 2009.

Lake, Kirsopp. *The Apostolic Fathers*. 2 vols. LCL. Cambridge: Harvard University Press, 1977.
Lacoue-Labarthe, Philippe. "Sublime." In *Encyclopædia Universalis*. Online ed. Paris, 2004.
Lagière, Anne. *La Thébaïde de Stace et le sublime*. Brussels: Latomus, 2017.
Lampe, Peter. *From Paul to Valentinus: Christian at Rome in the First Two Centuries*. Translated by Michael G. Steinhauser. Minneapolis: Fortress, 2003.
———. "Paul and the Church's Unity with Israel." Pages 64–66 in *Unity of the Church in the New Testament and Today*. Edited by Lukas Vischer, Ulrich Luz, and Christian Link. Translated by J. E. Crouch. Grand Rapids: Eerdmans, 2010.
Lanham, Richard A. *Handlist of Rhetorical Terms: A Guide for Students of English Literature*. Berkeley, University of California Press, 1968.
Légasse, Simon. *L'épître de Paul aux Romains*. LD 10. Paris: Cerf, 2002.
Leuchner, Thomas. *Ignatius adversus Valentinianos? Chronologische und theologiegeschichtliche Studien zu den Briefen des Ignatius von Antiochien*. VCSup 47. Leiden: Brill, 1999.
Lewis, C. S. *The Discarded Image: An Introduction to Medieval and Renaissance Literature*. Cambridge: Cambridge University Press, 1971.
Lindars, Barnabas. "The Rhetorical Structure of Hebrews." *NTS* 35 (1989): 382–406.
Livesey, Nina E. *Galatians and the Rhetoric of Crisis: Paul—Demosthenes—Cicero*. Salem, OR: Polebridge, 2016.
Locke, John. *An Essay Concerning Human Understanding*. Penguin Classics. London: Penguin, 2004.
Long, Thomas G. *Hebrews*. IBC. Louisville: Westminster John Knox, 1997.
Longinus. *On Great Writing (On the Sublime)*. Translated with an introduction by G. M. A. Grube. Indianapolis: Hackett, 1991.
———. *On the Sublime*. Translated by W. H. Fyfe. Revised by Donald Russell. LCL. Cambridge: Harvard University Press, 1995.
———. *On the Sublime*. Pages 77–102 in *Critical Theory Since Plato*. Revised by Hazard Adams. New York: Harcourt Brace Jovanovich, 1971.
Lotz, John-Paul. *Ignatius and Concord: The Background and Use of the Language of Concord in the Letters of Ignatius of Antioch*. PatSt 8. Frankfurt am Main: Lang, 2007.
Louw, Johannes P., and Eugene A. Nida, eds. *Greek-English Lexicon of the New Testament Based on Semantic Domains*. 2nd ed. New York: United Bible Societies, 1989.

Lowth, Robert. *Lectures on the Sacred Poetry of the Hebrews; Translated from the Latin of the Right Rev. Robert Lowth ... By G. Gregory ... to Which Are Added the Principals of Professor Michaelis, by the Translator and Others.* London: Johnson, 1753.

Lyotard, Jean-François. *Lessons on the Analytic of the Sublime.* Translated by Elizabeth Rottenberg. Stanford, CA: Stanford University Press, 1994.

———. "The Sublime and the Avant-Garde"; "Newman: The Instant." Pages 196–211, 240–49 in *The Lyotard Reader.* Edited by Andrew Benjamin. Oxford: Blackwell, 1989.

Mack, Burton L. *Rhetoric and the New Testament.* GBS. Minneapolis: Fortress, 1990.

Mader, Thomas F. "On Presence in Rhetoric." *College Composition and Communication* 24 (1973): 375–81.

Maier, Harry O. "Paul, Imperial Situation, and Visualization in the Epistle to the Colossians." Pages 171–94 in *The Art of Visual Exegesis: Rhetoric, Texts, Images.* Edited by Vernon K. Robbins, Walter S. Melion, and Roy R. Jeal. ESEC 19. Atlanta: SBL Press, 2017.

———. "The Politics of the Silent Bishop: Silence and Persuasion in Ignatius of Antioch." *JTS* NS 55 (2004): 503–19.

———. *The Social Setting of the Ministry as Reflected in the Writings of Hermas, Clement, and Ignatius.* SCJud 12. Waterloo: Wilfrid Laurier University Press, 2002.

Makkreel, Rudolf A. *Imagination and Interpretation in Kant: The Hermeneutical Import of the "Critique of Judgment."* Chicago: University of Chicago Press, 1990.

———. "Imagination and Temporality in Kant's Theory of the Sublime." *Journal of Aesthetics and Art Criticism* 42 (1984): 303–15.

Marshall, John W. "From Small Words: Reading Deixis and Scope in Romans." *JJMJS* 4 (2017): 1–20.

Martin, Troy W., ed. *Genealogies of New Testament Rhetorical Criticism.* Minneapolis: Fortress, 2014.

Maté, Gabor. *When the Body Says No: The Cost of Hidden Stress.* Toronto: Vintage Canada, 2004.

Minear, Paul S. *The Obedience of Faith: The Purposes of Paul in the Epistle to the Romans.* London: SCM, 1971.

Modiano, Raimonda. *Coleridge and the Concept of Nature.* Tallahassee: Florida State University Press, 1985.

———. "Coleridge and the Sublime: A Response to Thomas Weiskel's *The Romantic Sublime.*" *Wordsworth Circle* 9 (1978): 110–20.

Monk, Samuel Holt. *The Sublime: A Study of Critical Theories in Eighteenth-Century England.* Ann Arbor: University of Michigan Press, 1960.

Moo, Douglas. *The Epistle to the Romans.* NICNT. Grand Rapids: Eerdmans, 1996.

Moran, Michael, ed. *Eighteenth Century British and American Rhetorics and Rhetoricians: Critical Studies and Sources.* Westport, CT: Greenwood, 1994.

Morris, David B. *Religious Sublime: Christian Poetry and Critical Tradition in Eighteenth-Century England.* Lexington: University Press of Kentucky, 1982.

Mortensen, Klaus P. *The Time of Unrememberable Being: Wordsworth and The Sublime, 1787–1805.* Translated by W. Glyn Jones. Copenhagen: Museum Tusculanum, 1998.

Moss, Candida. *Ancient Christian Martyrdom: Diverse Practices, Theologies, and Traditions.* ABRL New Haven: Yale University Press, 2012.

Muir, John. "A Wind-Storm in the Forest." Pages 244–57 in *The Mountains of California.* New York: Century, 1894.

Murray, Bradley. "David Hume, On the Standard of Taste (pdf)." 2014. https://tinyurl.com/SBL4831g.

———. "Immanuel Kant, Critique of Judgment (pdf)." 2014. https://tinyurl.com/SBL4831f.

Mutschmann, Hermann. "Das Genesiscitat in der Schrift ΠΕΡΙ ΥΨΟΥΣ." *Hermes* 52 (1917): 161–200.

Myrone, Martin, ed. *John Martin: Apocalypse.* London: Tate, 2011.

Nicolson, Marjorie Hope. *Mountain Gloom and Mountain Glory: The Development of the Aesthetics of the Infinite.* Seattle: University of Washington Press, 1997.

Nickelsburg, George W. E. *1 Enoch 1: A Commentary on the Book of 1 Enoch, Chapters 1–36; 81–108.* Hermeneia. Minneapolis: Fortress, 2001.

Nickelsburg, George W. E., and James C. VanderKam. *1 Enoch 2: A Commentary on the Book of 1 Enoch, Chapters 37–82.* Hermeneia. Minneapolis: Fortress, 2012.

Nolland, John. *Luke 1–9:20.* WBC 35A. Dallas: Word, 1989.

Norden, Eduard. *Das Genesiszitat in der Schrift vom "Erhabenen."* Berlin: Akademie, 1955.

Nye, David E. *American Technological Sublime*. Cambridge: Massachusetts Institute of Technology, 1996.
Nygren, Edward J. *James Ward's Gordale Scar, An Essay in the Sublime*. London: Tate Gallery, 1982.
O'Gorman, Ned. "Longinus's Sublime Rhetoric, or How Rhetoric Came into Its Own." *RSQ* 34.2 (2004): 71–89.
Olbricht, Thomas H. "The Flowering of Rhetorical Criticism in America." Pages 79–102 in *The Rhetorical Analysis of Scripture: Essays from the 1995 London Conference*. Edited by Stanley E. Porter and Thomas H. Olbricht. JSNTSup 146. Sheffield: Sheffield Academic, 1997.
———. "The Foundations of Ethos in Paul and in the Classical Rhetoricians." Pages 138–59 in *Rhetoric, Ethic and Moral Persuasion in Biblical Discourse*. Edited by Thomas H. Olbricht and Anders Eriksson. ESEC 11. New York: T&T Clark, 2005.
———. *Informative Speaking*. Glenview, IL: Scott-Foresman, 1968.
———. "Response to James D. Hester and J. David Hester: A Personal Reflection." Pages 127–31 in *Genealogies of New Testament Rhetorical Criticism*. Edited by Troy W. Martin. Minneapolis: Fortress, 2014.
———. "Wuellner and the Promise of Rhetoric." Pages 78–104 in *Rhetorics and Hermeneutics: Wilhelm Wuellner and His Influence*. Edited by James D. Hester and J. David Hester. ESEC 9. London: T&T Clark, 2004.
Olbricht, Thomas H., and Jerry L. Sumney, eds. *Paul and Pathos*. SymS 16. Atlanta: Society of Biblical Literature, 2001.
Oravec, Christine L. "Sublime." Pages 757–61 in *Encyclopedia of Rhetoric*. Edited by Thomas O. Sloane. Oxford: Oxford University Press, 2001.
Otto, Rudolph. *The Idea of the Holy: An Inquiry into the Non-rational Factor in the Idea of the Divine and Its Relation to the Rational*. Oxford: Oxford University Press, 1959.
Perelman, Chaim, and Lucie Olbrechts-Tyteca. *The New Rhetoric: A Treatise on Argumentation*. Translated by John Wilkinson and Purcell Weaver. Notre Dame: University of Notre Dame Press, 1969.
Paley, Morton D. *Coleridge's Later Poetry*. Oxford: Clarendon, 1996.
Pernot, Laurent. *La Rhétorique dans l'Antiquité*. Paris: Librairie Générale Française, 2000.
———. "The Rhetoric of Religion." *Rhetorica* 24 (2006): 235–54.
Perler, Othmar. "Das vierte Makkabäerbuch, Ignatius von Antiochien und die ältesten Märtyrerberichte." *Rivista di archeologia cristiana* 25 (1949): 47–72.

Phibbs, John. *Place-Making: The Art of Capability Brown*. Swindon: Historic England, 2017.

Piehler, Paul. *The Visionary Landscape: A Study in Medieval Allegory*. London: Arnold, 1971.

Pirius, Rebecca. "Auto Theft Laws in Georgia." Criminal Defense Lawyer. 22 December 2020. https://tinyurl.com/SBL4831h.

Placher, William C. *The Domestication of Transcendence: How Modern Thinking about God Went Wrong*. Louisville: Westminster John Knox, 1996.

Pope, Alexander. *The Rape of the Lock and Other Major Writings*. Edited by Leo Damrosch. Penguin Classics. London: Penguin, 2011.

Porter, James I. "Lucretius and the Sublime." Pages 167–84 in *The Cambridge Companion to Lucretius*. Edited by Stuart Gillespie and Philip Hardie. Cambridge: Cambridge University Press, 2007.

———. *The Sublime in Antiquity*. Cambridge: Cambridge University Press, 2016.

Porter, Stanley E. *The Letter to the Romans: A Linguistic and Literary Commentary*. New Testament Monographs 37. Sheffield: Sheffield Phoenix, 2015.

Pound, Ezra. *How to Read*. New York: Haskell House, 1971.

Radcliffe, Ann. *The Mysteries of Udolpho*. Pages 221–527 in *Complete Novels of Mrs. Ann Radcliffe*. London: Folio Society, 1987.

Ray, John. *The Wisdom of God Manifested in the Works of Creation*. 2nd ed. London: Smith, 1692.

———. *Three Physico-Theological Discourses*. 2nd ed. London: Smith, 1693.

Reid, Nicholas. *Coleridge, Form and Symbol: Or the Ascertaining Vision*. London: Ashgate, 2005.

Richards, I. A. *Practical Criticism*. New York: Harcourt, Brace, 1929.

Richardson, Cyril C., trans. *Early Christian Fathers*. LCC 1. Philadelphia: Westminster, 1953.

Riesenfeld, Harald. "Reflections on the Style and the Theology of St. Ignatius of Antioch." *StPatr* 4/*TU* 79 (1961): 312–22.

Robbins, Vernon K. *Exploring the Textures of Texts: A Guide to Socio-rhetorical Interpretation*. Valley Forge, PA: Trinity Press International, 1996.

———. *The Invention of Christian Discourse, Volume One*. RRA 1. Dorset: Deo, 2009.

———. "Sociorhetorical Criticism: Mary, Elizabeth, and the Magnificat as a Test Case." Pages 29–74 in *Foundations for Sociorhetorical Explora-*

tion: *A Rhetoric of Religious Antiquity Reader*. Edited by Vernon K. Robbins, Robert H. von Thaden, and Bart B. Bruehler. RRA 4. Atlanta: SBL Press, 2016.

———. *The Tapestry of Early Christian Discourse: Rhetoric, Society and Ideology*. London: Routledge, 1996.

———. "Where Is Wuellner's Anti-Hermeneutical Hermeneutics Taking Us?" Pages 105–25 in *Rhetorics and Hermeneutics: Wilhelm Wuellner and His Influence*. Edited by James D. Hester and J. David Hester. ESEC 9 London: T&T Clark, 2004.

Robbins, Vernon K., and Roy R. Jeal, eds. *Welcoming the Nations: International Sociorhetorical Explorations*. IVBS 13. Atlanta: SBL Press, 2020.

Robbins Vernon K., and John H. Patton. "Rhetoric and Biblical Criticism." *QJS* 66 (1980): 327–37.

Robbins, Vernon K., Robert H. von Thaden Jr., and Bart B. Bruehler, eds. *Foundations for Sociorhetorical Exploration: A Rhetoric of Religious Antiquity Reader*. RRA 4. Atlanta: SBL Press, 2016.

Roberts, W. Rhys. "The Quotation from *Genesis* in the *De Sublimitate* (IX.9)." *CR* 9 (1897): 431–36.

Rodríguez, Rafael. *If You Call Yourself a Jew: Reappraising Paul's Letter to the Romans*. Cambridge: Clarke, 2015.

Rogger, Andre. *Landscapes of Taste: The Art of Humphry Repton's Red Books*. Classical Tradition in Architecture. London: Routledge, 2008.

Russell, Donald. A. *Criticism in Antiquity*. Berkeley: University of California Press, 1981.

———. "Greek Criticism of the Empire." Pages 297–329 in *Classical Criticism*. Vol. 1 of *The Cambridge History of Literary Criticism*. Edited by George A. Kennedy. Cambridge: Cambridge University Press: 1989.

———. "Introduction." Pages 145–58 in Longinus, *On the Sublime*. Translated by W. H. Fyfe. Revised by Donald Russell. LCL. Cambridge: Harvard University Press, 1995.

———. *"Longinus" On the Sublime: Introduction and Commentary*. Oxford: Oxford University Press, 1964.

Saint Girons, Baldine. *Le Sublime, de l'antiquité à nos jours*. Paris: Desjonquières, 2005.

Sanday, William, and Arthur C. Headlam. *A Critical and Exegetical Commentary on the Epistle to the Romans*. 5th ed. ICC. Edinburgh: T&T Clark, 1902.

Sanders, E. P. *Paul and Palestinian Judaism*. Philadelphia: Fortress, 1977.

Schoedel, William R. *Ignatius of Antioch: A Commentary on the Letters of Ignatius of Antioch*. Hermeneia. Philadelphia: Fortress, 1985.

Schoeni, Mark. "The Hyperbolic Sublime as a Master Trope in Romans." Pages 171–92 in *Rhetoric and the New Testament: Essays from the 1992 Heidelberg Conference*. Edited by Stanley E. Porter and Thomas H. Olbricht. JSNTSup 90. Sheffield: Sheffield Academic, 1993.

Screech, M. A. *Ecstasy and the Praise of Folly*. London: Duckworth, 1980.

Segal, Charles P. "ΥΨΟΣ and the Problem of Cultural Decline in the *De Sublimitate*." *HSCP* 64 (1959): 121–46.

Selby, Gary S. *Not with Wisdom of Words: Nonrational Persuasion in the New Testament*. Grand Rapids: Eerdmans, 2016.

Shaffer, Elinor S. "Coleridge's Theory of Aesthetic Interest." *Journal of Aesthetics and Art Criticism* 27 (1969): 399–408.

Shanks, Andrew. *Hegel and Religious Faith: Divided Brain, Atoning Spirit*. New York: T&T Clark, 2011.

Shaw, Philip. *The Sublime*. 2nd ed. New Critical Idiom. London: Routledge, 2017.

———. "Wordsworth and the Sublime." British Library, 2014. https://tinyurl.com/SBL4831b.

Shawcross, J. "Coleridge Marginalia." *Notes & Queries* 4 (1905): 341–42.

Sircello, Guy. "How Is a Theory of the Sublime Possible?" *Journal of Aesthetics and Art Criticism* 51 (1993): 541–50.

Skinner, Quentin. "Introduction: The Return of Grand Theory." Pages 1–20 in *The Return of Grand Theory in the Human Sciences*. Edited by Quentin Skinner. Cambridge: Cambridge University Press, 1991.

Smart, Christopher. "Christopher. "On the Immensity of the Supreme Being." Eighteenth Century Poetry Archive, 2015. https://tinyurl.com/SBL4831c.

Smillie, Gene. "'The One Who is Speaking' in Hebrews 12:25." *TynBul* 55 (2004): 275–94.

Smith, Adam. "The Principles Which Lead and Direct Philosophical Enquiries; Illustrated by the History of Astronomy." Pages 113–30 in *Essays on Philosophical Subjects*. Dublin: Wogan, Byrne, et al., 1795.

Son, Kiwoong. *Zion Symbolism in Hebrews: Hebrews 12:18–24 as a Hermeneutical Key to the Epistle*. Paternoster Biblical Monographs. Milton Keynes: Paternoster, 2005.

Spacks, Patricia Ann Meyer. *The Insistence of Horror: Aspects of the Supernatural in Eighteenth Century Poetry*. Cambridge: Harvard University Press, 1962.

Stowers, Stanley K. *A Rereading of Romans: Justice, Jews, and Gentiles.* New Haven: Yale University Press, 1994.
Talbert, Charles H. *Ephesians and Colossians.* Paideia. Grand Rapids: Baker Academic, 2007.
Taylor, Charles. *Sources of the Self: The Making of the Modern Identity.* Cambridge: Cambridge University Press, 1992.
Theobald, Michael. *Israel-Vergessenheit in den Pastoralbriefen: Ein neuer Vorschlag zu ihrer historisch-theologischen Verortung im 2. Jahrhundert n. Chr. Unter besonderer Berücksichtigung der Ignatius Briefe.* SBS 229. Stuttgart: Katholische Bibelwerke, 2016.
Thielman, Frank. *Ephesians.* BECNT. Grand Rapids: Baker Academic, 2010.
Thiessen, Jonathan. "Les lettres de l'apôtre Paul et la rhétorique du discours figuré." PhD diss., Université de Strasbourg, 2020.
Thonssen, Lester. *Selected Readings in Rhetoric and Public Speaking with Introductory Comments.* New York: Wilson, 1942.
Thonssen, Lester, and A. Craig Baird. *Speech Criticism, the Development of Standards for Rhetorical Appraisal.* New York: Ronald Press, 1948.
Thorsteinsson, Runar M. *Paul's Interlocutor in Romans 2: Function and Identity in the Context of Ancient Epistolography.* ConBNT 40. Stockholm: Almqvist & Wiksell, 2003.
Thurén, Lauri, ed. *Rhetoric and Scripture: Collected Essays of Thomas H. Olbricht.* ESEC 23. Atlanta: SBL Press, 2021.
———. "Where Is Rhetorical Criticism Taking Us Now?" Pages 333–50 in *Voces Clamantium in Deserto—Essays in Honor of Kari Syreeni.* Edited by Sven-Olav Back and Matti Kankaanniemi. Studier i exegetik och judaistik utgivna av Teologiska fakulteten vid Åbo Akademi 11. Åbo: Åbo Akademi University, 2012.
Tolkien, J. R. R. "On Fairy-Stories." Pages 38–89 in *Essays Presented to Charles Williams.* Edited by C. S. Lewis. Grand Rapids: Eerdmans, 1973.
Too, Yun Lee. *The Idea of Ancient Literary Criticism.* Oxford: Clarendon, 1998.
Usher, M. D. "Theomachy, Creation, and the Poetics of Quotation in Longinus Chapter 9." *CP* 102 (2007): 292–303.
Ussher, James. *Clio, or a Discourse on Taste; Addressed to a Young Lady.* 3rd ed. London: Davies, 1772.
Vallins, David, ed. *Coleridge's Writings Volume 5: On the Sublime.* New York: Palgrave Macmillan, 2003.

Vinzent, Markus. *Writing the History of Early Christianity: From Reception to Retrospection*. Cambridge: Cambridge University Press, 2019.

Vöhler, Martin. "Pseudo-Longinus, *Peri hypsous*." In *The Reception of Classical Literature*. Edited by Christine Walde. BNPSup 1/5. Online ed. Leiden: Brill, 2012. http://dx.doi.org/10.1163/2214-8647_bnps5_e1012470.

Wallas, Graham. *The Art of Thought*. Kent: Solis, 2014.

Waller, Marguerite. "The Empire's New Clothes: Refashioning the Renaissance." Pages 160–83 in *Seeking the Woman in Late Medieval and Renaissance Writings: Essays in Feminist Contextual Criticism*. Edited by Sheila Fisher and Janet E. Halley. Knoxville: University of Tennessee Press, 1989.

Walsh, George B. "Sublime Method: Longinus on Language and Imitation." *ClAnt* 7 (1988): 252–69.

Watson, Duane F. *The Rhetoric of the New Testament: A Bibliographic Survey*. Tools for Biblical Study 8. Leiderdorp: Deo, 2006.

Watson, Francis. *Paul, Judaism and the Gentiles: A Sociological Approach*. SNTSMS 56. Cambridge: Cambridge University Press, 1986.

———. *Paul, Judaism and the Gentiles: Beyond the New Perspective*. Grand Rapids: Eerdmans, 2007.

Webb, Ruth. *Ekphrasis, Imagination, and Persuasion in Ancient Rhetorical Theory and Practice*. Farnham: Ashgate, 2009.

Webster, Suzanne E. *Body and Soul in Coleridge's Notebooks, 1827–1834: "What Is Life?"* New York: Palgrave Macmillan, 2009.

Weiskel, Thomas. *The Romantic Sublime: Studies in the Structure and Psychology of Transcendence*. Baltimore: Johns Hopkins University Press, 1976.

Wesley, John. *The Complete Sermons*. Amazon CreateSpace, 2013.

West, M. L. "Longinus and the Grandeur of God." Pages 335–42 in *Ethics and Rhetoric: Classical Essays for Donald Russell on His Seventy-fifth Birthday*. Edited by Doreen Innes, Harry M. Hine, and Christopher Pelling. Oxford: Clarendon, 1995.

Whately, Richard. *Elements of Rhetoric*. London: Parker, 1851.

Wheeler, Kathleen. "Imaginative Perception in Coleridge's *Biographia Literaria*." *Coleridge Bulletin* NS 38 (2011): 1–16.

Witherington, Ben, III. *The New Testament Rhetoric: An Introductory Guide to the Art of Persuasion in and of the New Testament*. Eugene, OR: Cascade, 2009.

Wordsworth, William. "Lines Composed a Few Miles above Tintern Abbey on Revisiting the Banks of the Wye during a Tour, July 13, 1798." https://tinyurl.com/SBL4831d.

———. *Lyrical Ballads: With Pastoral and Other Poems*. London: Longman & Rees, 1798.

———. *Our English Lakes, Mountains, and Waterfalls as Seen by William Wordsworth 1770–1850*. London: Bennett, 1864.

Worthen, John. *The Life of William Wordsworth: A Critical Biography*. Blackwell Critical Biographies. Chichester: Wiley Blackwell, 2014.

Wuellner, Wilhelm. "Reconceiving a Rhetoric of Religion: A Rhetoric of Power as the Power of the Sublime." Pages 23–77 in *Rhetorics and Hermeneutics: Wilhelm Wuellner and His Influence*. Edited by James D. Hester and J. David Hester. ESEC 9. London: T&T Clark, 2004.

———. "Rhetorical Criticism in Biblical Studies." *Jian Dao* 4 (1995): 73–96.

———. "Where Is Rhetorical Criticism Taking Us?" *CBQ* 49 (1987): 448–63.

Young, Edward. *Young's Night Thoughts; or, Thoughts on Life, Death, and Immortality*. New York: Worthington, 1889.

Ziegler, K. "Das Genesiscitat in der Schrift ΠΕΡΙ ΥΨΟΥΣ." *Hermes* 50 (1915): 572–603.

Contributors

Murray J. Evans is professor emeritus of English at the University of Winnipeg.

Alan P. R. Gregory is principal of St. Augustine's College of Theology.

Christopher T. Holmes is John H. Stembler Jr. Scholar in Residence and director of biblical and theological studies, First Presbyterian Church, Atlanta, Georgia.

Roy R. Jeal is professor emeritus at Booth University College and research associate at Vancouver School of Theology.

Harry O. Maier is professor of New Testament and Early Christian Studies at Vancouver School of Theology.

Erika Mae Olbricht is senior instructor in the Department of English at Case Western Reserve University.

Thomas H. Olbricht (d. 2020) was Distinguished Professor Emeritus of Religion at Pepperdine University.

Vernon K. Robbins is professor emeritus of religion and Winship Distinguished Research Professor in the Humanities at Emory University.

Jonathan Thiessen is a classicist and biblical scholar. His PhD is from the Université de Strasbourg.

Ancient Sources Index

Hebrew Bible/Septuagint		2 Kings	
		1:15	145
Genesis	4, 65–66, 73–77, 82		
1	73, 75–77, 79	Psalms	78
1:2	162	18	203
1:3	74–75	18:6–16	146
1:9–10	74	19:1	224
1:10	74	32	16
7:11	x	50:6	224
8:2	x	95	78
15:1	145	97:5	149
15:5	220	97:6	224
21:17	145		
22:17	220	Ecclesiastes	
26:24	145	6:11 LXX	46
46:3	145	7:16	46
Exodus	79, 218	Isaiah	210
19	80	2:19–21	148
19:16–19	146	6:1–4	147
19:18	81	6:1–5	146
33:20	147	6:3	146
		6:5	144
Numbers		10:24	145
21:34	145	13:10	148
23:7–11	205	28:13 LXX	45
		29:6	146
Deuteronomy	79	34:4	148
4	80	37:6	145
		40:4	149
Joshua		41:10	145
11:6	145	44:8	145
		50	124
Judges			
5:4–5	81		

Jeremiah	210	Deuterocanonical Books	
1:8	145		
10:5	145	Sirach	
30:10	145	3:23	46
42:11	145	23:23	45
51:27	149		
		2 Maccabees	
Ezekiel		14:8	45
1:5–25	147		
1:22	147	4 Maccabees	188
1:28	144		
2:6	145	Pseudipigrapha	
37:7–8	148		
38:20	149	2 Baruch	
		10.2	142
Daniel		11.1	142
7	144	67.7	142
7:9	144		
7:13	144	1 Enoch	1, 6, 155, 158, 171, 219–20, 225
7:22	144	2.6	162
8:15–17	21	3.1–3	162
8:17	144	7	162
9:20–22	21	7.1–3	162
9:21	21	12–14	162
		14	146
Hosea		21	165
10:8	148	21.1–5	146
		21.1–6	162–63
Joel		21.1–10	6, 161, 175
2:1–11	149	21.6	163
2:30–31	148	21.7–10	162–63
		37–71	166
Amos		62	165, 167
8:9	148	62.1–5	166
		62.1–14	6, 175, 220
Zephaniah		62.11	166
1:15	148	62.13–14	166
		86.3–6	162
Haggai			
2:6	82	4 Ezra	
		3.1–2	142
Zechariah		3.28–31	142
8:13	145	16.44	142
8:15	145	16.46	142

Ancient Sources Index 251

Psalms of Solomon		Luke	1, 24–27, 33–34, 36–38, 99, 118
4.2	46	1–2	2, 13, 118, 120
		1:4	23, 37
Sibylline Oracles		1:26–38	2, 20
5.143	142	1:34	21
5.159	142	1:38	37
5.434	142	1:39–56	2, 26
		1:43	27
Ancient Jewish Writers		1:45	27
		1:46	27
Josephus, *Antiquitates judaicae*		1:48	27
6.55	45	1:49	27
11.36	45	1:55	27
		2:8–9	30
Josephus, *Bellum judaicum*		2:11	30
1.111	46	2:15–16	30
		2:15–20	2, 30
Philo, *De Iosepho*		2:17	30
216	45	2:18	30
		2:19	30
Philo, *De opificio mundi*		2:25–26	32
41.3	45	2:25–35	2, 32
		2:26	33
Philo, *De somniis*		2:30	33
2.69	45	2:30–32	32
2.132	46	2:33	32
		2:34	33
Philo, *Legum allegoriae*		2:35	32–33
1.30	47	2:41–51	2, 34
3.140	46	2:44	34
		2:46	34
Philo, *Quod Deus sit immutabilis*		2:47	35
44	47	2:48	35
		2:49	35
New Testament		2:50	35
		2:51	35
Matthew	25, 174	6:36	174
5:37	46		
5:47	46	John	99
24:29	148	3:3	115
		3:7	115
Mark			
8:34	222	Acts	
14:31	46	18:2	43
		21	48

Ancient Sources Index

Acts (cont.)
21:20–24	48
21:28–29	48

Romans	1, 42, 44, 61, 63, 99, 178
1	44
1:13	41
1:16	43, 47
2	61
2–3	3, 39–41, 43, 45, 60, 64, 120–21
2:1	44, 61
2:9	43, 47
2:10	43
2:17–24	60
2:17–29	46, 60–61
2:25–29	44
3	47, 49, 61, 63
3:1	44, 46–47, 61
3:1–2	44
3:1–9	60, 62
3:2–3	47, 62
3:3	44, 60
3:9	47
3:9–18	60
3:10–12	62
3:11–18	44
3:22	43
3:29	43
4:9	43
5:3–5	222
5:12	43
9–11	45
9:4	45
9:33	45
10:12	43
11:26	45
14	42
14–15	48
15:3	45
15:13	45

1 Corinthians	99
4:1	100

2 Corinthians	
4:7	100

Galatians	
5:2	46
5:2–12	48

Ephesians	1, 4, 103–7, 110
1–3	104, 108
1:2	108
1:4	106, 108
1:5	108
1:6	108
1:7	106, 108
1:9	107
1:13	108
1:14	108
1:20	106
1:20–23	108
1:21	109
2:1–4	109
2:2	107, 109
2:3	108
2:5	106
2:6	106
2:14	108
2:15	108
2:17	108
2:22	108
3:2–4	105
3:3	107
3:4	107
3:5	108
3:7	107–8
3:13	108
3:15	108
3:18–21	108–9
3:20	107
3:21	106
4–6	105, 108
4:2	108
4:3	108
4:4	108
4:7	108
4:13	108

4:15	108	11:7	79
4:17–20	109	11:11	79
4:24	108	12	81–82
5:1–2	108	12:1–2	84
5:2	106	12:12	84
5:19	9	12:18	80
5:21–6:9	108	12:18–21	79–80
5:32	107	12:18–24	79
6:11–12	109	12:18–29	3–4, 79, 82, 85
6:12	106–7, 109	12:19	80
6:14–17	109	12:21	80
6:19	107	12:22–24	80
6:23–24	106	12:25	79, 81
		12:25–29	83
Philippians		12:26	81
3:2–3	48	12:26–27	81
		12:27	82
1 Thessalonians	99	13:1–3	84
2:15–16	48	13:5	79
2 Timothy		Revelation	1, 5–6, 135–46, 148, 150–54, 217, 225
1:7	224	1	6, 136, 143, 218
		1:9–20	143
Hebrews	1, 4, 65–66, 78–79, 82–84, 122	1:11	144
1:1–2	78	1:12–16	144
1:5–14	78, 80, 83	1:17	141, 143–45, 218
2:1	83	2:7	143
2:3	83	2:10	141
3–4	83	2:11	143
3:7–4:13	78	2:17	143
3:8	78	2:26	143
3:12	78	3:5	143
3:15	78	3:12	143
4:7	78	3:21	143
4:14–16	84	4	6, 144, 146, 218
5:5–6	78	4:1	146
6:13–14	79	4:2–6a	146
6:17–18	79	4:5	146
7:17–22	78	4:5–6	147
8:8–13	79	4:6b–8	146
10:20	84	4:7	147
10:25	83	4:8	147
10:30	79	4:9–12	146
10:32–34	83	4:1–12	146
11:3	79		

Ancient Sources Index

Revelation (cont.)

Reference	Pages
6–16	6, 136, 148, 218
6:1–8:1	148
6:12–14	148
6:15	148
6:16	210
8:1–12	149
8:2–11:18	148
8:5	146
9	149
9:5	149
9:7	149
9:7–10	149
9:14–16	149
9:17	149
9:18	149
9:19	149
11:1	141
11:18	141–42
11:19	146
12	150
12–13	6, 136, 150, 152, 218
12:1	150
12:3	150
12:4	150
12:5–6	150
12:7–9	150
12:11	150
12:13–17	150
12:18–13:10	151
12:21	150
13	150–51
13:1	151
13:3	151
13:5	151
13:6	150
13:7	151
13:11	151
13:11–18	151
13:12	151
13:15	151
13:17	151
13:18	151
14:7	141–42
15:2	143
15:4	141–42
16:1–21	148, 150
16:9	150
16:11	150
16:17	149
16:18	149
16:19	149
16:20	149
16:21	150
18	218
18:10	141–42
18:15	141–42, 218
19:1	218
19:3	218
19:5	141–42
21:8	141, 143

Early Christian Writings

Eusebius, *Historia ecclesiastica*

Reference	Pages
5.1.40–42	188

Ignatius, *To the Ephesians*

Reference	Pages
6.1	178
14.2	178
15.1	178
15.2	178
19.1	178
19.1–3	186

Ignatius, *To the Magnesians*

Reference	Pages
8.2	178

Ignatius, *To the Philadelphians*

Reference	Pages
1.1	178
7.1	180
7.2	180

Ignatius, *To the Romans* 1, 7, 178, 183, 188

Reference	Pages
1.2	184
2.1	178, 186–87
2.2	187
3.3	184
4.1–2	183

Ancient Sources Index

5.1	184
5.1–3	180, 183
5.3	183
7.2	183

Martyrdom of Polycarp

13–15	188

Greco-Roman Literature

Anaximenes, *Rhetorica ad Alexdandrum*

20.5	57

Apsines, *Ars rhetorica*

10.13	57

Apuleius, *Apologia* (*Pro se de magia*)

14	69

Aristotle, *Rhetorica* 68

1.2.3	19
3.2	60
3.2.13	19
3.18	57
3.19	57

Arrian, *Epicteti dissertations*

3.5.2	46

Cicero, *De oratore*

3.203	57

Demetrius, *De elocutione*

279	57

Demosthenes, *In Midiam*

21.72	53

Dionysius of Halicarnassus, *Antiquitates romanae*

10.38.1	47

Dionysius of Halicarnassus, *De Demosthene*

54.5	57

Herodotus, *Histories*

2.29	53

Homer, *Iliad*

4.442	75
5.770–772	75
13	77
13.18	75
13.19	75
13.27–29	75
15.605	76
17.645–647	76
20.60	75
20.61–65	75, 77
21.388	75, 77

Isocrates, *Evagoras*

75	69

Longinus, *De sublimitate*

1.1	14, 16, 50, 53
1.3	14, 54
1.3–4	18, 53–54, 67–68, 137
1.4	51, 65–66, 72
1.4.9–10	179
2.2	56
3–5	55
3–7	67
3.5	55
6	55
6.1	14
7.1	23, 54
7.2	24, 26, 60
7.2–4	53
7.3	24, 54
7.3–4	60
7.4	24
8	67
8.1	16, 51, 55, 137
8.4	55
9	70, 76, 79, 82, 138
9–10	51
9–15	68
9.1–13.1	73
9.1–15.12	73

256   Ancient Sources Index

Longinus, De sublimitate (cont.)

9.2	185	22.4	182
9.4	75	23.1	56
9.5	75, 185	23.3	53
9.6	75, 82	24.2	56
9.6–7	77	25	53
9.7	185–86	26–27	56
9.8	75, 77, 82, 152	26.1–2	56
9.9	49, 65, 73–74	26.1–27.3	57
9.10	76	26.2	53
9.11	76	26.3	56
10	60	27.1	56
10.3	56	27.2	56
11	60	27.3	56
11–12	60	29.2	56
11.2	56	30–38	68
12	55	32.4	56
12.4	18, 51	33–36	51, 55, 84
15	20, 147	34.4	51
15.1–2	20–21, 56	35	50
15.8	21	35–36	52
15.9	18, 21, 26, 56, 182	35.2	72
15.12	73	35.2–4	52
16–29	68	35.3	19, 52
16.2	56	35.4	52
16.3	55	36.1–2	52
16.4	60	36.2	19
17.1–2	59–60	38	60
17.2	18, 56	38.5–6	56
17.3	56	39–43	68
18	57	39.1	56
18.1	53	41.2	56
18.1–2	57, 61	44	70, 72
18.2	56	44.1	70
19	58–59	44.2	71
19–21	58	44.2–3	71
19.2	59	44.3	71
19.3	59	44.6	71
20.2	53, 56	44.7	71
20.2–3	58	44.8	19, 71
21.1–2	58	44.11	72
21.2	56	44.12	55
22	59	Quintilian, *Institutio oratoria*	68
22.1	56, 59	4.1.63–69	57
22.3	182	5.11.5	57

8.4.8	60
9.2.6–16	57
9.2.38–39	57
12.10.61–65	181

Suetonius, *Divus Claudius*
25.4	43

Suetonius, *Nero*
16	43

Tacitus, *Annales*
15.44	43

Tacitus, *Dialogus ad oratoribus*
1	70

Theon, *Progymnasmata*
97.23–98.20	57

Xenophon, *Cyropedia*
7.1.37	53

Modern Authors Index

Addison, Joseph	198	Campbell, George	88–89, 92, 105
Agnew, Lois	90	Campbell, Ted A.	196
Aiken, Anna Letitia	198	Canuel, Mark	111, 125
Aiken, John	198	Caplan, Harry	60
Auerbach, Erich	123	Charland, Louis C.	200
Aune, David E.	142–45, 148–50, 152	Clarke, Michael	50
Baillie, John	192–93, 195, 198, 209	Clewis, Robert R.	111
Baird, A. Craig	87	Cohick, Lynn H.	104
Barbeau, Jeffrey W.	116	Coleridge, Samuel Taylor	1, 5, 16, 37–38, 93, 111–31
Barfield, Owen	114		
Barnes, Timothy D.	177	Conrad, Joseph	216
Barth, Markus	104	Corbett, Edward P. J.	88, 90–92
Battersby, Christine	167	Costelloe, Timothy M.	14–15, 111, 118, 189
Bauckham, Richard	144–45		
Baumgarten, Alexander Gottlieb	49	Craske, Matthew	208
Beecher, Henry Ward	87	Crockett, Clayton	198
Bernard, J. H.	158	Daniels, Stephen	ix
Bitzer, Lloyd F.	104	Das, A. Andrew	42
Blair, Hugh	4, 88–94, 100–103, 105–7, 109, 120, 189–90, 192–93, 206–7, 223–24	De Bolla, Peter	ix
		Dennis, John	8, 190, 192–93, 197–205, 207–8, 210, 223–24
Bloom, Harold	94	Derham, William	191–92
Blount, Brian K.	143–45, 147–49	Dodd, C. H.	45–46, 61
Boileau-Despréaux, Nicolas	40, 120	Dodds, E. R.	70
Boring, M. Eugene	144, 146	Doerr, Anthony	18
Brady, Emily	111, 118–19	Doran, Robert	67, 136–38, 153, 189, 217
Bremmer, Jan N.	177		
Brent, Allen	177, 183–84	Dunn, James D. G.	43
Brigance, William Norwood	87	Dyer, Bryan R.	83
Brown, Raymond E.	22	Edwards, Mark J.	178
Bruehler, Bart B.	1, 22	Evans, Donald D.	221
Burke, Edmund	8, 111, 123, 155, 167, 196–98, 207–8, 211–12, 223–24	Evans, Murray J.	1, 5, 9, 16, 37–38, 111–12, 116, 119–27, 129
Burke, Kenneth	17, 221	Faflak, Joel	171
Calvin, John	195, 224	Flaubert, Gustave	53

Modern Authors Index

Forsey, Jane 15
Frank, David 102
Fredriksen, Paula 48
Gager, John G. 73–75, 77
Gaudio, Michael xi
Gaventa, Beverly Roberts 33, 35–36
Gigerenzer, Gerd 19–20
Godolphin, F. R. B. 67, 136–37
Golden, James L. 88, 90–92
Gombis, Timothy O. 104
Goodspeed, Edgar J. 104
Gotlieb, Marc 50
Green, Joel B. 21, 23, 26, 33, 87
Gregory, Alan P. R. ix, 1, 7–9, 115–16, 123–24, 212–13, 216, 223–25
Griffiths, Jonathan I. 81
Grube, G. M. A. 67, 73, 137, 155
Güting, Eberhard 58
Hagaman, John 105
Hall, Robert G. 41
Halmi, Nicholas 115–16
Headlam, Arthur C. 39, 41
Heath, Malcolm 40, 67, 136
Hendrix, John Shannon 169–71, 220
Hertz, Neil 122
Hester, James D. 13, 88, 89, 98–101, 103, 107,
Hester, J. David 1, 9, 14, 17, 89, 98–101, 103, 107
Hill, James J. 66, 137
Hill, John 90
Holmes, Christopher T. 1, 3–6, 17, 65–68, 70, 73, 79, 122–23, 136, 217–18
Holmes, Michael W. 180
Holmes, Richard 112–13
Howell, Wilbur Samuel 88
Hübner, Reinhard 177
Hugo, Victor 222
Ingersoll, Robert 87
Innes, Doreen C. 67, 136–37
Jeal, Roy R. viii, 2, 8, 20–21, 104, 111, 118, 120, 169, 215–16, 225
Jewett, Robert 42, 44, 46
Jipp, Joshua W. 78, 80
Jonge, Casper C. de 41, 75–76

Joyce, James 224–25
Kahneman, Daniel 19–20
Kant, Immanuel 6–7, 49, 111, 123–26, 130, 155–61, 165, 167–69, 171–72, 174–75, 212, 219–21, 224
Keck, Leander E. 61
Keefe, Rosaleen Greene-Smith 89, 92–93
Kelhoffer, James A. 83
Kennedy, George A. 99, 105, 135
Kirwan, James 189
Koester, Craig R. 79, 83
Korn, Marianne 15
Kristeva, Julia 112, 122
Lacoue-Labarthe, Philippe 49, 53
Lagière, Anne 41
Lake, Kirsopp 178, 185–86
Lampe, Peter 42
Lanham, Richard A. 122–23, 126–27
Légasse, Simon 43
Leuchner, Thomas 177
Lewis, C. S. 114, 121–22
Lindars, Barnabas 79
Livesey, Nina E. 62
Locke, John 200
Lotz, John-Paul 184
Louw, Johannes P. 141
Lowth, Robert 190, 204–6, 223–24
Lyotard, Jean-François 198
Mack, Burton L. 135
Mader, Thomas F. 60
Magnuson, Paul 115
Maier, Harry O. 7, 20, 178–79, 216, 221–23
Makkreel, Rudolf A. 6, 155–61, 167–70, 172, 219–21
Marshall, John W. 46
Martin, Troy W. 135
Maté, Gabor 219
Mealand, David L. 58
Minear, Paul S. 42
Modiano, Raimonda 115, 117, 125, 128
Monk, Samuel Holt 189, 199, 207
Moo, Douglas 47
Moran, Michael 87

Morris, David B.	189, 204	Rogger, Andre	ix
Mortensen, Klaus P.	93	Russell, Donald A.	14, 16, 39, 65, 67–68, 87, 123, 136, 140, 179
Moss, Candida	178		
Muir, John	vii, xiii	Saint Girons, Baldine	50
Mutschmann, Hermann	73	Sanday, William	39, 41
Myrone, Martin	211–12	Sanders, E. P.	43
Nickelsburg, George W. E.	161, 164, 166	Schoedel, William R.	183
		Schoeni, Mark	41
Nicolson, Marjorie Hope	189	Screech, M. A.	138
Nida, Eugene A.	141	Segal, Charles P.	137
Nolland, John	21–24, 33, 35	Selby, Gary S.	14, 41
Norden, Eduard	73	Shaffer, Elinor S.	128
Nye, David E.	213	Shanks, Andrew	156, 172–75
Nygren, Edward J.	208	Shaw, Philip	14–15, 49, 94, 111, 189
O'Gorman, Ned	181	Shawcross, J.	117
Olbrechts-Tyteca, Lucie	103	Sircello, Guy	119
Olbricht, Thomas H.	vii, xi–xii, 1, 4, 9, 13, 17, 61, 98–99, 101, 103, 105, 107, 120, 223	Skinner, Quentin	111
		Smart, Christopher	209
		Smillie, Gene	81
Oravec, Christine L.	40	Smith, Adam	190
Otto, Rudolph	88	Son, Kiwoong	79
Paley, Morton D.	115	Spacks, Patricia Ann Meyer	189
Patton, John H.	135	Steele, Richard	198
Perelman, Chaim	99, 102–3, 110	Stowers, Stanley K.	42
Perler, Othmar	182–83, 188	Sumney, Jerry L.	61
Pernot, Laurent	41, 60	Talbert, Charles H.	104
Phibbs, John	ix	Taylor, Charles	198
Piehler, Paul	122	von Thaden Jr., Robert H.	1, 22
Pirius, Rebecca	163	Theobald, Michael	177–78
Placher, William C.	209	Thielman, Frank	104
Pope, Alexander	194	Thiessen, Jonathan	3, 48, 61, 120–21, 123
Porter, James I.	14–16, 18–19, 41, 50, 120, 135–36, 139–40, 144, 147, 152–53, 181, 186, 217, 219		
		Thonssen, Lester	87
		Thorsteinsson, Runar M.	42, 61
Porter, Stanley E.	42, 50	Thurén, Lauri	9, 98, 103
Pound, Ezra	15	Tolkien, J. R. R.	114
Radcliffe, Ann	194	Too, Yun Lee	65, 68–69, 123, 138
Ray, John	191–92	Usher, M. D.	76
Reid, Nicholas	116	Ussher, James	124, 197–99
Richards, I. A.	130, 221	Vallins, David	118
Riesenfeld, Harald	183	VanderKam, James C.	166
Robbins, Vernon K.	1–2, 6–7, 9, 13, 20, 22–24, 27–29, 98, 135, 219–21, 224	Veale, Lucy	ix
		Vinzent, Markus	177
Roberts, W. Rhys	33, 73	Vöhler, Martin	39
Rodríguez, Rafael	42, 61	Wallas, Graham	169

Waller, Marguerite	121
Walsh, George B.	137
Watson, Duane F.	135
Watson, Francis	42
Webb, Ruth	184
Webster, Suzanne E.	116
Weiskel, Thomas	117, 121
Wesley, John	195–96, 224
West, M. L.	76
Whately, Richard	88–89
Witherington, Ben, III	135
Wordsworth, William	viii–ix, xiii, 4, 88, 93–95, 97, 101–2, 106–7, 109, 112–13, 120, 123, 130
Worthen, John	93
Wuellner, Wilhelm	94
Young, Edward	8, 190–99, 203, 206, 208–10, 212, 223–25
Ziegler, K.	73

www.ingramcontent.com/pod-product-compliance
Lightning Source LLC
Chambersburg PA
CBHW020112010526
44115CB00008B/803